Solving
Discipline
Problems

Solving Discipline Problems

Strategies for Classroom Teachers

Second Edition

Charles H. Wolfgang
Florida State University

Carl D. Glickman
The University of Georgia, Athens

ALLYN AND BACON, INC.

BOSTON, LONDON,
SYDNEY, TORONTO

Library of Congress Cataloging-in-Publication Data

Wolfgang, Charles H.
  Solving discipline problems.

  Includes bibliographies and index.
  1. Classroom management.   2. School discipline.
I. Glickman, Carl D.   II. Title.
LB3013.W62 1986   371.1'024   85-19984
ISBN 0-205-08630-6

Printed in the United States of America

10 9 8 7   90 89 88

Dedicated to our children: **Ellen Louise Wolfgang,
Jennifer Sonya Glickman,** and **Rachel Adelle Glickman,**
for daily reaffirming our optimism about the
next generation.

Contents

Preface   xi
Acknowledgments   xiii

1   Introduction: Reaching the Breaking Point   1

    Why Is Disruptive Behavior Such a Problem Today?   3
    The Teacher's Never-Ending Task   4
    What Can Be Done?   5
    The Teacher as a Professional   6
    Getting Together on the Job   7

SECTION I: INTRODUCTION: TEACHER BELIEFS ON DISCIPLINE   9

2   Beyond Theory to Classroom Practice   13

    How Does Psychological Theory Help the Teacher?   14
    Three Schools of Thought   15
    Guidelines for Classroom Practice: The Teacher's Role   18
    Teacher Behavior: The Use of Power   20
    Organization of the Following Chapters   24

3   The Supportive Model: Gordon's Teacher Effectiveness Training   26

    Gordon and Rogerian Theory   27
    T.E.T. and the Teacher Behavior Continuum   29
    Summary   41

4   The Communication Model: Berne and Harris's Transactional Analysis   46

    Transactional Analysis   47
    The Theory   48
    TA and the Teacher Behavior Continuum   52

Games 60
Summary 62

5 The Valuing Model: Raths and Simon's Values Clarification   68

Teacher as Clarifier 71
Values Clarification and the Teacher Behavior Continuum 71
Reinforcement, Physical Intervention, and Isolation 77
What Happened to Simmie? 78
Summary 78

6 The Social Discipline Model of Rudolf Dreikurs   84

Dreikurs and Alfred Adler's Social Theory 85
Dreikurs's Methods and the Teacher Behavior Continuum 86
Summary 100

7 The Reality Model of William Glasser   107

Glasser and Reality Therapy 109
Glasser's Methods and the Teacher Behavior Continuum 110
The Classroom Meeting 118
Summary 122

8 The Behavior Modification Model   129

The Behavioral Position 130
The Basics of Reinforcement 133
Teacher Behavior Continuum and Behavior Modification 136
Summary 145

9 The Assertiveness Model of Lee and Marlene Canter   150

The Assertiveness Model 152
The Assertiveness Model and the Teacher Behavior
Continuum 155
Discussion of the Assertiveness Model 161
Summary 161

10 The Behaviorism/Punishment Model of Engelmann and Dobson   164

The Rationale for Physical Intervention 167
The Teacher Behavior Continuum with Punishment 169
Summarizing Engelmann and Dobson 178

11 **Strengths and Limitations of Today's Teacher-Student Interaction Models**   181

Relationship-Listening 181
The Supportive Model of Thomas Gordon 182
The Communication Model of Eric Berne and Thomas Harris's
Transactional Analysis 186
The Valuing Model of Louis E. Raths, Sidney Simon, and Others 188
Confronting-Contracting 189
The Social Model of Rudolf Dreikers 192
The Reality Model of William Glasser 193
Rules/Rewarders-Punishers 196
The Behavior Modification Model 197
The Assertiveness Model 199
The Behaviorism/Corporal Punishment Model 202
Summary 205

SECTION II: INTRODUCTION: BEYOND MODELS TO
            PROFESSIONAL DECISIONS   207

12 **Decision Making Based on an Eclectic Approach**   213

An Orderly Plan 224
Case Studies 224
Summary 235

13 **Decision Making Based on the Degree of Seriousness of Student Behavior**   236

Degrees of Crises 238
The Teacher's Helping Behavior 239
Summary 244

14 **Decision Making Based on Student Social Development**   246

Socialized Behavior: A Developmental Process 247
The First Seven Years of Social Development 248
Summarizing Developmental Theory 253
Rational and Moral Progression and Regression 255
The Passive Student 256
The Physically Aggressive Student 262
The Verbally Aggressive Student 266
The Social-Interaction-Through-Language Student 270
The Conceptualization-Through-Language Student 273
The Class as a Social Unit 275
Spheres of Competency 275
Summary 277

15 Decision Making Based on a Professional Team Approach   279

Staffing: A Team Process 282
Staffing Agenda: Steps and Procedures 285
Staffing—A Case Study 291
Summary of Staffing Procedures and Agenda 295

SECTION III: INTRODUCTION: DISCIPLINE AND CLASSROOM
             MANAGEMENT   297

16 Classroom Management: A Preventive Process   299

.   Kounin's With-It-Ness and Overlapping 301
Evertson and Emmer 306
Summary 312

17 Conclusion: A Better Tomorrow   314

Knowledge and Choices for Today's Teacher 314
The Professional Teacher 317
A Better Tomorrow 319

Appendix: Moral Reasoning: From Seven Years to Adulthood   320

Index   325

Preface

This book is for teachers! Teachers are on the frontlines in dealing with student misbehavior. Because teachers know their students, themselves, and their classrooms better than anyone else, they can make the wisest decisions about the most appropriate ways to respond to misbehaving students. The historic practice of having outside experts telling teachers what is best for them will no longer do.

If we as authors succeed in the pages to follow, teachers will come to realize that they are the true professionals holding the real power for taking discipline actions. This book, consequently, becomes a comprehensive resource guide of strategies, procedures, and possible actions.

The second edition of *Solving Discipline Problems* is updated in many ways. First, the popular *Assertiveness Model* has been added to the other models (Chapter 9). Secondly, new chapters have been added on selecting teacher discipline behaviors according to teacher values (Chapter 13) and degrees of seriousness of student misbehavior (Chapter 14). In addition, the chapter on using a professional team approach (Chapter 15) has been significantly altered to reflect the latest wisdom gained from recent case studies in public schools. Finally, a new chapter (16) on classroom management has been added to enable teachers to think more about classroom preventive practices.

The additions to and reorganization of this second edition remain true to the original purpose of trying to provide classroom teachers with a "rainbow" of discipline models and techniques to permit them to move beyond a singular approach in handling classroom behavior problems. Teachers are encouraged to make key decisions on what will be most helpful to them with their particular classroom and with their particular students.

Acknowledgments

We would like to acknowledge the persons who have helped make the second edition of this book a reality. Special mention to our reviewers Joyce Putnam and Sam Sinicropi who went beyond the call of duty in providing clear and constructive feedback to us. Also, thanks are extended to our editor Hiram Howard and the staff of Allyn and Bacon, Elydia Siegel and the staff at Superscript Associates, and Gayle Rogers for putting special attention into the production of this book. We would like to acknowledge also the teachers and other school personnel across the United States and Canada who have participated with us in workshops and courses in field testing our ideas. They have given us honest advice on what works in the classroom and, as a result, have greatly influenced the revisions contained in this new edition.

We would like to thank our spouses Mary Ellen Wolfgang and Sara Orton Glickman for being our partners. Finally, we mean to immodestly thank each other. Working from afar with concentrations on different levels of schooling has challenged us to share perspectives in creating a balanced book on classroom discipline. We are pleased to offer this book with the hope that it will increase the professional growth of teachers and the well-being of students.

"Don't worry, Alfred, it takes time to get a handle on class control."

Cartoon by Ford Button

1

Introduction: Reaching the Breaking Point

Mr. Erelan is a steady, easy-going, "salt of the earth" type of man who has been a seventh-grade teacher for nine years. At the age of thirty-two he has established himself as a good teacher in the eyes of his students' parents, his fellow teachers, and school administrators. He has a reputation as a strong classroom manager. Students have traditionally responded to his friendly, calm manner with appropriately restrained behavior. They banter easily with him and seem to have true affection and respect for him.

This year, however, has been a difficult one for Mr. Erelan. As a result of redistricting, the school where he teaches has many new students from the other side of town. Many of them come from low-income homes; they are also used to the tight-fisted discipline of their former school. Most of the new students respond well to Mr. Erelan, but one student, Sophia, is constantly challenging him. Sophia is an older student, having been retained one year. She is an indifferent learner, does not speak often, and is quick to lash out physically at others. Frequently she refuses to follow Mr. Erelan's directives. When Mr. Erelan tells Sophia to stop something she is doing (talking, dropping books, or bothering others), she ignores him and continues with her activities. When he resorts to physical restraint, Sophia loses all control and begins yelling, thrashing her arms, and flailing at him.

Mr. Erelan is near the end of his rope. Yesterday, Sophia struck one of her classmates, and when Mr. Erelan intervened, she swore at him. This morning, when she entered the classroom, she immediately grabbed a fellow student's comic book and tore it to shreds. Mr. Erelan ran over, saying "Sophia, go sit in the corner," but Sophia refused. When he started to pull her out of her seat, Sophia exploded, knocking her chair to the floor, striking out at Mr. Erelan and then spitting at him. She finally broke away, ran out of the classroom, and disappeared down the corridor.

Mr. Erelan felt he had had enough. He told the class that he needed to step out of the room for a minute. Slipping into the hall, he leaned against the wall and tried to regain his composure. He thought of how hopeless the situation with Sophia had become. He felt totally incapable of helping her. Not only that, but her behavior prevented him from working with any of the other students. He could not bear to think about having the entire school year disrupted by Sophia and her problems.

Does this example seem exaggerated? Unfortunately, it is not. It is a rare classroom teacher who has not had to deal with a Sophia or, even worse, with many Sophias. We venture to say that the reader can readily identify one or more children in his or her own classroom who are providing a similar experience and creating similar concerns. What prompts us to say this? The National Education Association (NEA),[1] reports that in 1981, 36 percent of teachers said they would probably not go into teaching if they had to decide again. This percentage is nearly twice the percentage of teachers who felt that way in 1976 and nearly three times the percentage of such teachers in 1971. A major reason given for this response was "negative student attitudes and discipline."

Growing discontent with disruptive behavior in the classroom has been cited by the Gallup Poll as the public's number one school concern.[2] A leading educational journal has devoted an entire issue to this subject,[3] and a new term, "the battered teacher,"[4] has been coined. All of this documentation, however, does not bring the issue home as clearly as seeing a teacher like Mr. Erelan standing alone in a school hallway, trying to compose himself.

Being teachers ourselves, we have had firsthand experiences with depression stemming from feelings of inadequacy in coping with a particular child. We know the reality of having this child constantly in one's thoughts day and night, of losing sleep in dread of facing the next school morning, and hoping that a weekend or vacation could last forever. Again, it might be thought that we are overstating the problem, and perhaps to some individual readers we are; however, in our experiences as teachers of children and of other teachers we are convinced that this is the most common issue faced by those who work with children. We are assuming throughout this book that the reader has had or can anticipate a similar plight and wishes to learn of various ways not only to cope with disruptive children but to become a *proactive* agent in helping these children grow and attain more socialized behavior. We hope that in this way teachers will gain some personal satisfaction and a better night's sleep as well.

WHY IS DISRUPTIVE STUDENT BEHAVIOR
SUCH A PROBLEM TODAY?

In an earlier time (according to the cited NEA report) when teachers seemed to be more satisfied with their profession, a teacher might have been able to get along by using techniques learned from experiences with his or her public school teachers or from experiences gathered through an under-graduate teacher-training program. Teachers by and large worked with staid, homogeneous populations of students who could be expected to behave as previous youngsters did. Students in any one particular school generally came from the same family backgrounds, the same socioeconomic class, the same race, and often the same culture and religion. Techniques that worked with one child could be expected to have similar effects with others.

As the saying goes, "The times have changed." Public schools now contain a heterogeneous mix of youngsters. With increased mobility of families, we have in almost every neighborhood, families that come from various geographical regions and various cultures. Court-ordered desegregation has furthered this change. Also, public laws have added to the heteroge-neous school mix, putting children with special needs, who were once separated from the regular classroom, into the regular classroom (main-streaming). It can be safely said that as classrooms have become more heterogeneous, teachers have become increasingly discontent with their lives. More behavioral conflicts have erupted, with teachers discovering that their once "sure methods" no longer are working.

Please do not misunderstand us. We believe that heterogeneity is a healthy trend, one that is compatible with a democratic society. We do not advocate solving the issue of conflict in the classroom by suggesting that we retreat to homogeneous classrooms. This would be a simplistic effort to try to turn back the clock as well as to nullify some of this nation's hard-won civil and social advances. Instead, the answer lies in accepting the fact that working with diverse children who have different needs and styles is desir-able and that teachers need to be educated in ways of making their own behaviors more compatible with such diversity.

We can compare the interaction of a symphony conductor with the orchestra to a teacher working in today's heterogeneous classroom. If the conductor gives the same signs to each musician, regardless of the tone and timbre of instrument played, then the sound that emanates from all the players would be, at best, monotonous and flat or more totally discordant. Trained and competent conductors know how to give different signals to various musicians to elicit the full quality of each instrument and player. As a result, the listener hears a dynamic mix of intensity and diversity that merges into an exciting blend of harmonious sound. So it can be with the classroom teacher. The use of the same approach to every child would be stifling and inadequate. A vital classroom of developing children is created by a teacher who varies strategies suitable for each youngster. The end result is an optimal environment of individual children working cooperatively with each other.

THE TEACHER'S NEVER-ENDING TASK

Working with students is a never-ending process. Teachers truly care about their students and want to provide them with the best possible learning experiences. However, unlike some professionals, educators have difficulty gaining a sense of satisfaction from what they do. If one has a wall to build, then one can go about doing the necessary construction, and in time the wall is done. However, a child is never "finished." Teachers can never be satisfied that a child has reached his or her optimal level. The teacher must always strive to improve each student's situation. No wonder teaching is such a demanding profession, and one where the teacher finds it extremely hard to close the classroom door at four in the afternoon and forget about school until the next morning! Children are never "done." This endless process is the ultimate beauty and ultimate frustration of our profession.

When a teacher encounters an extremely disruptive student, whatever sense of class achievement that has been previously attained begins to erode. Not only is the particular child's school life unhappy, but his or her actions scream for the teacher's constant attention. Such attention pulls the teacher away from what he or she desires to do with the other children. The teacher is caught betwixt and between. Is it fair to give one child so much attention that it works to the disadvantage of the others? Or should the disruptive child be simply ignored or even isolated in another area? The reality of most schools requires that the teacher attend to the disruptive child. The teacher then must live with the guilt engendered by not spending as much time as he or she would want to with the other students. This guilt continues to compound. After all, if the teacher has decided to focus energy and attention on one child at the sacrifice of the others, the expectation would be to attain positive results and be able to return in short course to the rest of the classroom. To focus one's energies on one child and then to see no improvement, or even perhaps to witness a deterioration of the situation, brings the teacher to the breaking point and to the previously mentioned stage of helplessness.

WHAT CAN BE DONE?

Let us attempt to answer this question honestly. A cavalry of soldiers and horses is not likely to come charging down the hill to the teacher's rescue. Unless a disruptive child suddenly moves out of town (perhaps with the teacher paying the moving expenses!), it is most likely that the child is in the teacher's classroom to stay. The guidance counselor, the school psychologist, the school nurse, and the principal may offer some help, but it is the teacher who bears the brunt of the responsibility for the child.

The teacher must call upon many internal resources and skills to deal with the situation. The teacher has been through an undergraduate teacher training program and perhaps a graduate program as well. He or she may think back to courses in child psychology or classroom management. In most cases, such courses deal with the general dimensions of children's behavior and do not offer much help in specific application. On the other hand, the teacher may have been in a program that did stress certain specific applications such as behavior modification, student-centered counseling, or value clarification. If the teacher has been trained in a specific approach, or in no approach, the same problem will still exist. The teacher has a limited range of techniques for dealing with the limitless range of behaviors in children.

The more resourceful teacher who is aware of his or her limitations will try to extend his or her "bag of tricks" by keeping current on the latest expert advice. The teacher may browse through a bookstore for professionals or talk with colleagues about the newest approach. More than likely (as evidenced by the huge number of books sold), a glossy paperback will be purchased— one that gives assurance on its cover of providing "the answer" to working with children. Whether that book is entitled *T.E.T.: Teacher Effectiveness Training*, *Discipline Without Tears*, *Schools Without Failure*, *Transactional Analysis*, *Behavior Modification*, or is some other popular book, the teacher will have in hand a concrete approach to use. Again, however, the teacher remains limited. The specific approach that is read about and then implemented may or may not work. *The reason the newly learned technique may not work is that such popular books espouse one approach to working with all children.* It is our conviction that children are different and what works for one child will not be the same as the approach that works for another.

For this reason, what we will attempt to do in this book is to provide teachers with a practical demonstration and illustration of each of the major approaches to working with disruptive children. We do this by providing an eclectic *Teacher Behavior Continuum* (TBC) that encompasses all of the various behaviors and shows how the continuum can be used in different ways for different youngsters. In other words, our purpose is to acquaint the teacher fully with what is now known about working with today's children. In so doing, we hope to replace existing feelings of helplessness and not knowing what to do with a particular troublesome child with the sense of confidence and professionalism that emerges when one knows of the spectrum of strategies available and is thus able to make a suitable decision for each child.

THE TEACHER AS A PROFESSIONAL

As we have mentioned, ours is not a "how to" book in the sense of giving a teacher a step-by-step approach to be slavishly followed when dealing with disruptive children. Our definition of professionalism is crucial for understanding how this book is to be used. We define a professional as one who gathers information about a problem, has a knowledge base of possible alternative strategies, is aware of the consequences of employing each strategy, and then chooses the strategy that is most logically appropriate. This process stems from an underlying belief structure or philosophy pertaining to long-range goals for children.

We realize that this definition sounds rather vague, so we will try to apply it by looking at how a "professional" teacher would attack the problem created by a disruptive child. First, he or she would compile information on the nature of the student and the specific behaviors exhibited by the child. Secondly, this information would be checked against a spectrum of alternative ways to approach the student. The teacher would then carefully match each approach with what the predicted outcomes and consequences would be. This would be followed by choosing the most congruent approach. Finally, the teacher would use that approach only as a temporary stage of action, and would plan further steps leading to his or her ideal of how children should eventually be treated in the classroom setting.

To clarify our definition of "professional" further, we will contrast it with the term "technician," and show how a book written for technicians would be quite different. A "technician" is an individual trained to employ one exact approach to solving a problem. A technician does not need to judge alternatives, results, or long-range goals. He or she simply needs to do what is prescribed. The techician need not speculate about consequences before acting; he or she simply needs to act. As an automobile moves down an assembly line, the "door hinge" technician needs simply to make the proper hinge placement and secure the door. The teacher-technician, when confronted by a disruptive student, simply gives the same command or takes the same action that he or she has always given or implemented.

We believe that in contrasting these two terms we have shown what we mean by a "professional" teacher. We further assume that if the reader were already a *complete* "professional" in dealing with disruptive children, he or she would have not selected this book. Obviously, it would be nice if we were all "complete," but it seems clear that the reasons to write this book do exist, as does the need for its application.

We as authors do not believe in training teachers as technicians; we believe in educating teachers as professionals. We assume, as stated earlier, that teachers need to be educated in multieclectic approaches for dealing with children in our new, diverse classroom environments. It is the teacher who knows his or her own goals better than any outside "expert" and is the one who is most competent to decide and select those strategies most suitable for specific children. We will offer guideposts and case studies, but the ultimate decision is and should be the teacher's own. When a teacher is instructed to use only one approach, it suggests a denigrated view of that individual's competence. Teachers possess the capacity to make decisions from alternatives. Often, all that is lacking is the information about alternatives. This lack is created by the reluctance of the "experts" to give teachers credit for the ability to decide for themselves. Most experts try to force-feed their approach as the "right" one, and in so doing, they degrade both teachers and others who espouse different approaches. Fritz Redl criticized the experts in this way:

> All sides have pitched "belief" versus "belief," leaving the classroom teacher alone on the job in the process. Well, then, why the heck don't we forget about our theoretical disputes or convictional competitions and get together on the job?[5]

GETTING TOGETHER ON THE JOB

What this book intends to do is treat teachers as professionals in exploring the very troublesome area of classroom discipline and student management. We will discuss in Section One the *Teacher Behavior Continuum* (TBC) and various operating models of discipline. In Section Two, we will provide four ways to make decisions about which behaviors, techniques, and skills to use. In Section Three, classroom management will be studied. It's time for us all "to get together on the job" to help students.

NOTES

1. National Education Association, *Status of the American Public School Teacher 1980–81* (Washington, D. C.: National Education Association, 1982), p. 74.

2. George Gallup, "The 16th Annual Gallup Poll on the Public's Attitudes Toward the Public Schools," *Phi Delta Kappan*, September 1984, pp. 23–28.

3. "Special Issue: The Problems of Discipline and Violence in American Education," *Phi Delta Kappan*, January 1978.

4. Alfred Bloch, MD, "The Battered Teacher," *Today's Education*, March–April 1977, pp. 58–62.

5. Fritz Redl and David Wineman, *When We Deal With Children: Selected Writings* (New York: Free Press, 1972), p. 259.

Introduction: Teacher Beliefs on Discipline

The following ten chapters will explore three distinct schools of thought and eight operational models of discipline. Before reading about the various approaches and models, the reader may find it helpful to clarify his or her own beliefs.

Beliefs on Discipline Inventory*

This inventory is designed for teachers to assess their own beliefs on classroom discipline. It enables teachers to assess to what extent they believe in the Human Relations—Listening; Confronting-Contracting; and/or Rules/Rewards-Punishment approach to discipline. Our hypothesis is that teachers believe and act according to all three approaches of discipline, yet usually one predominates in their beliefs and actions.

Forced Choices

Instructions: Select either A or B. You may not completely agree with either choice, but choose the one that is closer to how you feel.

1. A. Although children think, the decisions they make are not yet fully rational and moral.
   B. Students' inner emotions and decision-making processes must always be considered legitimate and valid.
2. A. Generally, I assign students to specific areas or seats in the classroom.
   B. Generally, my seating (or work area) assignments are open to negotiation.
3. A. No matter how limited the students' opportunities may be, students should still be given the responsibility to choose and make decisions.
   B. Teachers need to realize that, in addition to their effect on students during school hours, students are greatly influenced by their own families, the neighborhoods where they live, their peers, and television.
4. When the high noise level in a classroom bothers me, I will more likely:
   A. Discuss my discomfort with the students and attempt to come to a compromise about noise levels during activity periods.

*Developed by Roy T. Tamashiro, Webster College, and Carl D. Glickman, University of Georgia

B. Allow the activity to continue as long as the noise is not disturbing or upsetting any student.

5. If a student breaks a classmate's portable tape player that the classmate brought to school, I, the teacher, will more likely:
   A. Scold both students, one for disrespecting other people's property, and the other for breaking a rule that prohibits bringing radios and tape players to school.
   B. Avoid interfering in something that the students (and possibly their parents) need to resolve themselves.

6. If students unanimously agree that a classroom rule is unjust and should be removed, but I, the teacher, disagree with them, then:
   A. The rule should probably be removed and replaced by a rule made by the students.
   B. The students and I should jointly decide on a fair rule.

7. When a student does not join in a group activity:
   A. The teacher should explain the value of the activity to the student and encourage the student to participate.
   B. The teacher should attempt to identify the student's reasons for not joining and should create opportunities that respond to those reasons.

8. During the first week of class, I will more likely:
   A. Let the students interact freely and let the students initiate any rule making.
   B. Announce the classroom rules and inform students how the rules will be fairly enforced.

9. A. The students' creativity and self-expression should be encouraged and nurtured as much as possible.
   B. Limits on destructive behaviors need to be set without denying students their sense of choice and decision.

10. If a student interrupts my lesson by talking to a neighbor, I will more likely:
    A. Move the first students away from the others and continue the lesson because time should not be wasted on account of one individual.
    B. Tell students how angry I feel and conduct a dialogue about how the first students would feel about being interrupted.

11. A. A good educator is firm but fair in taking disciplinary action on violators of school rules.
    B. A good educator discusses several alternative disciplinary actions with the student who violates a school rule.

12. When one of the more conscientious students does not complete an assignment on time:
    A. I will assume the student has a legitimate reason and that the student will turn in the assignment when she or he completes it.
    B. I will tell the student that she or he was expected to turn in the assignment when it was due, and then, with the student, we will decide on the next steps.

Scoring Key and Interpretation

Circle your responses on the following table and tally the totals in each table:

Table I		Table II		Table III	
2A	1A	4B	1B	2B	4A
3B	5A	6A	5B	3A	6B
7A	8B	9A	8A	7B	9B
11A	10A	12A	10B	11B	12B

Total number of responses in Table I _____
Total number of responses in Table II _____
Total number of responses in Table III _____

A high percentage of responses in Table I represents a leaning towards the Rules/Rewards-Punishment approach to discipline; in Table II, towards the Human Relatons–Listening approach; and in Table III, towards the Confronting-Contracting approach to discipline.

By examining which table contains the largest number of responses, you can identify the approach to discipline that dominates your beliefs. The table with the second largest total of responses represents your second most prominent belief. Of course, the table with the fewest total responses represents the discipline approach that you least believe in.

If you have an equal number of responses in each table (or close to equal), this may indicate that your approach to discipline is eclectic rather than clearly identified with any one of the discipline models.

Naturally, this brief summary is not definitive. However, it ought to give you a general picture of how strongly you believe in each of these three discipline approaches.

With a clarification of your own beliefs in hand, you may now want to read about how these beliefs are translated into discipline actions.

2

Beyond Theory to
Classroom Practice

        To know fully what one does as a teacher, one needs to understand the framework and consequences of behavior. Different teacher behaviors are compatible or incompatible with certain psychological theories. A teacher who chooses a certain behavioral strategy with students should be aware of the underlying psychological consequences of that choice. All too often, we unwittingly practice behaviors that are contrary to our own beliefs. Unless we behave towards students in ways that are reasonably compatible with our own values and ideals, we are working at cross purposes with our inner selves. In other words, what we desire in student behavior will not materialize until we choose those strategies that are most consistent with our own beliefs in achieving those ends. We cannot possibly know what is most congruent in these contexts until we understand the psychological basis for each of our actions. Therefore, we have a vital need for a psychological perspective in knowing what approaches to use.

        This may sound rather abstract, but let us personalize the discussion. One of us was a teacher of sixth-grade students in a small, rural potato-farming community in New England. (To simplify matters, we will refer to this individual in the third person.) All through teacher-preparation courses, he had learned to value student independence and problem solving. When it came to behavior, he believed that children should learn self-discipline and should be free to choose their own courses of action. All of this sounds fine, but within weeks of starting his initial teaching job, this nice, idealistic teacher was screaming his head off at students. He found himself exerting physical pressure to prevent the students from constantly moving out of their seats. The teacher was becoming more frustrated and more punitive in his behavior, while the students were raging further and further out of control. The teacher felt guilty. Something was obviously wrong, but what was it?

Unfortunately, at this time the teacher did not have enough psychological perspective to reorient his behavior. On one hand, he intrinsically valued self-discipline for children, but on the other hand he was using techniques that made it impossible to achieve self-discipline. He was taking more and more control away from the students. One may think, "The fool, why did he not use other approaches?" The answer is twofold. First, he was not totally aware of the inconsistency in his actions; secondly, even if he had been, he did not know of other, more consistent approaches. So what was he left with? He was left with a defeatist attitude and the conviction that his students simply weren't capable of controlling themselves. These feelings led to a justification for continuing to use the very teacher behaviors that made such convictions and prophecies self-fulfilling. With such teacher behavior, his students would never learn to exercise choice and independence. The infamous vicious circle was off and spinning.

HOW DOES PSYCHOLOGICAL THEORY HELP THE TEACHER?

If the teacher can view his or her own behaviors as indicative of a certain psychological position, it will help clarify the need to change either these beliefs or actions. In knowing the various major psychological theories, the teacher additionally gains a greater working knowledge of alternative approaches that he or she may use at different times in working with individual students. We should point out that we do not expect teachers always to use those behaviors that are totally consistent with their own philosophy. To expect such rigid consistency is unrealistic. Rather, we would expect teachers to use approaches drawn from various theoretical bases but eventually to move in the direction of their own beliefs, or to use approaches consistent with stages of student development.

We understand that the mere use of the terms "theory" or "psychological foundation" turns many readers off. The memories of sitting through courses dealing in theory have often been experiences of perceived irrelevance and consequential boredom. Much of what was learned in college was regurgitated on the final exam and then forgotten. This kind of experience is lamentable, as a solid grounding in educational psychology is of immediate relevance to anyone who works with children. Theories about how students learn, how they behave, the curriculum materials to be used, and the instructional methods to be employed do not originate in a vacuum. Whether we are aware of it or not, they come out of various psychological orientations. Unfortunately, the determinations about which materials, methods, and so forth that teachers use are usually made by those outside of the classroom. Decisions about these matters are usually made by commercial companies, school boards, or central office personnel. The teacher is not expected to choose but simply to practice whatever is dictated by others. The lack of teacher input in these decision-making processes is unfortunate. Often those persons outside of the student and teacher process are mandating the "what" and "how" of teaching, and are making decisions about materials and curriculum based on superficial criteria (such as cost, public appeal, popularity) without giving proper thought to the ultimate psychological outcome of their choices.

What we are proposing is that, at least in the realm of student management, we return the power of decision making to those on the "firing lines," the classroom teachers. To make wise choices, the teacher needs knowledge of the rudimentary psychological underpinnings of the alternatives. With this in mind, we invite the reader to follow us through a simplified discussion of psychological theories of child development.

THREE SCHOOLS OF THOUGHT

We have taken various psychological interpretations of child development and categorized them into three basic beliefs:

1. The child develops from an inner unfolding of potential.
2. The child develops as a result of external conditions.
3. The child develops from the interaction of inner and outer forces.

The first explanation presupposes that the child has an inner drive that needs to find its expression in the real world. The second explanation disavows any such inner force and instead emphasizes what the outer environment (of people and objects) does to the human organism to cause it to develop in its peculiar way. The third explanation presupposes that internal and external forces are constantly interacting and focuses on what the individual does to modify the external environment as well as what the external environment in return does to shape him or her.

Using these explanations of social learning, we have labeled three schools of psychological thought. They are Relationship-Listening, Confronting-Contracting, and Rules/Rewards-Punishment. The student of classical psychology may be ruminating at this point, trying to remember where in his or her studies have such psychological schools of thought been encountered. The answer is simple. They probably haven't been. These terms and categories, although not entirely original, have been so identified by us to give clarity to the practical applications of teacher behaviors that will be described later. To reassure the bewildered psychology student, the more familiar schools of psychological thought will be found in our subsequent explanations.

Relationship-Listening

Relationship-Listening encompasses humanistic and psychoanalytical thought. These psychologists share a belief in the inner person. The humanists believe that within every child is an inner rationality which is constantly striving to improve that child.

As Carl Rogers, who is perhaps the most popular proponent of the humanist movement, has written:

> Human beings have a natural potential for learning . . . this potentiality and desire for learning, for discovery, for enlargement of knowledge and experience can be released under suitable conditions. It is a tendency which can be trusted, and the whole approach to education . . . builds upon and around the student's natural desire to learn.[1]

The psychoanalysts might find themselves feeling uncomfortable being grouped with the humanists, but their founder Sigmund Freud was a pioneer of the "inner person" concept. The psychoanalysts, however, do interpret these inner elements quite differently from the humanists. They believe that instinctual inner drives can be destructive and must be raised to a conscious level in order for the individual person to channel and control these forces in a constructive manner.

Briefly, we can conclude that Relationship-Listening advocates agree that the child's outward behavior should not be the primary focus for understanding his or her development. Instead they look to inner feelings. Behavior is only symptomatic of inner processes. Any increased growth is found in facilitating expression of those inner dynamics.

Rules/Rewards-Punishment

Rules/Rewards-Punishment encompasses experimental behaviorist psychologies. These psychologists hold to the premise that human development can be explained through an understanding of the quantity and quality of external stimulation. They believe observable behavior is the only key to understanding a person's social growth and that adjustment in human behavior comes about through the changes in outside conditions. (To them, there simply is no inner or emotional dimension to human growth.) As B. F. Skinner, the leader of behavioristic theory, wrote:

> An experimental analysis shifts the determination of behavior from autonomous man (free to decide for himself) to the environment—an environment responsible both for the evolution of species and for the repertoire acquired by each member. . . . It is the autonomous inner man who is abolished and that is a step forward.[2]

Confronting-Contracting

The Confronting-Contracting school of thought includes practitioners of social, gestalt, and developmental psychologies. Although they may differ in their particular emphasis, they all concur that an explanation of development must take into account a multitude of factors. The whole child can only be understood by the interrelationship of all the parts. A child must be viewed as part of his or her total environment, in terms of what goes on both internally and externally. Growth is seen as a result of the constant interplay between child and society. Jerome Bruner, America's foremost cognitive developmentalist, wrote:

> One finds no internal push to growth without a corresponding external pull, for, given the nature of man as species, growth is as dependent upon a link with external amplifiers of man's powers as it is upon those powers themselves.[3]

Similarly, Alfred Adler, with his emphasis on living in a group, described the socialization process this way:

> We always come upon the outstanding fact that throughout the whole period of development, the child possesses a feeling of inferiority in its relations both to parents and the world at large . . . this feeling of inferiority is the cause of his continual restlessness as a child, his craving for action, his playing of roles, and pitting of his strength against that of others. . .[4]

Both Bruner and Adler take note of the dynamics that occur between child and environment. Bruner refers to external amplifiers; Adler refers to the world of other people.

GUIDELINES FOR CLASSROOM PRACTICE: THE TEACHER'S ROLE

Our terms Relationship-Listening, Confronting-Contracting, and Rules/Rewards-Punishment should become clearer as we describe the popular applications of the various psychologies of social learning theory to the classroom. Writers who share the common assumptions within each of our three categories propose different roles for the teacher in relation to his or her troublesome student. Relationship-Listening writers emphasize the role of the teacher as being supportive to the student's own attempts at problem solving. Confronting-Contracting writers emphasize a parity relationship between teacher and student in arriving at joint solutions. Rules/Rewards-Punishment writers stress the role of the teacher as planner and organizer of the environment for shaping the student's behavior.

Relationship-Listening

Relationship-Listening proponents have an abiding faith in the student as master of his or her own destiny. The function of the teacher is to provide a facilitating environment so that children can give vent and free expression to their feelings. The teacher empathizes with the child as he or she wrestles with inner emotions. This view is evident in the writings of Carl Rogers *(Freedom to Learn)*;[5] Virginia Axline *(Play Therapy)*;[6] Clark Moustakas *(The Authentic Teacher)*;[7] Thomas Gordon *(Teacher Effectiveness Training)*;[8] Thomas Harris *(I'm OK—You're OK)*;[9] and Louis Raths, Merrill Harmin, and Sidney Simon *(Values and Teaching)*.[10]

Clark Moustakas expressed this application of beliefs when he wrote:

> Personal interaction between teacher and child means that differences in children are recognized and valued. . . . Relations must be such that the child is free to recognize, express, actualize, and experience his own uniqueness. Teachers help to make this possible when they show they deeply care for the child, respect his individuality, and accept the child's being without qualification.[11]

The Relationship-Listening advocates believe in a supportive, facilitating environment where the teacher is present to accept and empathize with the student in his or her inner struggle.

Confronting-Contracting

In this view, the child is not seen as developing solely from either inward unfolding or from the conditioning of outside forces. Instead, it is felt that development occurs with the simultaneous pushes and pulls from within and without. Boundaries must be established and students must be made aware of behaviors from others that enhance or detract from their functioning in society.

The role of the teacher is to be one of constant interaction with the child. He or she allows freedom of behaviors up to a circumscribed point. A child who transgresses acceptable boundaries then comes into conflict with the teacher. The teacher takes command and jointly forces a mutually acceptable resolution. This theoretical view is broadly evident in the writings of Rudolf Dreikurs (*Discipline Without Tears*, 1972)[12] and William Glasser (*Schools Without Failure*, 1969).[13]

Dreikurs's work (1972) is indicative of the interactionalists' position. He stated:

> Conflicts cannot be resolved without shared responsibility, without full participation in decision-making of all the participants in a conflict. Democracy does not mean that everybody can do as he pleases. It requires leadership to integrate and to win mutual consent.[14]

The Confronting-Contracting theory of coping with child behavior is based on the teacher being able to assume the role of a clarifier, a boundary delineator, and finally an enforcer. These theorists believe that children should take responsibility for their actions but need the active involvement of a kind but firm teacher. The child and/or teacher may decide on the remedy. Regardless of action, a solution acceptable to all must result.

Rules/Rewards-Punishment

The Rules/Rewards-Punishment writers share the assumption that a child develops according to the conditions of his or her environment. It is only with the implementation of a logical system of conditioning serving as reinforcement that socialized behavior can be assured.

The teacher is thus the controller of the environment. His or her task is to select the appropriate conditioners in direct commands, positive and negative reinforcements, and/or concrete punishments to insure the proper learning behavior. Examples of such theory are evident in the writings of James Dobson (Dare to Discipline);[15] Lloyd Homme (How to Use Contingency Contracting in the Classroom);[16] Garth Blackham and Adolph Silberman (Modification of Child and Adolescent Behavior);[17] Siegfried Engelmann (Preventing Failure in the Primary Grades);[18] Saul Axelrod (Behavior Modification for the Classroom Teacher);[19] Charles Madsen and Clifford Madsen (Teaching Discipline);[20] and Lee Canter and Marlene Canter (Assertive Discipline).[21]

Saul Axelrod (1977) echoes the Rules/Rewards-Punishment point of view. He wrote:

> By accepting a position as a teacher, a person has not only a right but an "obligation" to modify student behavior. Children enter the schools without the necessary social and academic skills to function independently and productively in adult society. . . . Teachers who do not bring about suitable changes in student behavior are failing to live up to the responsibilities of the profession.[22]

There is no recognition of either the child's inner emotions or the child's capability of rational decision making. The teacher takes command over the child's disruptive actions and makes immediate use of directive techniques to channel the child into constructive behavior. In order to keep a child learning efficiently, misbehavior is dealt with by selective reinforcement until the undesirable behavior is extinguished and the desired behavior is obtained. The split in this school of thought is between those who advocate control of behavior by use of positive and negative reinforcement alone and those who advocate the additional use of punishment.

TEACHER BEHAVIOR: THE USE OF POWER

After years of observing teacher behavior, we have found seven typical techniques that teachers utilize in dealing with misbehavior.[23] If you were to reflect on your own classroom experiences as a teacher, you might be able to identify your own immediate response to sudden misbehavior. Whether it is a book flying over your head, a scuffle, or abusive language, you probably would react in some of the following ways:

Silently Looking On: Some teachers 1) simply look over at the offender as if to say, "I see what you're doing but I know that you can take care of yourself," 2) observe the behavior and collect information on the entire situation before acting, or 3) gaze directly at the student with a penetrating frown.

Nondirective Statements: Some teachers immediately reflect the episode back to the student ("John, I saw you throw the book"; or "You must be angry to throw that book";), or they reflect internally about what their next steps should be.

Questions: Other teachers react with such questions as, "What do you think you're doing?" or "Jimmy, why are you doing that?"

Directive Statements: The habitual response of many teachers is immediately to correct the child with such statements as "Stop that," "Get back into your seat," or "Don't do that again!"

Modeling: There are teachers who react to disruptive situations by moving over to the student, taking him or her by the arm, returning with the student to his or her seat and concretely showing the student what he or she should be doing. For example, the teacher opens the book to the correct page, puts the pencil in the student's hand, and begins to work on the next problem. Other teachers might elect to point out a well-behaved student as an example to be followed.

Reinforcement: Some teachers attempt to ignore the disruptive behavior and reward the student's next appropriate behavior with praise or privileges. Other teachers will punish the student by removing privileges, sending a note home, and so forth.

Physical Intervention and Isolation: Teachers who have experienced much frustration often will physically remove the student from the situation. This is done by isolating a student to a place in the room or out in the hall. Some teachers exert physical pressure by grabbing, shaking, or paddling the student.

We could categorize behaviors in other ways, but for purposes of this book we believe that these seven categories encompass most of the individual variations of teacher action. A few teachers use all seven, some use four or five, and many use only two or three.

The seven behaviors have been listed in a purposeful way. After delineating these seven behaviors, the authors noted that each behavior reflects a certain power relationship between teacher and student. Some teacher behaviors obviously provide the student with a great amount of time and opportunity for self-improvement. Other behaviors clearly give the teacher immediate control over the student. With these differences in mind, we conceptualized a power continuum. At one end of the continuum, strategies are used whereby the child has the most control of his or her behavior and the teacher has minimal control (this has been illustrated by the use of a capital *C* for child and a lowercase *t* for teacher); in the middle and at the other end of the continuum, the teacher subsumes the child's power (note the use of a lowercase *c* and a capital *T*). The seven teacher behaviors are inserted along this continuum as shown in Figure 2–1.

The reader can see how teacher behaviors such as silently looking on and nondirective statements will encourage the child to find his or her own solutions, while behaviors such as questions, directive statements, and modeling tend to diminish the child's control and increase the teacher's power until finally modeling, reinforcement, and physical intervention move the source of power from the child and give it fully to the teacher. Therefore, what we have is a continuum of teacher behaviors that reflects a graduated scale of teacher control.

Now here comes the tricky part, so read carefully! As stated earlier, in describing major psychological theories of managing children, we have found and identified three distinct perspectives of the developing child. These are Relationship-Listening advocates, who believe that the child develops by having a supportive environment that encourages his or her own problem solving; the Confronting-Contracting advocates, who believe that a child develops through a constant give-and-take relationship with others; and the Rules/Rewards-Punishment advocates, who believe that the child develops only by the conditioning of outside forces. Therefore, the application of these various theories emphasizes teacher behaviors that reflect the corresponding degrees of power possessed by child and teacher. The Relationship-Listeners stress the use of teacher behaviors on the left of our

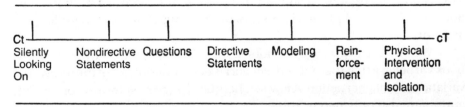

FIGURE 2–1. Teacher Behavior Continuum (TBC)

continuum, the Confronting-Contractors stress teacher behaviors that cluster in the middle, and on the right side the Rules/Rewarders-Punishers see the teacher as having maximum power over the students' actions. This is illustrated with writers in Figure 2–2.

The techniques or methods imbedded in each major psychological school of thought can be understood accordingly. At the child-centered end of the continuum, the Relationship-Listeners use minimal teacher power. The teacher uses an empathetic glance and reflective questions. The teacher utilizes only supportive and accepting behavior towards the child in order to maximize the chances of a child working through his or her own misbehavior.

The Confronting-Contractors have the teacher move in more boldly by the act of drawing attention to the behavior through nondirective statements, questions, and directive statements. They strive for a solution wherein the teacher and child attempt to find an integrative answer to the inappropriate behavior. Confronting-Contractors employ some of the techniques of the Relationship-Listeners and Rules/Rewarders-Punishers, but they are wary of any unilateral control of behavior by either student or teacher.

On the teacher-centered end of the continuum, the Rules/Rewarders-Punishers have the teacher take control of the situation. The student corrects his or her behavior as the result of commands, explicit teacher modeling, rewards, and/or being physically restrained or isolated. In all, the Rules/

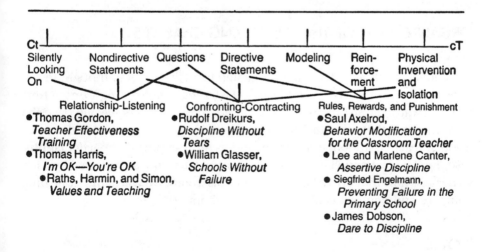

FIGURE 2–2.   Teacher Behavior Continuum (TBC)

Rewarders-Punishers look for a tangible and immediate way to correct the misbehavior of the student.

Although these are somewhat simplistic explanations, the Teacher Behavior Continuum (TBC) will provide the reader with a "handle" for understanding the following sections, where detailed explanations of some of the most popular student-management approaches will be provided. The TBC also establishes a framework for a teacher to reflect on his or her own teacher behaviors and to compare the TBC with one's personal belief about children and their development.

Most of the popular approaches address in some way all seven behaviors on our continuum, and we will include an explanation of how each behavior is portrayed within those contexts. Some specific teacher behaviors from the TBC will prove to be more vital tools than others for a teacher implementing a specific approach. Often, those behaviors that are not central to a specific application are given very different interpretations by that individual. For example, the Relationship-Listeners stress silently looking on, nondirective statements, and questions, yet they also speak of modeling, reinforcement, isolation, and physical intervention. However, they explain these latter behaviors quite differently from the interpretations heeded by the Confronting-Contractors and Rules/Rewarders-Punishers. For each popular application and its aligned proponents we will go through the seven teacher behaviors of the continuum and show specific strategies and interpretations, and thus permit the highlighting and comparison of each model.

ORGANIZATION OF THE FOLLOWING CHAPTERS

What follows will be a delineation devoted to each school of thought in the next three chapters; i.e., Relationship-Listening, Confronting-Contracting, Rules/Rewards-Punishment. Within each of these chapters we will describe in some detail the actual techniques suggested by two (or more) of the more popular teacher-student interactive models representing that particular philosophy. The reader will be shown the central techniques suggested by each writer and how they are to be used in the classroom. We will at the same time compare and contrast each model with others.

NOTES

1. Carl Rogers, *Freedom to Learn* (Columbus: Charles E. Merrill Publishing, 1969), pp. 157–58.

2. B. F. Skinner, *Beyond Freedom and Dignity* (New York: Knopf, 1971), pp. 214–15.

3. Jerome S. Bruner et al., *Studies in Cognitive Growth* (New York: John Wiley and Sons, 1966), p. 6.

4. Alfred Adler, *The Practice and Theory of Individual Psychology* (Totowa, New Jersey: Littlefield Adams, 1972), p. 33.

5. Rogers, *Freedom to Learn*.

6. Virginia M. Axline, *Play Therapy* (New York: Ballantine Books, 1969).

7. Clark Moustakas, *The Authentic Teacher* (Cambridge, Massachusetts: Howard A. Doyle Publishing, 1972).

8. Thomas Gordon, *T.E.T.: Teacher Effectiveness Training* (New York: Peter H. Wyden Publishing, 1974).

9. Thomas A. Harris, *I'm OK—You're OK: A Practical Guide to Transactional Analysis* (New York: Harper & Row, Publishers, 1969).

10. Louis E. Raths, Merrill Harmin, and Sidney B. Simon, *Values and Teaching: Working with Values in the Classroom* (Columbus: Charles E. Merrill Publishing, 1966).

11. Moustakas, *The Authentic Teacher*, p. 31.

12. Rudolf Dreikurs and Pearl Cassel, *Discipline Without Tears* (New York: Hawthorn Books, 1972).

13. William Glasser, *Schools Without Failure* (New York: Peter H. Wyden Publishing, 1969).

14. Dreikurs and Cassel, *Discipline Without Tears*, p. 71.

15. James Dobson, *Dare to Discipline* (Wheaton, Illinois: Tyndale House Publishing, 1970).

16. Lloyd Homme, *How to Use Contingency Contracting in the Classroom* (Champaign, Illinois: Research Press, 1970).

17. Garth J. Blackham and Adolph Silberman, *Modification of Child and Adolescent Behavior*, 2nd ed. (Belmont, California: Wadsworth Publishing, 1975).

18. Siegfried Engelmann, *Preventing Failure in the Primary Grades* (New York: Simon and Schuster, 1969).

19. Saul Axelrod, *Behavior Modification for the Classroom Teacher* (New York: McGraw-Hill, 1977).

20. Charles H. Madsen and Clifford K. Madsen, *Teaching Discipline: A Positive Approach for Educational Development*, 2nd ed. (Boston: Allyn and Bacon, 1974).

21. Lee Canter and Marlene Canter, *Assertive Discipline: A Take-Charge Approach for Today's Educator* (Seal Beach, California: Canter and Associates, 1976).

22. Axelrod, *Behavior Modification*, p. 158.

23. Charles F. Wolfgang, *Helping Aggressive and Passive Preschoolers Through Play*. (Columbus: Charles E. Merrill Publishing, 1977).

3

The Supportive Model: Gordon's Teacher Effectiveness Training

The scene is a fifth-grade classroom after school dismissal, and one child has remained behind. He approaches the teacher.

Student: "I hate this school!"

Teacher: "School is making you very unhappy."

Student: "Yes. I'm going to go back to my old school."

Teacher: "You're unhappy with this new school and you would like to go back to your old one."

Student: "Yeah, I never get to play. Every recess Tommy and Jeff pick the team, and they never pick me. No one likes me in this 'dumb' school."

Teacher: "You don't get picked for the teams and it makes you feel that no one likes you."

Student: "Bill and Mike don't get to play either. And we are going to get that ball first, and we won't let anyone else play! But, we tried that yesterday and Jeff knocked us down and took the ball—and, you know, the playground teacher wouldn't do anything about it! If I brought my ball from home they wouldn't do that!"

Teacher: "The other boys take the school ball away from you and they would not be allowed to do that if the ball was yours."

Student: "Yes. Could I bring my ball from home to use?"

Teacher: "Yes, if you think that would help."

Student: "Then I can start my own team and not let Tom and Jeff play!"

Teacher: "You could start your own team and not let Tom and Jeff play."

Student: "Well, I would, if they let me pitch."

"Douglas, what I think I hear you saying . . . "

John Anfin, from *Phi Delta Kappan*

This dialogue is an example of one child's attempt to adjust and find his place in a new school, and it is typical of hundreds of similar problems that students bring to teachers. We see the teacher using the techniques suggested in Thomas Gordon's problem-resolution model called *T.E.T.: Teacher Effectiveness Training*. The teacher did not advise, judge, or criticize this child on how to solve the problem, but instead simply listened carefully to the child's statements, appeared interested, and showed understanding of the student by mirroring the student's feelings and perceptions. Each time the student spoke, more of what was bothering him emerged and the parameters of his problem became clearer. Intellectually the child explored ways of solving his problem and finally was able to decide on a course of action. The *T.E.T.* techniques provide many helpful tools for the classroom teacher, and it will be our purpose to explore the theoretical roots and principles of such an approach and then show how these techniques relate directly to our own Teacher Behavior Continuum.

GORDON AND ROGERIAN THEORY

T.E.T.: Teacher Effectiveness Training,[1] created by Thomas Gordon, is based on a school of thought first conceptualized and popularized by Carl Rogers in his books entitled, *Client-Centered Therapy*,[2] *On Becoming a Person*,[3] and

Freedom to Learn.[4] Rogers's therapeutic concepts were a departure from the highly deterministic Freudian psychology therapy of innate inner aggressive drives. Although the belief in the inner person remained, Rogers did not accept the position that the child is inherently ruled by destructive forces. Instead, he aligned with A. H. Maslow's belief that the child is born "prior to good and evil,"[5] a belief that would suggest that what a child grows to become will be a summation or embodiment of the child's experiences. The child does have an inherent capacity, but it is a capacity of being rational and capable. Rogers believes that given empathetic understanding, warmth, and openness one will choose what is best for oneself and will become a fully functioning person, constructive and trustworthy. The child is seen as "exquisitely rational," and it is believed that problems arise from the conflict that occurs when that inherent rationality is stifled. It is felt that this "stifling" happens in the classroom when teachers set about to order, direct, or force a student to behave according to the teacher's will.

The underlying assumption of Rogerian theory is that each person is unique and thus it is impossible for one person to make appropriate decisions for another. Any two people in a given situation will experience that situation in different ways. This is because we experience and interpret stimuli based on our prior encounters, goals, expectations, and attitudes. Each person will "screen" the event according to who he or she is as a person, and this screening, to a great extent, occurs at the unconscious level. Life, then, according to Rogerian theory, is a process of continually changing situations and continually changing problems in which we must make a multitude of decisions based on our individual experiences and perceptions. Many of these factors about making decisions ourselves are hidden from our consciousness. Therefore, within the Rogerian theoretical framework the process or goal for the individual experiencing problems is consciously to process his or her difficulties through the vehicle of language. By expressing one's feelings and concerns, an individual can make decisions that will result in the most appropriate rational solution.

Let's return to our earlier example of the student who "hates school." This first expression of "I hate this school!" was just the tip of the iceberg. Underneath there was a collection of fears and disappointments. "I hate school" might be more adequately interpreted as a message reading, "Dear Teacher, I'm very unhappy in this school because I have problems. Will you listen to me and help me?" The Rogerian teacher hears this wider message and does not fall into the trap of denying the child's underlying message by lecturing or advising the student; i.e., "Oh, come on, this is one of the best schools in the state. You ought to appreciate what you have and how lucky you are!" or, "Well, young man, that attitude will never do. You must change your behavior if you want to get along here."

The teacher, as we saw, took an empathic, nonjudgmental position and simply mirrored the student's statements. This mirroring enabled the student to feel that the teacher followed what he was saying, that not only was he being permitted to talk but that he was being encouraged to continue and to expand on his feelings and ideas. The teacher believed that, given a supportive climate, the student would be able to express his problem(s) and feeling(s), and then suggest his own solutions. Whether the solutions are successful or not is not as important as the student being able to trust his own capacities to master his problems eventually.

This theory holds that a faith in one's own problem-solving capacity relates directly to the idea of "self-concept." Self-concept can be defined as a set of ideas that one holds about oneself as a person. You may see yourself as basically competent or incompetent in meeting life's continual challenges. It is only with the opportunity to wrestle with your own daily problems that you become master of your own destiny. In the "I hate school" example, the child has been able to enhance his self-concept by realizing that he can define his own problems and make attempts to solve them. If the teacher had lectured or advised the student, the opposite effect might have occurred and the child's self-concept would have been weakened in the process.

Based on this theoretical position, the teacher's role is primarily one of being a supportive, noncritical facilitator with a total commitment to the rational ability of a child to identify and solve his or her own unique problems. With this understanding we may now turn to the techniques of Thomas Gordon and observe how he has operationalized Rogerian theory into specific teacher practices, as described in *T.E.T.: Teacher Effectiveness Training*. We will follow Gordon's procedures, using the Teacher Behavior Continuum (TBC) as our organizer in comparing the central elements or behaviors. Again, please keep in mind that these behaviors are (1) silently looking on, (2) nondirective statements, (3) questions, (4) directive statements, (5) reinforcement, (6) modeling, and (7) physical intervention and isolation. As previously stated, the ranked order of these behaviors suggests an increasing use of power by the teacher and a decrease on the part of the student. It should be obvious that, given Gordon's theoretical framework, he will stress those behaviors (1, 2, and 3) that give most control to the child. With this in mind, let us begin.

T.E.T. AND THE TEACHER BEHAVIOR CONTINUUM

Silently Looking On

Central to the *T.E.T.* model is the expression of open and authentic communication between teacher and student. By definition, the word "communication" suggests an exchange of ideas between people. Obviously, there is a difference between talking and hearing versus communicating. Communicating is a process whereby each party understands what the other has to say and formulates responsive messages in a way to create further understanding. Of course, all teachers will "hear" what a child says. The child who screams an obscenity is clearly heard, but, according to Gordon, the child is often not understood in terms of the meaning of the "real" message and the impact of strong feelings being expressed. Stress is placed on the teacher to use the least control possible in the process of understanding a student. That minimal control is described as *silently looking on* as the teacher *critically listens* to what a student is trying to say.

The first step on the Teacher Behavior Continuum is for the teacher simply to look at a misbehaving child. The look should be one of saying, "I see what you are doing. I have trust in your ability to correct yourself. If you need my help, I am here." The student who cannot achieve his or her own immediate solution to the problem should then be encouraged to verbalize the issue. The teacher gives the student much time and encouragement to express what is troubling him or her, with the teacher nodding or using various gestures to encourage the child to continue.

Student: "Janie is a stuck-up snob. She wouldn't go to the game with us!"
Teacher: "Uh-huh." (Teacher nods while looking at the child.)

Gordon, in *T. E. T.: Teacher Effectiveness Training*, states, "Saying nothing actually communicates acceptance. Silence—critical listening—is a powerful nonverbal message that can make a student feel genuinely accepted and encourages him to share more and more with you. A student cannot talk to you about what is bothering him if you are doing the talking."[6]

Questioning (Skipping Nondirective Statements Temporarily)

At times while students are talking to us, they seem to have trouble beginning, or, once started, they pause in the middle of what they are saying and cannot appear to get started again. In these instances, it may be necessary to use what Gordon called "door openers or reopeners." Examples would be such questions as "I'm interested, would you like to talk more about that?" or "Would you like to go on?" Such "door openers" (questions) are of a non-evaluative nature. They encourage the student to explore his or her feelings more fully.

Teacher: "Hello, Tommy. I think I see a worried look on your face. Would you like to talk about it?" (This is the use of *questioning* as a "door opener.")

Student: "Someone stole my pencil. This has happened three times this week!"

Teacher: "*Uh-huh.*" (Nods while *silently looking on*—critical listening.)

Using these supportive questions as "door openers" is quite different from using those kinds of questions that Gordon calls "roadblocks to communication." The latter are questions that probe, crossexamine, or accuse and are of little help to a student trying to find his or her own solutions. For example, "How much time did you spend on this project?" or "Did you ask permission before you did that?" are all questions that impose the teacher's will and dominance. These are really camouflaged directive statements that say, "You are wrong. You need me to tell you what to do." Gordon is adamantly opposed to the use of questions or direct statements that diminish the student's capacity to alter rationally his or her own behavior. On the other hand, making nondirective statements is seen as a more active way of helping the student.

Nondirective Statements

The question now arises as to exactly how we can use language to communicate with students most effectively. The most important use of language by the teacher within the *T.E.T.* model is called "active listening." To employ silence, to acknowledge responses by silently looking on, or to use "door openers" as questions has a positive but limited use and, in general, reflects passive behavior on the teacher's part. Effective communication between teacher and student involves a much more *active* response by the teacher through "active listening" and the use of *nondirective statements*. The teacher can actively communicate to the student that he or she is being understood by summarizing or mirroring the student's feelings or problems as the teacher comprehends them.

It may be helpful to look more closely to see how true communication really works, or, in short, "Why people talk." Gordon says that people talk when they have an internal need, either physical or emotional, and that people encode that need in the form of spoken language so that they can be understood by others. Unfortunately, many needs, especially those related to feelings, are difficult to express in language. If we return to the first example in this chapter, which begins with a student saying "I hate this school," we realize it was only after much active listening that we discovered the child's real feelings and problems. The student first attempted to "encode" his feelings by stating, "I hate this school," which was a "unique coding" and revealed only the surface of the deeper problems that he was facing. We must not take such "uniquely coded" statements at face value, but permit the child to continue expressing through language while we mirror with "active listening" (*nondirective statements*) our understanding of what the child is attempting to say. For example, a student who has just been expelled from gym class and returns to the homeroom teacher might be dealt with as follows:

Student: "I hate folk dancing . . . that sissy stuff is for girls."

Teacher: "You don't like folk dancing because you think it is sissy stuff." (*Nondirective statements* as "active listening.")

Student: "Yes. Mrs. Jones in music class makes us folk dance on Fridays."

Teacher: "Uh-huh." (Nods while *silently looking on*—"critical listening.")

Student: (Drops eyes and gives no further verbal response.)

Teacher: "Would you like to tell me more about that?" (*Questioning* as a "door opener.")

Student: "Yeah, Mrs. Jones is unfair.!"

Teacher: "Mrs. Jones has done some things that you feel are unfair." (*Nondirective statements* as "active listening.")

Student: "Yeah, she made us dance boy-girl and boy-girl, and there weren't enough girl partners and she made me be a 'girl,' and all the boys laughed."

Teacher: "You felt angry with Mrs. Jones for making you take a girl's part, and then you felt silly when the boys laughed."

In the preceding dialogue, we see the teacher helping the student express feelings that were "uniquely encoded" and unclear at first ("I hate folk dancing..."), and through "critical and active listening" the teacher finally hears the student's central problem and the feelings that were deeply troublesome.

Now that the teacher has some understanding as to what the problems of his or her student are, what should the teacher do? Should the teacher tell the student how he should respond to the music teacher? Gordon would say "no." He would describe such a response as another "roadblock," called "advising, offering solutions or suggestions."[7] Should the teacher confront the music teacher? Should the teacher call in the principal or guidance counselor? *T.E.T.* provides a helpful construct for the teacher to use in answering these questions and for defining what the teacher's response should be.

The central key to these issues in *T.E.T.* is, "Who owns the problem, the teacher or the child?" As shown in Figure 3-1, all behaviors of the student can be placed on a "window" and divided into three areas: (1) those behaviors that indicate the student is having a problem (i.e., other students will not pick him as a team member); (2) a no-problem behavior (i.e., a child works quietly at his desk); (3) those behaviors by the student that have a direct and concrete effect on the teacher, causing the teacher to "own" the problem (i.e., student interrupts while another child is being helped.)[8]

When the problem belongs to the student ("I can't find my pencil" or "Mrs. Jones won't let me do so-and-so"), the role of the teacher is to use critical listening (*silently looking on*) and "door openers" (*questions*), and to mirror periodically the child's concerns or messages with active listening (*nondirective statements*). If the problem is owned by the teacher, in that it has a concrete effect on the teacher, then he or she may introduce an "I" message. This is a matter-of-fact *directive statement* containing the word "I" that expresses to the student the description of the student's behavior and how it is having a negative effect on the teacher. It also tells the student how the teacher feels about these actions; for example: "When gym equipment is left in the aisle, I might trip, and I'm afraid I might fall and be hurt." The "I" message must contain the sequence of "behavior, effect, feeling." Once an "I" message is expressed and the student has heard how his or her behavior is interfering with the teacher's needs, the teacher returns to critical listening (*silently looking on*), active listening (*nondirective statements*), and, if need be, to using "door openers" (*questions*). The following dialogue provides examples of each of these behaviors.

Teacher: "Carol, when lunch papers are left on the table instead of being thrown away, I must pick them up before the next lunch group can be seated. I find this frustrating!" ("I" message)

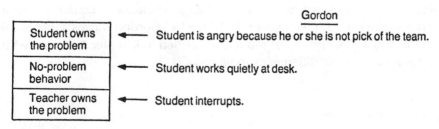

FIGURE 3-1. Problem of Ownership

Student: "I'm always getting picked on! Everyone *always* picks on me!"

Teacher: "You feel that everyone is making unfair demands on you." (active listening, *nondirective statement*)

Student: "Well, everyone picks on me."

Teacher: "Uh-huh." (critical listening, *nondirective listening*)

Student: (Silence)

Teacher: "Would you like to tell me more?" ("door openers," *questions*)

Student: "Well, Mrs. Jones makes me pass out the papers and erase the boards, and Miss Anderson makes me clean out the hamster cages three weeks in a row. And no one else gets jobs but me."

Teacher: "You feel that it is unfair for you to be given extra jobs by teachers, and therefore you do not need to clean up after yourself at lunchtime." (active listening, *nondirective statement*)

Student: "Well, it is unfair, but I guess I could throw my lunch papers away. Gee, I didn't know it was such a problem for you. But, I'm going to tell Mrs. Anderson, 'No more hamster cages for me!' "

The preceding dialogue reveals a problem clearly owned by the teacher. The student's *behavior* (leaving behind lunch papers) had a concrete effect on the teacher (the teacher had to pick them up and it interfered with her ability to seat other children), and in turn the teacher described her feelings (frustrated). We can also see that the teacher did not use any forms of power-related behavior to manipulate the outcome. After delivering an "I" message, the teacher returned the problem to the student, and the teacher maintained a nonjudgmental stance.

There are other behaviors engaged in by students about which a teacher might hold very strong feelings. However, when these are investigated closely it may be found that they do not have a concrete effect on the teacher, and then an "I" message would have little impact. How a student styles his or her hair, or the issue of wearing short dresses, or students holding hands in the halls, or poor posture, or the choosing of friends all may evoke strong feelings in a teacher, but these student behaviors involve clashes in values and cannot be said to affect the teacher directly. They are simply matters of personal taste. Gordon warns against trying to change students to conform with a teacher's values by "I" messages or "roadblocks." Gordon suggests the use of values clarification, one of our models described in Chapter 5, to deal with problems concerning differences in values.

Directive Statements

We can imagine some of our readers shaking their heads in amazement and thinking, "Do you mean to say that this fellow Gordon says for us never to tell students what to do? He must be some kind of a crazy guy!" Never fear. Actually, Gordon does believe that there are times when teachers must use very strong directive statements with students, such as the giving of orders, directions, or commands. When *directive statements* are used correctly they are described by Gordon as strong "influencing attempts" by the teacher. If a student is in some immediate danger, naturally it is appropriate for the teacher to command, "Turn down that flame, quickly, it's in danger of exploding!" or "Don't jump now, someone is climbing underneath!" or "Watch your head!" Such "influencing attempts" are generally acceptable to students, and they are willing to comply. We see no true conflict arising between teacher and student as a result. The difficulty occurs when teachers overuse commands or direct too strongly. Then, in reaction, students begin to resist and the teacher and student find themselves in conflict. When this occurs, such *directive statements* again become roadblocks, and the teacher will need to return to "active listening" to reestablish the relationship.

Gordon cites the following examples of directive statements that should be avoided by teachers.

1. *Ordering, commanding, directing.* Example: "You, stop playing with your pencil and finish that test right now."
2. *Warning, threatening.* Example: "You had better straighten up, young man, if you want to pass this course."
3. *Moralizing, preaching, giving "shoulds" and "oughts."* Example: "You know what happens when you hang around with 'that gang,' you get into trouble. You ought to choose your friends more wisely."
4. *Advising, offering solutions or suggestions.* Example: "What you need to do is to make a list and then put yourself on a time schedule to get these things done on time."
5. *Teaching, lecturing, giving logical arguments.* Example: "Let's look at what is going to happen. If you do not bring your gym clothing you will not be able to take PE and you will fail that class."

(Each of the preceding roadblocks presents a teacher's solution to a student's problem. The next five communicate judgments, evaluations, and, at times, putdowns.)

6. *Judging, criticizing, disagreeing, blaming.* Example: "You're just not the student that your sister was."
7. *Name-calling, stereotyping, labeling.* Example: "You're always acting like the class clown. When are you going to grow up?"
8. *Interpreting, analyzing, diagnosing.* Example: "You're always trying to find the easiest way to get around your homework."
9. *Praising, agreeing, giving positive evaluation.* Example: "You are the best

student I have in this class. I'm sure you will want to be chairperson of this committee."

10. *Reassuring, sympathizing, consoling, supporting.* Example: "I also found that course difficult when I first tried it, but once you get into it you'll find it easier."[9]

The last two roadblocks (numbers 9 and 10) are examples of strong reinforcing techniques that are central to some of the models that will be summarized in following chapters. It is interesting to note that certain strategies held to be of utmost importance to some experts are scorned by others. Gordon's interpretation of reinforcement must be closely read to understand the later differences with other writers.

Reinforcement

The resolution of conflict within the *T.E.T.* models relates to Gordon's definition of two types of authority and how the teacher uses his or her power with students. *Type I authority* is desirable and is based on a person's expertise, knowledge, and experiences. An individual obtains the power inherent in Type I authority by being judged as one who is wise and expert enough to be listened to by students, and is an individual sought after for advice. *Type II authority* is undesirable. It is aligned with a power-based position that enables a teacher to (1) dispense certain benefits that students need or want (reward or positive reinforcement) or (2) inflict discomfort or painless punishment on students (negative reinforcement). Later we will discuss how the Rules/Rewarders-Punishers use reinforcement and rewards as a central tool in their techniques to get students to change. The Relationship-Listener writers such as Gordon dramatically disagree with such an approach. Gordon sees the use of both positive and negative reinforcements as a manipulation and misuse of power by a teacher which will eventually produce defensive reaction mechanisms in students to deal with such authoritarian power. Gordon would suggest that if we see the following behavior in our students, we may need to investigate our use of power. These following behaviors indicate the use of Type II authority:

- rebelling, resisting, defying
- retaliating
- lying, sneaking, hiding feelings
- blaming others, tattling
- cheating, copying, plagiarizing
- bossing, bullying, pushing others around

- needing to win, hating to lose
- organizing, forming alliances
- submitting, complying, buckling under
- apple polishing
- conforming, taking no risks, trying nothing new
- withdrawing, dropping out, fantasizing, regressing[10]

Finally, even the teacher who has Type I authority and uses silently looking on, nondirective statements, door openers, and "I" statements will still run into conflict with an individual child. The occasions will be less frequent but still inevitable. The *T.E.T.* model provides a resolution for such conflict. Gordon has defined conflict as a collision occurring between teacher and student where their *behaviors* interfere with each other's attainment of their own needs and thus *both parties own the problem*. For example:

Teacher: (Returns to the classroom to discover a student taking a pencil from the teacher's desk.) "When pencils are taken from my desk, I cannot find one to do my work and I must pay to purchase new ones. This has happened a number of times, and I find it annoying." ("I" message; *directive statements*)

Student: "Well, each time I return from music class I find someone has taken my pencil. This has happened three weeks in a row."

In this example both teacher and student own the problem and they find themselves in conflict. Gordon suggests that such problems are usually resolved by using two methods that result in either the teacher or the student winning. In *Method I*, the teacher wins by using authority and power, and the student loses.

Teacher: "Well, you're just going to have to learn that you cannot be permitted to steal from the teacher's desk. For the remainder of this week you will not be permitted to go for recess (or to the pep rally)." (Judging, criticizing, blaming, and punishing are creating an obstacle to the student's rational capacity to solve his or her problems.)

We can restate the dialogue to show *Method II*, where the student wins and the teacher loses.

Teacher: "Someone has taken your pencil."

Student: "Yes, and if you had not left class to go to the teacher's lounge to smoke a cigarette, you would have been here to prevent someone from taking my pencil. My father is really angry, and he said if I have one more thing stolen from my desk he is going to come to see the principal."

Teacher: "Well, uh, I don't ever want you to take things from my desk again."

This is an example of *Method II*, where the student "wins" when the teacher gives up or ignores the student's actions. These win-lose methods both center on a "power-struggle" between teacher and student, and in each case the loser goes away feeling resentful and angry. Many teachers unknowingly use one of these methods. Some teachers use both, which is even more destructive as the teacher swings from an authoritarian position to one of being permissive. They appear highly erratic and unpredictable and leave the student confused. Gordon proposes an alternative solution called *Method III*, "no lose," where the conflict is resolved without the teacher or student using or losing power.

Teacher: "Someone has taken your pencil." ("active listening"; *nondirective statement*)

Student: "Well, I probably shouldn't have taken yours, but I really need a pencil for the test next period—and someone keeps stealing mine."

Teacher: "Can you think of how we may solve this problem for now so we will both have our pencils and both feel OK."

Student: "Well, it only happens on Tuesday when I go to music class. I could take my pencil with me, but I don't use pencils in music class, and I really don't want to carry it around."

Teacher: "Taking your pencil to music class does not seem to be the solution. ("active listening"; *nondirective statement*)

Student: "Yeah, I wonder if I could put my pencil somewhere else in the classroom on Tuesdays when I go to music, somewhere where it will be safe. And, I'm going to bring this problem to our class meeting to see if we can get people to stop taking my pencil."

Teacher: "It sounds like you have begun to solve your problem." ("active listening"; *nondirective statement*)

Student: "Could I put it in your desk?"

We can see that *Method III*, "no lose," is a conflict-solving process in which the teacher does "active listening" and uses "I" messages until he or she fully hears what the child's problems and needs are, and then they "put their heads together" until a solution can be found that is acceptable to both. *Method III* creates a "no lose" result, and no power struggle is involved. The solution can be suggested by either the student or the teacher, but the final agreement must be acceptable to both members involved with the conflict.

Method III, a final departure point for Gordon, is a central beginning point for the Confronting-Contractors (Dreikurs and Glasser), who see all student misbehavior as affecting others. These writers would agree with the general steps described here, but not with the teacher's behaviors. Gordon also suggests that to create a "no lose" climate, the teacher can introduce the "scientific method," involving the following six steps developed by John Dewey, as a format for *Method III*.

   Step 1. Defining the Problem: With the use of active listening and "I" messages, the teacher helps a student or an entire class focus on a problem that affects them. During this defining step, one should not attempt to provide a solution or make an evaluation, but instead simply attempt to get everyone involved, to clarify their needs.

   Step 2. Generating Possible Solutions: During this second step, the goal is to "brainstorm" many different solutions for the problem, again without attempting to make an evaluation of the ideas presented. Early evaluation of solutions will limit creativity, and the teacher might need to use "I" messages to keep the discussion guided towards brainstorming.

   Steps 3 and 4. Evaluating and Deciding on Solution(s):   Having made a list of the possible solutions in Step 2, the teacher and student, or group, need to go over each solution to determine which ones can be agreed upon by all involved. If the teacher or student cannot live with the solution being considered, they can express this through "I" messages. It is important that all solutions be considered fully, and the teacher will have to use much active listening to achieve this end.

   Steps 5 and 6. Implementing and Evaluating Solution(s):   During the final steps, a clear agreement must be established as to who will do what and when they will begin. At this time, those involved should set a time to meet again to re-evaluate the results.[11]

   In using the *Method III* ("no lose") conflict-solving process, Gordon suggests that there are some problems outside the teacher's "area or spheres of freedom." He provides a chart that looks much like a target with a bull's-eye, and places the teacher in the center.[12] This center area represents activities such as classroom organization, rules, assignments, and so forth, that are within the teacher's "area of freedom." In turn, each circle moving out from the center is labeled "school principal," "district superintendent," "local laws," "state laws," and "federal laws." Each new circle represents a higher level of authority that can limit the teacher's freedom to make certain decisions. For example, the state law requires compulsory education for all students, so if by *Method III* the teacher and class were to decide that school attendance should be elective, there would be no way to implement their decision. This issue is simply outside their realm of decision making. In other words, there are certain social constraints within which both the student and teacher must live.

Although *T.E.T.* rejects the systematic use of *reinforcers*, which we will see described in the Rules/Rewards-Punishment models, Gordon does acknowledge the need to create a classroom that is supportive of various activities. He suggests the classroom environment can be modified in a systematic and creative way to alleviate student disruption. It can be changed to enrich the learning space and activities. In modifying the environment, time is another variable that relates to certain student problems. The effective teacher knows that at certain times in the day it is better to introduce difficult concepts to students, while at other times students tend to be irritable, which can make such learning difficult. Time, within the *T.E.T.* model, is organized and viewed in three ways: (1) diffused time, (2) individual time, and (3) optimum time.[13]

When students are working closely with others in a busy classroom, they need to use a lot of energy for screening out stimuli in order to concentrate on such work as reading or working a math problem. *Diffused time* is the time period in which the student works in close social contact. The student can only function effectively for a limited time in such a stimulating environment before becoming fatigued. It is necessary, therefore, for students to have some *individual time* where they can be by themselves for a short period (for example, a "quiet corner" or an individual study carrel). The third classification, *optimum time*, is a period during the day when a student is able to meet individually with the teacher or a fellow student. If this time is not provided for, the child might attempt to fulfill his or her need for personal attention by being disruptive. This misbehavior forces the teacher to deal with the student and in turn gives the one-to-one contact that is desired. With these time classifications in mind, the teacher is encouraged to plan the day deliberately to create a balance of all three forms of time to maintain a teaching-learning environment that maximizes a "hassle-free" climate for child growth.

Modeling

Although the use of modeling is a technique more systematically used by the Confronting-Contractors, the *T.E.T.* model acknowledges its importance. For the teacher using *T.E.T.*, the rule of thumb is, "Do it, don't talk about it! Practice, don't preach!" In other words, the teacher, by his or her every action, is modeling to the students behaviors that reflect the teacher's values. Greater problems arise when the teacher attempts to "teach" students to behave in one way while he or she behaves in an opposite manner. The injunction to "Do as I say, not as I do" produces a double standard that is easily recognized by students. Gordon would suggest that we as teachers look closely at our school and class rules and ask, "Do the rules allow the adults to behave in one way while denying the same behavior to nonadults?" Can teachers hit students (corporal punishment) while acts of fighting among students are severely punished? Do teachers "cut" the lunch line, while students must wait their turn? Are teachers permitted to smoke in school while students are not? Such questions require us to introspect closely and ask ourselves what exactly are the values that we are modeling. A teacher's modeled behavior has a powerful effect on student behavior.

   T.E.T. also addresses the modeling of behavior that a teacher uses while resolving a conflict with a student. Do we retreat to *Method I* power behaviors that enable only the teacher to employ his or her authority to win? Or, do we give in and use *Method II*, wherein we become permissive and lose to the student? The *Method III* ("no lose") technique of problem-solving models the type of authentic behavior that helps relationships between teacher and students. A youngster, having seen *Method III* ("no lose") techniques modeled by the teacher, may then begin to use similar techniques with adults and peers.

Physical Intervention and Isolation

The use of such physical behaviors by the teacher as inhibiting a disruptive child by removing him or her from the classroom is not explicitly dealt with in *T.E.T.*. We may infer, though, that such strong measures would not be acceptable within the *T.E.T.* framework, except in a case where a student physically endangered him- or herself or others. A reasonable teacher would be justified in intervening to keep students safe. The use of isolation or physical force to coerce students would be an extreme form of a "roadblock" to communication and would be clearly rejected by *T.E.T.*.

SUMMARY

By using the Teacher Behavior Continuum (TBC) in Figure 3–2 we may now summarize and outline the "tools" that Gordon has provided to the teacher in his *T.E.T.: Teacher Effectiveness Training* model. Those tools are classified

Silently Looking On	Nondirective Statements	Questions	Directive Statements	Modeling	Reinforcement	Physical Intervention and Isolation
(1) Critical Listening (silence)	(4) Active Listening (mirroring feelings) "You're worried about getting an exam soon."	(3) Door Re-openers "Do you want to talk more about it?"	(6) Influencing "Watch your step"	(a) Method III "no lose"	(c) Reorganizing space	
(2) Acknowledgement-type Responses (gesture)	(5) "I" messages "When I find papers left on the floor . . . " (behavior, effect, feeling)			(b) Daily actions	(d) Reorganizing time (diffused, individual, optimum)	

Supportive Model

Author: Thomas Gordon

(numbers) overt behavior
(letters) covert behavior

FIGURE 3–2. Teacher Behavior Continuum (TBC)

into overt and covert teacher behaviors in Figure 3—2. The overt behaviors are those outward actions taken by teachers that can be clearly observed and defined. These are (1) critical listening or (2) acknowledging responses and gestures, (3) door openers or reopeners, (4) active listening (mirroring feelings), (5) "I" messages, and finally (6) strong "influencing."

The covert behaviors suggested by *T.E.T.* are actions that run through the teacher's mind in reflecting, planning, predicting, and preventing, and do not deal with direct action or conflict resolution between student and teacher. These covert actions can be listed as (a) planning *Method III* ("no lose") conflict resolution, (b) modeling teacher behavior consistent with expected student behavior, (c) reorganizing classroom space, and (d) reorganizing classroom time (diffused, individual, and optimum times).

NOTES

1. Thomas Gordon, *T.E.T.: Teacher Effectiveness Training* (New York: David McKay, 1974).
2. Carl R. Rogers, *Client-Centered Therapy: Its Current Practices, Implications, and Theory* (Boston: Houghton Mifflin, 1951).
3. Carl R. Rogers, *On Becoming a Person: A Therapist's View of Psychotherapy* (Boston: Houghton Mifflin, 1961).
4. Carl R. Rogers, *Freedom to Learn* (Columbus: Charles E. Merrill Publishing, 1969).
5. Abraham H. Maslow, *Toward a Psychology of Being*, 2nd ed. (New York: D. Van Nostrand, 1968), p. 3.
6. Gordon, *T.E.T.: Teacher Effectiveness Training*, p. 61.
7. Gordon, *T.E.T.*, p. 48.
8. Gordon, *T.E.T.*, p. 40.
9. Gordon, *T.E.T.*, pp. 51—52.
10. Gordon, *T.E.T.*, p. 200.
11. Gordon, *T.E.T.*, pp. 227—34.
12. Gordon, *T.E.T.*, p. 275.
13. Gordon, *T.E.T.*, pp. 169—75.

REFERENCES

Related Readings

Clark, D. H., and Kadis, A. *Humanistic Teaching*. Columbus: Charles E. Merrill Publishing, 1971.

Holt, John. *Freedom and Beyond.* New York: E. P. Dutton, 1972.

> *For information about how school districts can offer the Teacher Effectiveness Training Course to their teachers, write to School Programs, Effectiveness Training, Inc., 531 Stevens Avenue, Solana Beach, California 92075.*

INSTRUCTIONAL MEDIA

The following can be ordered from:
    American Association for Counseling and Development
    5999 Stevenson Avenue
    Alexandria VA 22304

Films

Be an Effective Teacher
Thomas Gordon

> 55 minutes; two reels, 16mm. color and sound. Sale price $400; rental fee per day of use $40.
>
> *This film on teacher effectiveness training (T.E.T.) provides a sound basis for promoting a learning environment in the classroom. In reel one, role-play demonstrations portray the T.E.T. approach in action through active listening when the child has the problem and "I" messages when the teacher has a problem. In reel two, conflict resolution skills are presented and Gordon discusses the origins and underlying philosophy of the central concepts, as well as the techniques of implementation. (order no. 77533C)*

Carl Rogers on Education (Part I)

> 30 minutes; 16 mm. color and sound. Sale price $300; rental fee per day of use $30.
>
> *Carl Rogers describes how people acquire significant learning and indicates the directions in which the educational system must change to have a real impact on students. The film covers such topics as: the role of the student in formulating his or her own curriculum, the circumstances under which learning will be a lasting and meaningful process, the activities a teacher should engage in to be a facilitator of learning and the qualities in the interpersonal relationship between facilitator and students that foster and encourage the learning process. (order no. 77526C)*

Carl Rogers on Education (Part II)

> 30 minutes; 16 mm. color and sound. Sale price $300; rental fee per day of use $30.
>
> *Carl Rogers continues his analysis of the educational system by focusing on the following topics: implementing "freedom to learn" within the restraints and obligations imposed upon teachers in the usual educational setting, coping with the different expectations students have of what they want or need from a teacher, the role of the educational system in transmitting society's values and in helping*

young people resolve value questions, the characteristics in young people that are fostered by teachers who facilitate "freedom to learn" (order no. 77527C)

The following can be ordered from:
Media Five
2211 Cahuenga Boulevard
West Los Angeles CA 90068

T.E.T. in High School
Thomas Gordon
29 minutes; color, Sale price $395; rental fee per day of use $45.
Demonstrates the "no lose" method of resolving conflicts and improving human relations in the secondary-level classroom.

4

The Communication Model: Berne and Harris's Transactional Analysis

Mr. Tyler, the kindergarten teacher, turns to discover a large pool of paint at the feet of a five-year-old girl standing before the painting easel. Sally, a bold little girl, has spilled paint on the floor for the third time this week. She looks at the spreading paint, wraps the end of her smock around her hand and hugs it like a blanket. At the same time, she sucks her thumb and looks away from Mr. Tyler's gaze. Mr. Tyler's immediate inclination is to say words to this effect: "Sally, why in the world do you always make such a mess? You never pay attention to what you're doing." Instead he pauses. He is a teacher trained in Transactional Analysis. He knows that Sally's behavior indicates she is being the *Child*, impulsive and irresponsible. Mr. Tyler realizes that if he goes ahead with his retort he would be perpetuating the *Child* in Sally by taking the role of admonishing *Parent*. Instead, he must speak as the rational *Adult*, and in so doing, hope to bring out Sally's *Adult* as well. With these thoughts, he says: "Sally, paints are hard to control but you can clean them up. What do you need to clean up this mess?"

What were all of the verbal options open to Mr. Tyler? The following are a number of responses that the teacher might have made:

Questions

Who made this mess? *(Parent)*
What do you need to clean this up? *(Adult)*
Why is it that I always have to clean up your mess? *(Child)*

46

Directive Statements

See this mess you made because you never pay attention to what you're
   doing. *(Parent)*
Paints are hard to control but you can clean them up. *(Adult)*
I'm so mad, I'm not giving you any more paint! *(Child)*

TRANSACTIONAL ANALYSIS

We have all heard teachers make these kinds of statements to children as well
as to each other. Transactional Analysis (generally referred to as TA) provides
the teacher with a helpful framework for viewing what is said to and by
students and to ascertain whether their verbal interactions are conducive to
dealing with misbehaving students. Transactional Analysis was first presented in *Games People Play* by Eric Berne[1] and *I'm OK—You're OK* by
Thomas A. Harris.[2] These books primarily dealt with communication between adults. Later, these same principles and concepts were used to help
adults deal with children in such books as *Born to Win* by James and
Jongeward,[3] *TA for Tots*[4] and *TA for Kids*[5] by Alvyn M. Freed, and *Games
Students Play* by Ken Ernst.[6]

If we place ourselves in the shoes of the teacher encountering the
kindergarten child described in the beginning of this chapter, we can think
about the many occasions when we would like to have retracted what was
said and rephrased it in a more positive manner. However, according to TA,
there are many different persons in ourselves. It is believed that our inner
energy is often diverted into opposing factions. First delineated by the early
works of Sigmund Freud, this idea of inner energy was tied to the existence of
three constructs: (1) the *Id*, representing our instinctual selfish needs or
drives, (2) the *Superego*, representing a restrictive force over these selfish
drives, and (3) the *Ego*, which serves as a referee balancing the forces of
hedonism and repression to attain enlightened self-interest. The teenager
finds a sporty-looking car parked at the corner with the keys in the ignition.
The *Id* says, "Go on, take it for a ride. What a thrill!" The *Superego* shouts, "No,
you will be arrested. You and your parents will be embarrassed and
ashamed." In a healthy individual, the refereeing *Ego* resolves the dilemma
with thoughts such as, "I will not take the car now, but if I want a car like this,
then I will work overtime, save my money, and by the summer I will be able to
purchase my own car." Life for every individual is a dynamic process of

interplay of urges and checking forces. These concepts, although interesting and maybe helpful for the highly trained psychoanalyst, have been generally too abstract to be useful to the classroom teacher who must deal with everyday behavior. Such TA writers as Berne and Harris have attempted to operationalize these Freudian concepts into ways that adults can use readily. A TA model for teachers has been developed that describes direct actions and behaviors to be used in their work with students of all ages.

THE THEORY

Theorists in the process of documenting the basis for the principles of TA have leaned heavily on research done on memory processes and the experiments done by such neurosurgeons as Dr. Wilder Penfield.[7] Such experiments have involved stimulating the various parts of the brain with mild electrical waves. It was discovered that such shocks elicited from the subject a recall of historical events and feelings. Subjects reported feelings that "they were there," and they could relive past incidents. From these experiments it was hypothesized that day-to-day experiences serve as stimuli that evoke memories of past situations and cause the person to relive the events with vivid images and feelings. The brain can be thought of as a recorder of experiences. All events from birth onward are put on "tape" and are stored for instant retrieval. One might recall walking past a restaurant and smelling the aroma of fresh bread and roast turkey. The mind is quickly flooded with images and feelings about Thanksgiving dinner as a child. It is almost as if the person were a child again. Obviously other stimulations can trigger negative recordings. The smell of wood burning could conjure up recollections of a traumatic house fire or the smell of oil could bring to mind a car accident.

Life is a process of dynamic urges and counter-checks. We all have a stored memory of our past experiences that can be quickly invoked with the accompanying vivid images and feelings.

The central principle of TA is called the social "transaction."

Eric Berne states:

> The unit of social intercourse is called a transaction. If two or more people encounter each other ... sooner or later one of them will speak, or give some other indication of acknowledging the presence of the others. This is called the *transactional stimulus*. Another person will then say or do something which is in some way related to the stimulus, and that is called the *transactional response*.[8]

From a classroom perspective, the transaction just described would be either the teacher initiating action toward the student and the student acting back, or the student acting toward the teacher and the teacher responding. What teachers or students "do" or "do back" is to a great extent a reflex response whereby the student or teacher hears a "tape" of a similar past experience and simply "acts" it out in reality. For example, a classroom teacher needs to move his or her students to the auditorium, and this present situation triggers a memory-bank response: 'Boys, line up; girls, line up." This act of verbalization has never been thought out consciously by the teacher. It is simply what he or she has experienced in his or her own school experiences as a student. The teacher simply "replays the tape" and says to the students what was said to him or her as a student. What TA can do for the teacher is to provide another repertoire of words that will bring out positive and constructive responses from the students.

Berne closely observed people's outward behavior and actions as they replayed their internal "tapes." He frequently saw a metamorphosis occur before his very eyes. At one moment a person's manner, appearance, words, and gestures were indicative of a confident "adult" who could respond to information in a business-like, rational manner. At the next moment the same person might change and employ the "childish" actions of being impulsive, demanding, and whining. Soon the person might change again to become a harsh "parent": judgmental, sounding off with advice, and evaluative. After extensive observations Berne concluded that in all people there exist three states of being. One state is that of a "little person" much like a three-year-old, which he called the *Child*. The second state is an imitation of all the stored-up experiences a person has had as a child of his or her own parents; this state is called the *Parent*. The third state is called the *Adult*. The *Adult* is quite different from the other two states and is rational, responsible, and objective. These three states, *Child*, *Parent*, and *Adult*, are more readily understood and applied than the previous Freudian terms of the *Id*, *Superego*, and *Ego*. Following are more detailed explanations of each of Berne's states.

Parent

The *Parent* state is based on all the "tapes" we have stored from those experiences we have had with our parents or parent substitutes which we recorded in total when we were very young. They are recorded as "truths" because, as helpless children, we were totally dependent on our parents for security and lacked the intellectual ability to evaluate our parents' actions. In these tapes are recorded not only the external admonitions and rules as heard from parents when they were stern, but also the pleasures given to us by a happy and proud parent. The *Parent* contains a controlling side and a nurturing side. Much of a parent's rules were for the child's own safety; e.g., "Don't run into the street." Difficulty arose, however, when a parent told us to do one thing while he or she did another. Our memories record both the verbal and behavioral experience. "Don't tell lies!" exhorts the parent, but the child often catches the adult telling lies; e.g., "Tell the salesman at the door I'm not at home." Usually these unedited contrary tapes hidden in our *Parent* state contain imperatives and extremes about what the child should or should not do. The words and terms "never," "always," and "never forget that" come out of the *Parent* state.

Child

While we are recording the external rules as part of our *Parent* state, we are simultaneously recording the same internal feelings as part of our *Child* state. Since the child does not have the vocabulary or intellectual ability to question and evaluate his or her experience, the "seeing, hearing, and feeling data" become our *Child*. Because a young child is far from behaving in socially decreed ways, the *Child* takes great joy in exploring, testing, and generally getting into the world with ceaseless energy and noise. In turn, when these explorations conflict with parental values, the child must give up much of his or her desires for unlimited exploration to win parental approval. Because of the frustration caused by the parent's demands for a civilized child, the young child begins to feel that, "I'm not OK." These "not OK" feelings are permanently recorded in our *Child* state and can never be erased from memory. We can all remember (at least a few times, and in some cases, many times) when we have felt inadequate in controlling ourselves, even when we knew that we were acting wrong. We might uncontrollably and irrationally explode at someone. The *Child* has taken over.

The *Child*, however, also has a positive side. On these tapes are the "OK" recordings of good feelings that go with exploring, touching, and feeling. "OK" feelings come from memories of being held warmly and closely, or the carefree times playing in the park, or the glorious feelings of licking a cold, smooth ice cream cone. All tapes of positive and negative feelings have been recorded before the age of five, and they will always be there to be replayed.

Adult

As the young child moves out of toddlerhood, he or she begins to store information for use in understanding future events. The child begins to think and the rational abilities of categorizing and generalizing begin to develop. As early as ten months old the child is able to do things that provide both awareness and thoughts about himself or herself. These beginning *Adult* data are quite different from the *taught* concept of life in the *Parent* stage and the *felt* concept of life in the *Child* stage. The *Adult* develops a thought concept of life based on information gathered and rationally processed. The *Adult* as a rational state in the early years of life is weak and can be easily displaced by the demands of the *Parent* or *Child*.[9]

It is the task of the *Adult* to test the rules and information of the *Parent*. Through experience, the *Adult* discovers it is true that one "should not run into the street" *(Parent)* and this information in the *Parent* can be trusted and is dependable. The "not OK" feelings first associated with these early reprimands, although now seen as justified by the *Adult*, are still not erased, and such "not OK" feelings can still swell up. An individual always needs the rational *Adult* to turn off these "not OK" feelings. It is also the *Adult's* job to determine when the *Child*'s feelings can be expressed. As a mature person, the *Adult* knows that it is acceptable to cry at a wedding but not appropriate to scream at the school principal (even when the "son-(daughter)-of-a-gun" deserves it!).

The general day-to-day job of the *Adult* is to "check out" old information found in the *Parent* and to update and validate it for future use; e.g., does drinking coffee really stunt growth? Hopefully, if the information in the *Parent* is found to be accurate by the *Adult*, the person is free to obey the messages—"Walk on the right side of the hall," "Don't go down one-way streets," "Fasten the seat belt"—and there is no further need to expend energy debating these issues. This saves the *Adult* from having to "reinvent the wheel" and make every decision from "scratch." If the information from the *Parent* is prejudicial ("Don't play with any children that have slanted eyes") and the information gained by the *Adult* is contradictory ("My teacher has slanted eyes and she treats me warmly and is always helpful"), the youngster must use a lot of energy to try to resolve the differences between *Parent* information and *Adult* information. When such *Parent* information wins out, we have the roots of prejudice and mistrust of others with a view that certain others are "not OK."

The premise of TA is that all individuals need to feel adequate. Within them are three states or forces; if the *Adult* state is given ample opportunity to develop, then the youngster will become a rational and wise person who will be understanding of others and him- or herself. He or she will be able to use the other states of *Parent* and *Child* in a constructive manner.

The *Adult* force tests the rules and information of the *Parent*. The *Adult* also determines when the feelings of the *Child* can be expressed. When there is little conflict between the *Parent*, *Child*, and *Adult*, the student has a lot of energy left to explore and to use the world creatively. Harris states that creativity is born from curiosity in the *Child* when it provides the "want to" and the *Adult* provides the "how to."

A student who constantly misbehaves does so because of an untenable tension among the three inner forces. If the *Child* holds the greater influence, the student has an attitude of "I'm not adequate but others are." If the *Parent* holds the greater influence, the youngster has an attitude of "I am all right, the rest of the world is to blame for every problem that occurs." If the student is severely caught by both *Parent* and *Child* working against each other with little adult intervention, we have the most severe attitude of "I am inadequate and so is everyone else. Everything is hopeless."

The teacher's job is to approach the misbehaving student in ways that affirm the attitude that the child is capable and that he or she can also trust the rest of the world. This is done by interacting with the child in two ways. The first way affirms the positive and valid dimension of the inner *Parent* and *Child*. The second way is to appeal to the child's *Adult* by approaching the student with the teacher's own *Adult*. These two ways are forms of "stroking."

Stroking is the expression of affection given to one individual by another with the use of physical or verbal behaviors. All of one's life could be viewed as an attempt to acquire such strokes.

Let's stop for a moment. We can sympathize with the reader when such words as "transaction," *Child*, *Parent*, *Adult*, and "stroking" are reeling off these pages. What does this mean? How, as a teacher, can I use this information? We admit that such terms, although perhaps less obtuse than *Id*, *Ego*, and *Superego*, are nonetheless still difficult to explain and summarize in a few pages. You have persevered long enough; we will now plunge into applications. We hope that the TA terminology will become clearer as we give examples and move through our Teacher Behavior Continuum. Remember, though, the basic aim of TA is to promote rational thought (the *Adult*), to affirm the positive aspects of restraint (the *Parent*), and to facilitate creativity (the *Child*).

TA AND THE TEACHER BEHAVIOR CONTINUUM

Silently Looking On

First of all, teachers need to find clues that will help them decide what internal state they are operating from and what internal state the particular student with whom they wish to deal possesses. Teachers need this vital information to ascertain the most appropriate approach to use in dealing with a disruptive student. Nonverbal clues can be found in facial expressions, vocal tones, and body gestures.

The following clues signal that the *Parent* is in control: "Furrowed brow, pursed lips, the pointing index finger, head-wagging, the 'horrified look,' foot-tapping, hands on hips, arms folded across chest, wringing hands, tongue-clucking, sighing, patting another on the head ..."[10] There are also nonverbal actions that are unique to each teacher and to which students can easily see and interpret as, "Oh, oh, here comes the *Parent*." Usually students will have great fun mimicking our idiosyncratic mannerisms when we are not in sight.

Following are nonverbal clues that indicate the *Child* is in charge: "Tears; the quivering lip; pouting; temper tantrums; the high-pitched, whining voice; rolling eyes; shrugging shoulders; downcast eyes; teasing; delight; laughter; hand-raising for permission to speak; nail-biting; nose-thumbing; squirming; and giggling."[11]

Finally, how will the *Adult* look? The face will not be blank or dull, but the face, eyes, and body will be moving continually with short periods of non-movement as we or the student listen closely to what is being said.[12]

Just as there are many nonverbal clues that enable us to view the transaction of teacher and student, we find similar clues in key phrases or spoken words. *Parent* clues are in the use of words like the following: "I am going to put a stop to this *once and for all*; I can't for the life of me...; Now always remember ...; ('always' and 'never' are *almost always Parent* words ...)." The evaluative words *may* identify the *Parent* such as: "... stupid, naughty, ridiculous, disgusting, shocking, asinine, lazy, nonsense, absurd, poor thing, poor dear, no! no! sonny, honey ..., How dare you? cute, there there, Now what?, Not again!" The automatic or the unthinking use of "should" and "ought" are again near giveaways to the *Parent* state.[13]

The *Child* state's verbal clues can be seen in the following words: "I wish, I want, I dunno, I gonna, I don't care, I guess, when I grow up bigger, biggest, better, best (and many similar superlatives)."[14]

Finally, language can give us clues that the *Adult* state is in control: "How much, in what way, comparative, true, false, probable, possible, unknown, objective, I think, I see, it is my opinion. Basic vocabulary words such as why, what, where, when, who, and how."[15]

The teacher, after observing both his or her own behavior and the student's, is now ready to make an assessment of strategies and plan an appropriate action. This assessment or analysis of stages has to be primarily reflective. As Mr. Tyler did with Sally, the teacher needs to ask, "Is the child's behavior indicative of the *Child*, the *Parent*, or the *Adult*? Is my behavior indicative of the *Child*, the *Parent*, or the *Adult*?" After an assessment of the answers to these questions, the teacher is prepared to change his or her behavior with nondirective statements, questions, and directive statements that are more in keeping with constructive purposes and will elicit the child's rationality.

Let's see how this assessment might work. A middle-school teacher may have just undergone the following experience. The scene is a junior high school classroom of low achievers.

Teacher: (Looks at watch, takes a deep breath, and lets it out slowly with a hissing sound, glances at student, and frowns.)

Student: (Glances at teacher, returns frown, pushes papers aside, and crosses arms across chest.)

Teacher: Do you have work to do? (In a tone of disgust.)

Student: Unfortunately I do.

Teacher: I cannot believe your work. You're so immature. Of all the eighth-grade classes that I have had in my ten years of teaching, your class is the worst!

Student: I can believe it! This class is terrible. I can't get any work done.

Teacher: I've told you over and over again that you have to do your work or you're not going to pass this course.

Student: (Nods.) Yeah. Well, this is a waste of time.

Teacher: You and some others need to be taught a lesson in this class. You people never should have been promoted to the seventh grade. But you know the administration. Anything to please the parents.

Student: Yeah, anything.

The teacher may walk away from this interchange knowing that little has been accomplished. Certainly the student is not about to finish his or her work any quicker than before. By reflecting on the transactions, the teacher might be able to find out why nothing was accomplished, and later, in a similar situation, be able to take a different tack. In analyzing this transaction and the exchange of "strokes" between these two people, we see the *Parent*. The teacher is scolding and judging while the student is agreeing with an "I could care less" attitude. The conversation is carried on without any attempt to get the facts or to test the reality of the participants' statements. They appear to enjoy their "misery" while exchanging "Aren't things awful for both of us" messages. This occurs because such blaming permits each participant to feel "OK" by blaming the present situation on others.

The teacher using TA to analyze the situation may later be able to approach the student through the use of the *Adult* state.

Teacher: (Looks attentively at student and smiles.)

Student: (Looks up at teacher, looks bewildered, and then frowns and crosses arms.)

Teacher: Is the work too difficult to do?

Student: No, there's too much of it.

Teacher: How much can you get done by the end of class?

Student: Only one page (out of eight).

Teacher: Oh come now, the most you can do is one page?

Student: Yeah.

Teacher: All right, if they're not too hard to do, when will you finish the rest of the pages?

Student: Tomorrow.

Teacher: Well, then, if you have to do these pages as extra homework I guess it's all right. However, if you don't have them done by tomorrow then we'll have to decide how we can make sure they get done.

The reader will notice that the teacher has avoided using the evaluative, belittling *Parent* and the stubborn, emotional *Child*. By responding as the *Adult*, the game of "ain't it awful" cannot be played. The student continued to try to be the *Parent* and place the blame elsewhere. The teacher remains the *Adult*, keeping the problem focused and realistic.

Before we proceed to nondirective statements, we must stress that the teacher act as an *Adult* and appeal to the child's *Adult*. This, however, does not mean that there aren't instances when a teacher and student cannot respond to each other as *Parent* to *Parent* or *Child* to *Child*. These are acceptable transactions (although limited in promoting rationality) in affirming (or stroking) each person as adequate. For example, the student finally finishes all his work and laughs with uncontrollable glee and says, "See, 'teach,' I told you I could do it!" The teacher responds with a spontaneous victory gesture. In this case we have a *Child-to-Child* transaction that sends positive vibrations back and forth. Here is another example: The student looks up in the middle of his work and says, "I know that I have to finish this work no matter how hard it is!" The teacher responds with "Yes, that's right. You have to finish that work." What we have is a *Parent*-to-*Parent* transaction that, again, is complementary and productive.

Although the adult state of rationality is prized, other complementary transactions are valuable. What is to be avoided are crossed transactions that create pain and difficulty between people. For example, the student asks, "What time is lunch?" and the teacher replies, "You're always thinking of eating. Why don't you finish your work and stop thinking about your stomach?" This is a case of the student's *Adult* being violated by the teacher's *Parent*. Harris gives many examples of various interactions called complementary, crossed, and ulterior. An ulterior transaction is more subtle because it involves a surface message that is different from the real intent. In this chapter we will stick to 1) the use of *Adult* messages to promote rationality and 2) complementary messages that promote positive self-concepts.

Nondirective Statements

Although the use of nondirective statements by teachers is not as central a tool as seen in the previous chapter on *T.E.T.*, it is a viable *Adult* technique for a teacher to use in having a student explain his or her behaviors and thoughts.

Student: I hate those kids. They are driving me crazy!" *(Child)*
Teacher: The students are doing things that you do not like. *(Adult)*

The statement by the student is coming from his or her *Child*, while the teacher's nondirective statement can be thought of as a response coming from the *Adult*. In other words, the teacher is dealing with reality and his or her words reflect for the student the "facts" as the teacher interprets them. Generally, then, nondirective statements communicate from the *Adult* states and help students to verbalize and clarify the true meaning of their actions.

Questions

The use of questions can become more effective if teachers can analyze the messages they send as "OK" or "not OK" with the help of the *Parent*, *Adult*, *Child* construct. To demonstrate, we return to the introductory example: the kindergarten teacher turns to discover a large pool of paint at the feet of a five-year-old standing before the painting easel. The teacher's question-responses could have come from these alternatives.

Questions

1. Who made this terrible mess?
(Parent to Child)

teacher   student
(P)   (P)
(A)   (A)
(C)   (C)

This question indicates that the teacher is making an evaluative *Parent* statement (terrible) and treating the student as a wayward *Child*.

2. What do you need to clean this up?
(Adult to Adult)

teacher	student
(P)	(P)
(A) ————————→	(A)
(C)	(C)

This question indicates that the teacher is acting in a constructive "Let's get to it!" manner. The teacher is responding to the student in a way that indicates that the student is capable of solving this temporary problem. It is one *Adult* speaking to another.

3. Why is it that I always have to clean up your mess?

teacher	student
(P)	(P)
(A)	(A)
(C)	(C)

This question indicates that the teacher is acting from his or her own childish impulse to see every act as being personally related to self. The teacher is seeking an answer to the egocentric perception that "everything wrong always happens to me." He or she asks the question as if the student has an evaluative, authoritative *(Parent)* answer. The teacher, if thinking rationally, would know that the student is not capable of supplying such an answer.

Now let's reverse this situation. What are the alternative replies that a teacher can make to a student's question? Often, in a classroom, students bait their teacher with hostile questions. For example, Billy receives his test paper, looks at his grade, and yells out, "Why didn't you tell me beforehand that you were going to grade this test?!" The student's *question* was from a "you (teacher) are not OK" posture by sending a message from the student's *Parent* to the teacher's *Child*. (Alternative questions could have emanated from the student's *Adult*, such as, "What criteria did you use in order to give a grade?" or from the *Child*—"I'm never any good at taking your tests.") The "Why didn't you tell me?" question is judgmental and implies that something is wrong with the teacher's rational abilities.

The teacher can respond from one of three states. If he or she responds as a *Parent* with, "Well, you're the only one that didn't hear the directions.

Maybe you had better start listening!" then the teacher has intensified the battle by inferring that it's not his or her fault that the student can't hear. With a statement such as this, the teacher can hardly expect the student to discuss the issue rationally.

If the teacher responds as a *Child* with, "I'm at my wit's end. I do not know what I'm doing!" then the teacher has affirmed the student's *Parent* question. The teacher has said in effect that the student is right and that the teacher is inadequate. Such a response encourages the student to continue with the attitude that he or she is "OK" and it's the teacher who is always wrong.

On the other hand, if the teacher responds as an *Adult* with, "I thought I did explain that this paper would be graded. Everyone else seemed to know it. Perhaps you weren't listening or were absent on the day I told the class. Let me check," then the teacher has presented the facts as known and has encouraged the student to look for the reasons for the apparent miscommunication. The teacher has turned the student's baiting question into a learning experience that is profitable for both.

Directive Statements

We have seen that there are questions and then there are questions! The same can be said for directive statements. The following are all directive statements.

1. You are so loud all the time, you can't keep your mouth shut! Shut your mouth for once in your life!
2. You make me so mad. All you want to do is drive me crazy. Please keep quiet!
3. I can't teach the class when you talk so loudly. If you have something to say, raise your hand and I'll listen to you.

Here are three direct statements with the same purpose in mind, to keep the student quiet, yet they are very different. The first statement tries to shut the student up by sending an evaluative *Parent* (I'm OK; you're not) message. The second one attempts to quiet the student by pleading with the student for mercy. It is a *Child* (I'm not OK; you are) message to a *Parent*. The third is a reasoned statement that looks at cause and effect and a possible solution. It is an *Adult* (I'm OK; you're OK) message to another *Adult*.

In commanding disruptive children, a teacher could analyze his or her own verbalizations to see what hidden messages they might contain. Are the commands reinforcing the *Child*, *Parent*, or the *Adult*?

It is misleading to think that a teacher should never use *Parent* or *Child* directive statements. These are healthy and natural when used in appropriate situations. For example, when informing children about "hard and fast" classroom rules, the teacher should be the authoritarian *Parent*.

- Do not go up the left side of the stairs!
- Be in your seat when the bell rings!

Where the *Parent* gets into trouble is when such statements become destructive and emotionally "loaded" between teacher and student ("You must have a vacuum between your ears. I've told you a thousand times, you're supposed to be in your seat when the bell rings!").

Child statements that are natural are those that reflect uncontrolled enthusiasm.

- "Jimmy, you make me feel terrific when you behave that way!"
- "Wow, what a super kid. I must be a super teacher!"

Such instances of *Child* states illustrate strong positive emotions between teacher and student. *Child* states become destructive when emotions of anger, vindictiveness, and apathy emerge and overwhelm rational restraint (i.e., "Go away! I can't stand the sight of you!").

Reinforcement

Reinforcement of desirable behavior through a reward system is not directly mentioned in the TA model. The idea of conditioning a student's behavior is foreign to the Relationship-Listening position. Instead, the Transactionalists use the notion of "stroking." Every person needs to be accepted as "OK." Children who have a "not OK" image and who are expending their inner energy in conflict need the greatest affirmation of self-worth. As Harris wrote, a parent (or teacher) working with a child with problems should "whenever in doubt, stroke." The greater the percentage of time that classroom teachers give and receive "strokes" through complementary messages, the greater the chances of students having a positive image and thus being able to go about the business of correcting their own behavior.

We have seen in the previous sections of this chapter how a teacher's verbalizations can affirm or denigrate a child's image. The teacher should be conscious of and verbalize complementary messages.

Modeling

Harris suggests that teachers should teach TA to their students. It is his opinion that if students and teachers had a common language for analyzing behavior, it would be easier for them to clarify and correct their own actions. As he wrote:

> Education is heralded as the greatest medication for the ills of the world. Those ills, however, are deeply embedded in behavior. Therefore *education about behavior* through an easy-to-understand system like P-A-C, [*Parent, Child, Adult*] could well be the most important thing we can do to solve the problems which beset us and threaten to destroy us.[16]

The teacher can therefore demonstrate Transactional Analysis through lectures, role playing, and discussions. Alvyn Freed has written a book for teachers and parents that tells the TA story to children.[17] Teachers can read the story to their students. Such stories can help students recognize their own inner feelings and categorize their verbalizations.

Physical Intervention and Isolation

The use of physical intervention and isolation is the antithesis of what TA proposes. An approach that is based on revealing inner patterns through analyzing coded messages between people and on having the child ultimately be responsible for his or her own solutions would regard such use of the teacher's power as being detrimental to a child's development.

GAMES

The study of the games that misbehaving children use is a powerful tool for the teacher. By understanding such games, the teacher can put together all the gathered knowledge of TA into a comprehensive plan.

Many children continue to see themselves as "not OK." They will act in ways to receive attention from their teacher. They have generally not received warmth and positive attention, and rather than go unrecognized altogether, they resort to "acting out" in order to receive a negative reaction such as "cold pricklies," which further reinforce their "not OK" scripts and serve as an excuse for not improving behavior. Children manifest this misbehavior in the form of individual "games." Ken Ernst has classified many of these games into such categories as "Uproar," "Chip on the Shoulder," "Stupid," "Clown," "Schlemiel," and "Make Me."[18]

"Uproar":   These children engage in "knuckle-cracking, gum-popping, finger-tapping, pen-clicking, hair-combing, dress-straightening, pencil-sharpening, paper-rattling, clock-watching, turning around, wiggling, coming in late, acting stupid, and trying to sidetrack the lecture." When admonished by the teacher, such students say they are being picked on and shortly resume the game with another form of distraction.

"Chip on the Shoulder":   The student that plays the game of "Chip on the Shoulder" will at times throw things, be verbally abusive, and generally cause a classroom disturbance that appears to be similar to the child playing "Uproar." The student in "Uproar" is constantly looking for ways to "bug" the teacher's *Parent,* while the student playing "Chip on the Shoulder" only causes a disturbance when he or she is called upon or some demand is made to perform. This behavior is simply a cover for "I'm not OK" feelings, whereby the student fears being considered "dumb," and rather than running that risk, the student decides to be a "devil" by striking out.

"Stupid":   The game of "Stupid" is played by children who are performing a host of acts that make them appear "dumb." They collect an audience and get others to make fun of them, while they show their delight with nervous smiles. These students may "accidentally" do the wrong assignment, injure themselves while using school equipment inappropriately, or participate in a host of similar acts that eventually get them called "Stupid" by peers.

"Clown":   The "Clown" is generally well liked by teacher and students, and can be found mimicking the actions of teachers or others to the delight of his or her peers. Usually this is done when the teacher's back is turned.

"Schlemiel":   This student repeatedly bumps into others, knocks things over, and disrupts others' belongings and activities. They quickly volunteer to help "clean up the mess," and succeed in making things worse. Generally they respond to criticism with, "Well, it was only an accident," or "I was only trying to help."

"Make Me":   Students playing "Make Me" simply refuse to do assignments or to perform the requirements necessary. When questioned by the

teacher they will lay down the challenge of "Make Me." The "Make Me" student puts the teacher in the position of a persecutor or a rescuer.

Although there are various treatments for each diagnosis, generally the teacher can use the following strategies:

- First, *analyze the game that the student is playing.* What is the student looking for? (What kinds of strokes? From whom?) What state is the student operating from and to which of the teacher's states is the student directing messages? *(Child? Parent? Adult?)*
- Second, *don't play the game!* Come back as the *Adult.* Allow the child to see the game for what it is.
- Third, give "strokes" or attention *that affirms the child's worth.*
- Fourth, *allow the child to find his or her own solution.*

Taking the example of the "Stupid" game, let's apply the strategies.

Hector is bumbling, incoherent, and "dumb," or at least this is how he appears. Whenever called upon, he vacantly stares, says something unintelligible or nonsensical, and then sheepishly grins to himself as the other students roll their eyes and giggle. The teacher should:

1. Identify that Hector is acting stupid as part of his "I'm not OK" self-perception. The frustration and impatience that he causes the teacher is also evidence of a "not OK" perception of the teacher. Hector is acting as the helpless, bad *Child* and is appealing to the domineering bad *Parent* to correct and control him.
2. Act as the *Adult* and not as the rescuing or scolding *Parent.* The teacher should meet with Hector in private and tell him that the "game is up." The teacher will not persecute or rescue Hector when he raises his hand. He will be called on, and if no intelligible answer is forthcoming, nothing will be said or done to him.
3. Meet with Hector after class, if he is embarrassed to answer correctly in front of the class. Then he can tell the teacher the answers that he "would" have given in the classroom. The teacher should give "strokes" by touching, smiling, or verbalizing.
4. Allow Hector to decide when to venture forth with correct answers in class.

SUMMARY

We can now refer to the Teacher Behavior Continuum (Figure 4–1) and summarize Transactional Analysis. Covertly, the teacher needs to use the

Ct | | | | | | | cT

Silently Looking On	Nondirective Statements	Questions	Directive Statements	Modeling	Reinforcement	Physical Intervention and isolation
(a) Diagnosis of teacher and student internal states	(1c) Use as an *Adult* response to clarify student's explanation, *Adult* to *Adult*.	(1a) Ask student *Adult* questions, *Adult* to *Adult*.	(1b) Reply to student's actions with *Adult* statements, *Adult* to *Adult*.	(3) Teach and demonstrate the principle of TA to the student.	(2) Affirm the student as "OK" with complementary transactions, *Child* to *Child*, *Parent* to *Parent*, *Adult* to *Adult*.	
—The teacher is acting as *Child, Parent, Adult?*				Lecture, role playing, story telling.	Avoid cross transactions, *Parent* to *Child*, *Child* to *Parent*, etc.	
—The student is acting as *Child, Parent, Adult?*						

Communication Model (TA)

Authors: Eric Berne, Thomas A. Harris, and others

(numbers) overt behaviors
(letters) covert behaviors

FIGURE 4–1. Teacher Behavior Continuum (TBC)

Parent, Child, Adult construct to analyze the teacher and student transaction (letter *a*). When dealing with disruptive behavior, the teacher then overtly sends messages from his or her *Adult* to the student's *Adult* by the use of questions, directive statements, or nondirective statements (1a, 1b, 1c). The teacher must continue to "stroke" the student with complementary transactions that affirm the "I'm OK, you're OK" perception (2). The teacher helps the student to analyze his or her behavior by teaching TA (3). Finally, the teacher allows the student to make his or her own solutions.

NOTES

1. Eric Berne, *Games People Play: The Psychology of Human Relations* (New York: Grove Press, 1964).

2. Thomas A. Harris, *I'm OK—You're OK: A Practical Guide to Transactional Analysis* (New York: Harper & Row, Publishers, 1969).

3. Muriel James and Dorothy Jongeward, *Born to Win: Transactional Analysis with Gestalt Experiments.* (Boston: Addison-Wesley, 1971).

4. Alvyn M. Freed, *TA for Tots (and other Important People)* (Sacramento: Jalmar Press, 1973).

5. Alvyn M. Freed, *TA for Kids, (and Grown-Ups, Too).* Transactional Analysis for Everyone Series, (Sacramento: Jalmar Press, 1971).

6. Ken Ernst, *Games Students Play, and What to do About Them.* (Mellbrae, California: Celestial Arts, 1973).

7. William Penfield, "Memory Mechanisms," *A.M.A. Archives of Neurology and Psychiatry*, ed. L. S. Kubie et al., 67 (1952): 178−98.

8. Harris, *I'm OK—You're OK*, pp. 29−30.

9. Harris, *I'm OK—You're OK*, pp. 43−50.

10. Harris, *I'm OK—You're OK*, pp. 65−66.

11. Harris, *I'm OK—You're OK*, p. 67.

12. Harris, *I'm OK—You're OK*, p. 67.

13. Harris, *I'm OK—You're OK*, p. 66.

14. Harris, *I'm OK—You're OK*, p. 67.

15. Harris, *I'm OK—You're OK*, pp. 67−68.

16. Harris, *I'm OK—You're OK*, p. 161.

17. Alvyn M. Freed, *TA Stories for Kids*, (Mellbrae, California: Celestial Arts, 1977).

18. Ernst, *Games Students Play, and What to Do About Them*, pp. 13−36.

REFERENCES

Berne, Eric. *Games People Play: The Psychology of Human Relations.* New York: Grove Press, 1964.

Bry, A. *The TA Primer: Transactional Analysis in Everyday Life*. New York: Harper & Row, 1973.

Ernst, Ken. *Games Students Play, and What to do About Them*. Mellbrae, California: Celestial Arts, 1973.

Freed, Alvyn M. *TA for Kids (and Grown-Ups, Too)*. Sacramento: Jalmar Press, 1971.

Freed, Alvyn M. *TA for Teens (and Other Important People)*. Sacramento: Jalmar Press, 1973.

Harris, Thomas A. *I'm OK—You're OK: A Practical Guide to Transactional Analysis*. New York: Harper & Row, Publishers, 1969.

James, Muriel, and Jongeward, Dorothy. *Born to Win: Transactional Analysis with Gestalt Experiments*. Boston: Addison-Wesley, 1971.

Muriel, V. & Jongeward, D. *The People book: Transactional Analysis for Students*. Menlo Park, California: Addison-Wesley, 1975.

> For information on the International Transactional Analysis Association (ITAA), which holds study groups, seminars, and institutes and publishes the quarterly Transactional Analysis Journal, write to the International Transactional Analysis Association (ITAA), 1772 Vellejo Street, San Francisco, California 94123.

INSTRUCTIONAL MEDIA

Films

The following can be ordered from:

Media Five
3211 Cahuenga Boulevard, West
Los Angeles, California 90068

Games We Play in High School
Eric Berne

> 29 minutes; color. Sale price $395; rental fee $45 per week.

> *Concepts of Transactional Analysis are introduced as a means of improving secondary discipline, human relations, and learning. Describes techniques and games students and teachers play in the classroom.*

The OK Classroom
Thomas Harris

> 29 minutes; color. Sale price $395; rental fee $45 per week.

> *Discusses Transactional Analysis concepts, explains special meanings of the terms: Parent, Adult, Child, Transaction, Strokes, Life Positions, and Games. Documentary examples of theory in action.*

The following materials are available from:

University of California, Extension Media Center
2223 Fulton Street
Berkeley, California 94720

Transactional Analysis

30 minutes; color. Sale price $300; rental fee $30.

Introduces the use of TA in management, illustrates the reasons for people's actions in organizations, and shows how to promote productive employee behavior. Uses interviews, dramatic re-enactments, and animation to explain and demonstrate such principles of TA as game playing, the three types of trans-action-stroking, trading stamps, and life scripts.

The following materials are available from:

Social Studies School Service
10,000 Culver Boulevard, Department 33
P.O. Box 802
Culver City, CA 90230

Filmstrips

Transactional Analysis or Who's OK?
Eric Berne

1 color filmstrip, 1 LP record, guide $25; 1 color filmstrip, 1 cassette, guide $25.

An outline of the basic concepts of transactions analysis. Shows the characteristics of the "parent," "child," and "adult," and how the origins of the "parent" and "child" in early life can carry the message of "not OK." Shows how mental problems caused in this fashion can be corrected by the "adult" within each person by an appreciation of the true relationships among the different facets of the personality. Multi-Media Productions.

Games People Play
Eric Berne

1 color filmstrip, 1 cassette, guide, $25.

A discussion of the basic theory of fixed social responses, "games." Shows how childhood insecurities grow into poses to win greater security in life. Describes in detail such poses as the joker, the drunk, the tyrant, and the adapter, showing them to be isolating shields that prevent human growth. Encourages the individual to understand the games he or she plays and to replace them with honesty. Multi-Media Productions.

Sound Filmstrips

Getting it Together with Transactional Analysis

6 color filmstrips, 6 cassettes, guide, $143.

Translates the basic concepts of TA into behaviors readily recognized by students. Students' interactions with parents, teachers, and peers are dramatized to illustrate the functioning of parent, adult, and child ego states. Visuals are colorful, vivid, and contemporary in style. Pomfret House.

Simulation

OK: An interaction Unit on Transactional Analysis for the Secondary Classroom.

35 student guides, teacher's guide, $16.

A four-phase student introduction to transactional analysis, the problem-solving technique developed by Eric Berne to increase self-acceptance. Through brief lectures and numerous classroom activities, students enter the phases of ego states—the three basic personality parts of parent, adult, and child; strokes—the units of recognition that fulfill basic human needs; psychological games and discounts—the human responses to a lack of positive strokes; and staying OK—a model by which students can understand their mood changes and then react to control their feelings. Players: 25—35. Time: 3 weeks.

Workbook

Winning with People: Group Exercises in Transactional Analysis
Dorothy Jongeward and Muriel James

1—4 copies $4.95 each; 5 copies and over $4.45 each.

A workbook designed to introduce the basic concepts of transactional analysis in a group situation. By alternating text and exercises which involve the student, the book introduces such ideas as life scripts, the personalities people develop, and contracts for change. Exercises include developing negative and positive reactions, analyzing ulterior transactions, and investigating contamination of adult thinking through such influences as prejudice and advertising. Illustrated. 8½" × 11". Addison-Wesley. 118 p.

5

The Valuing Model: Raths and Simon's Values Clarification

Miss Jansen stops her sixth-grade social studies lesson and tells the students to put their books away and take out paper and pencils. It is time to do an exercise on personal values. Miss Jansen spends twenty minutes, twice a week, on these types of lessons. Today's lesson will be role playing around a common dilemma that students might face. She walks to the front of her desk, leans against it, and begins:

"Class, I'm going to tell you a story, and after the story you are to write down what you would have done it you were Peter."

This story is about Peter and his best friend Bob. Both boys have decided that they need a new baseball for the upcoming ball game. Together they have two dollars. They go into the local discount store that is advertising a sale on baseballs. The boys immediately head for the sports department. At the baseball table, they see a sign saying that some baseballs are for sale for only one dollar and fifty cents. Looking at the balls, Bob discovers that all the balls on sale are gone. The only ones left are the higher-priced ones costing three dollars. Peter says to Bob, "Heck, let's go; we don't have enough money." Bob says, "Wait, there's an empty box left over that is marked at the sale price. Let's take one of the three-dollar balls out of its box and put it into the lower-priced box. No one will ever know." Peter is not sure, but before he can act, Bob has made the exchange and is walking to the check-out counter. Bob yells to Peter to hurry up with the money. Peter runs to the counter, Bob hands him the box, and the cashier asks for a dollar and fifty cents. Peter pays, gets his change, and walks out the door with his purchase. At that moment, a large man grabs Peter by the arm, turns him around, and says, "Son, let me see that box." Peter glances up at the man and sees a badge on his coat that reads *Store Detective*. Peter looks quickly for Bob, but his friend has disappeared.

68

Miss Jansen looks up and tells her students to think very carefully about what they would tell the detective if they were Peter. After waiting two full minutes, she asks them to write down their answer on a piece of paper. She then asks if two students would like to act out what they would have done. Ernie, who prides himself in being glib and cocky, volunteers to play Peter. Roberta, a rather quiet child, volunteers to be the detective. They come to the front of the room and begin their play. Roberta grabs Ernie's arm and says, "Hey, boy, why did you steal that baseball?" Ernie responds, "I did not steal anything. The ball was in this box and I paid the price that is printed on it." Roberta says angrily, "You are a liar. You changed the box!" Ernie retorts, "I did not! I paid the price on the box. Prove that I didn't."

Miss Jansen stops the scene and asks Roberta, "You think that Peter was wrong to pay for that ball?" She turns to Ernie and asks, "What is another way that Peter might have acted?" Ernie replies, "He could just put the blame on Bob; after all, Bob made him do it." Miss Jansen turns to the class and asks, "How much is Bob to blame and how much is Peter to blame?" She then says to Roberta and Ernie, "OK, you two sit down. Let's have two more students come up and show us a different way that this scene could be portrayed."

The reader might recognize the above classroom lesson as a values-clarification exercise. Miss Jansen is attempting to provide students with activities that allow them to take an individual look at their own ways of behaving. Such activities help them explore their attitudes, aspirations, purposes, interests, and behaviors. Additionally, they learn to understand what some of the alternative values are that other people possess. Such a process enables students to choose a future course of action consciously from a selection of alternatives.

A value is defined by Raths, Harmin, and Simon as the outcome of a three-part process whereby the student is engaged in

Choosing:

1. freely
2. from alternatives
3. after thoughtful consideration of the consequences of each alternative

Prizing:

4. cherishing, being happy with the choice
5. willing to affirm the choice publicly

Acting:

6. doing something with the choice
7. repeatedly, in some pattern of life[1]

What does all this have to do with disruptive behavior in the classroom? Many teachers unwittingly give us the answer. It is common to hear a frustrated teacher lament the unscrupulous behavior of a student with such statements as "Kids today have no values. They have no sense of right or wrong." Louis Raths, Sidney Simon, and Merrill Harmin would agree with such thinking. They view the causes of much misbehavior as the result of a student not knowing or not thinking about his or her values and therefore not being able to live in accord with a guide of personal judgments.

Louis E. Raths, who developed the theoretical basis for today's popular techniques in values clarification, delineated three types of misbehavior. There is misbehavior that results from 1) a student's mental or physical capabilities, 2) a student's emotional experiences, and 3) a student's lack of values. For example, a student who bullies others or outsmarts others is taking advantage of his or her physical or mental assets. The student who cringes with fear every time he or she is corrected might be reliving the emotional trauma of being severely scared or beaten as a child. On the other hand, there are students who cheat, lie, or steal who do so because they do not possess any values criteria that would suggest that what they are doing is wrong. As Raths, Harmin, and Simon put it:

> We have found that several kinds of problems children often exhibit in school and at home are profitably seen as being caused by values, or, more precisely, by a lack of values. To put this another way, we have found that, when children with certain behavior problems are given value experiences of a particular kind, these problems often ease in intensity and/or frequency. In short, there is strong support for the notion that values must be added to the possible explanations of children's behavior problems.[2]

The students who can be most helped through values-clarification techniques are those who are very *apathetic, flighty, uncertain,* or *inconsistent,* or who are *drifters, overconformers, overdissenters,* or *role players*."[3]

Unlike the other behavior management models in this book, the values-clarification model does not provide immediate steps for the teacher to take when dealing with a student engaged in a disruptive act. Rather, values clarification is a technique to be used over a long period of time. Those students who misbehave due to a "values vacuum" need the frequent and ongoing opportunities to be engaged in values activities. One does not acquire or change values from one minute to the next. It is only after much time and much exploration that change comes about. For these reasons, the reader should keep in mind that the values-clarification model is proposed to be helpful over the "long run," and the reader will need to consider other models in this book for remedying immediate disruptive situations.

TEACHER AS CLARIFIER

The role of the teacher is to guide students through an exploration of their own values. This is done through informal teacher and student verbal exchanges as well as formal group exercises. The teacher must remain nonjudgmental and not press a student to accept the teacher's own values. The values-clarification authors believe that values are, by their very nature, personal. If a student is to act according to a private code of behavior, then the student needs to internalize that code by his or her own free will. Forcing one to accept a teacher's values is a losing proposition, as the student will rebel, neglect, and not be committed to such an external imposition. The Relationship-Listener's faith in the student's ability to make wise and productive choices permeates all the writings of the values clarificationists. As Raths, Harmin, and Simon wrote:

> We have presented a view of the concept of value that is based on a particular notion of human potential, one which emphasizes man's capacity for intelligent, self-directed behavior.[4]

The teacher's role as a Relationship-Listener who believes in the student's ability to choose wisely is an active one. The teacher must set up situations that make a student look at his or her own present values, consider alternatives, and make future choices. It is those procedures for setting up such situations that we will explain along the Teacher Behavior Continuum. It is mainly in the categories of *Silently Looking On, Questioning*, and *Modeling* that the teacher receives the most help.

VALUES CLARIFICATION AND THE TEACHER BEHAVIOR CONTINUUM

Let's introduce a typical student misbehavior that could be the result of a lack of values.

Simmie is an eleven-year-old girl who comes from a broken home. She lives with her Dad. Her other brothers and sisters live with their mother in another state. Simmie has to fend for herself, as her dad works nights and sleeps during the day. She usually sees her father only a few minutes each day. Her behavior in school is erratic. Some days she works attentively and is a "model" student; on other days she is "off in her own world"—spacy, dreamy, and inattentive. She is mostly calm and aloof with other students, but once in a while she completely "flies off the handle," screaming obscenities and gouging others with teeth and fingernails.

As we explain the values-clarification procedures along the Teacher Behavior Continuum, we will include specific applications to Simmie that will help to clarify her values and eventually improve her behavior. Let's begin.

Silently Looking On

The teacher needs to be aware of spontaneous moments when students indicate their existing values. In such one-to-one contacts, the teacher needs to listen carefully to what the student is saying before moving into *questions*. Indicators[5] of a student's values are expressions of:

1. *Attitudes*—"I think that ..." "I don't feel that ..."
2. *Aspirations*—"Some day, I want to be ..." "When I get older ..."
3. *Purposes*—"When I finish this, I'm going to buy a ..." "I want to make a ..."
4. *Interest*—"It feels great when I'm ..." "I love doing ..."
5. *Activities*—"After school, I do ..." "On vacations, I spend my time ..."

When the teacher *silently looks on* and hears a student making such statements, he or she can be prepared to probe the student's underlying values. The teacher needs to keep in mind the seven-step criteria of a true value: 1) choosing freely, 2) choosing from alternatives, 3) choosing after thoughtful consideration of the consequences of each alternative, 4) prizing and cherishing, being happy with the choice, 5) willing to affirm the choice publicly, 6) acting and doing something with the choice, 7) acting repeatedly in some pattern of life.

Simmie often comes to school and strikes up a conversation with Lucerne. Their teacher, Mr. Jordan, has often overheard her talking about how "out of sight" various Hollywood male movie stars are and that some day she "would love to live in California and learn to surfboard." The teacher takes such statements as *value indicators* of interest (male movie stars), aspirations (live in California), and activities (learn surfing).

Nondirective Statements

Nondirective statements are not delineated by the values clarificationists. Yet, in working with students, it is important to listen to their opinions and ideas and not to interject with one's own. When a student talks, the teacher should really listen (similar to Gordon's "active listening"), and to do so, he or she can use nondirective statements to paraphrase and encourage a student to continue.

> One morning Simmie passes the teacher at the door and says, "Wow, am I glad to be here at school." Mr. Jordan looks directly at her and says, "You are glad to be at school." Simmie replies, "You betcha, it's such a hassle getting out of the house without waking Dad and getting yelled at. I wish we had a bigger house." The teacher listens and replies, "You want to live in a larger house so you won't need to bother your dad." Simmie looks up and says, "No, not exactly. It's not Dad; it's just that the house is so crummy and messy. I don't want to talk about it." With that she breaks the conversation and sits down. Mr. Jordan returns to preparing himself for class.

It is important to note that the teacher did not press Simmie beyond her wishes to talk. When the student refuses to initiate conversation or asks to go no further, the discussion is at least temporarily halted. On many occasions a teacher can help a student think of his or her values by a simple nondirective statement (or a question) and leave it at that.

The teacher must take care not to interject his or her own thoughts and opinions. Nothing would have turned Simmie away further from the values-clarification process than after saying, "I wish we had a bigger house," Mr. Jordan had said, "Oh, I know. We all like bigger things, but we are too materialistic in this society. We should be happy with what we have." Such an interjected "pearl" might make the teacher feel like the "fountain of wisdom," but it would have left Simmie with the feeling that the teacher "has all the answers and what I think is unimportant."

Questions

Perhaps the most important tool that the values-clarifying teacher has is an abundance of questions to ask. If the student, in either an individual or group situation, indicates a willingness to continue the conversation, the teacher can formulate questions around the seven-step criteria of a value.[6]

1. *Choosing freely*
   —Where do you suppose you first got that idea?
   —How long have you felt that way?
   —Is there any rebellion in your choice?
   —How many years will you give to it? What will you do if you're not good enough?

2. *Choosing from alternatives*
   —What else did you consider before you picked this?
   —How long did you look around before you decided?
   —Did you consider another possible alternative?

3. *Choosing thoughtfully and reflectively*
   —What would be the consequences of each alternative available?
   —Have you thought about this very much?
   —Just what is good about this choice?

4. *Prizing and cherishing*
   —Are you glad you feel that way?
   —How long have you wanted it?
   —What good is it?

5. *Affirming*
   —Would you tell the class the way you feel some time?
   —Would you be willing to sign a petition supporting that idea?
   —Do people know you feel that way?

6. *Acting upon choices*
   —What are your first steps, second steps, and so on?
   —Have you made any plans to do more than you already have done?
   —Where will this lead you? How far are you willing to go?

7. *Repeating*
   —What are your plans for doing more?
   —Has it been worth the time and effort?
   —How long do you think you will continue?

Mr. Jordan has given class instructions to complete the sentence, "If I had three wishes to be granted, I would ask for . . ." After waiting five minutes, he asks if anyone would like to share his or her answer. Simmie responds immediately.

Simmie: "1) Be a movie star, 2) marry a handsome actor, and 3) live in Hollywood."

Mr. Jordan: "Where do you suppose you got those ideas?" (Choosing freely.)

Simmie: "From watching movies and reading magazines."

Mr. Jordan: "Are there other things that you have thought about?" (Choosing from alternatives.)

Simmie: "Yeah, once I was going to be a high-fashion model, but I'm not tall enough."

Mr. Jordan: "What is so good about being a movie star, marrying someone handsome, and living in Hollywood?" (Prizing and cherishing.)

Simmie: "I'd be famous and rich."

Mr. Jordan: "Could you be famous and rich doing something else? (Choosing thoughtfully and reflectively.)

Simmie: "Yeah, I guess so. I don't know doing what."

Mr. Jordan: (to the class) "Does anyone have any other ways that someone could become famous and rich?" (Choosing from alternatives.)

From this dialogue, the reader should get a sense of how Mr. Jordan is using questions to probe and explore the validity of Simmie's professed value. The teacher does not use the seven categories of questions in any rigid or all-inclusive manner. Rather, questions are to be used to probe a particular aspect of values at a time. There will be occasions when one will use a single kind of question as well as occasions when one will use all seven. The teacher will, with a student, eventually move into the final consideration of a true value: Is the student willing to act upon it (acting upon choices and repeating)? For example, is Simmie willing to work at being an actress, to take drama lessons, write scripts, practice diction, and so forth? If not, then she does not possess a true value and must look at the other choices open to her.

Directive Statements

When a teacher is engaged in values clarification, he or she should avoid the use of directive statements. If a student asks a teacher for his or her opinion, then the teacher should respond freely. However, this is quite different from telling the student what he or she should believe. At times an adult will, in actuality, be making a directive statement under the guise of questioning. For example, questions such as, "Don't you think that people should never do that? or "You can't possibly believe that is proper behavior, can you?" are value-laden. They are thinly veiled attempts to have the student comply with the teacher's views. All such value influences (questions or directive state-ments) are not designed to facilitate a student's own thinking.

Modeling

The use of the entire class for the discussion of individual values is an invaluable tool for value formation. Remember that part of the criteria for value clarification is choosing from alternatives, being knowledgeable about consequences, and choosing freely. If a student is to form his or her own true standards of conduct, the student must be aware of what the choices are in formulating those standards. By doing values-clarification exercises in a group, the student can listen to differing points of view and therefore have a greater source of information upon which to base the most rational decision. For these reasons, formal exercises for the teacher to use for the entire class are suggested. The teacher provides instructions, allows the individual stu-dent to reflect or write down his or her thoughts, and then asks if anyone would like to share his or her thinking. Students are not coerced to speak out. A quiet student who does not participate is still hearing various ideas and eventually may choose one (modeling) as his or her own.

We have already seen Mr. Jordan use such an approach by asking the class to complete the sentence, "If I had three wishes . . ." A few days later he asks the class to rank in order[7] the following statements:

1. I would rather live
    _____ in the country
    _____ in the suburbs
    _____ in the middle of a large city
2. Which would you *most* not want to be?
    _____ poor
    _____ sickly
    _____ ugly

After the students have made their rankings, he asks if anyone would discuss ranking for statement number two. Many hands are raised and a lively debate ensues among those who would least want to be poor, sickly, or ugly. This time Simmie does not participate. Instead, she intently listens to the most attractive girl in the class explain why she would least want to be sickly. The girl explains, "Your health is most important. If you feel good, then you can always do something later on about being poor or ugly, but if you're sick, it keeps you from doing anything. Besides, look at all the poor or ugly people who became great. Eleanor Roosevelt and Winston Churchill weren't any great shakes to look at. Look at how poor so many famous actors and actresses were when they began. People such as Elizabeth Taylor, Paul Newman, and Woody Allen made it because they were healthy and could work hard. You gotta be concerned about your health first." Simmie shakes her head in disapproval throughout the girl's explanation, yet she listens to every word.

There are literally hundreds of different values-clarification exercises that have been written for teachers to use. They can be found in the reference books at the end of this chapter. Some of them are listed here as examples.

- *I-Urge Telegrams:*[8] The student writes an imaginative telegram to someone whom he or she wants to influence.
- *What's in Your Wallet?*[9] The student takes out three items that show different things that he or she values. The student can voluntarily explain or write down his or her choices.
- *I Am the Jury:*[10] The student listens to a case involving a brilliant honor student who is caught selling one five-dollar bag of marijuana. The listener has to decide on the penalty and give reasons for the choice.
- *Your Personal Coat of Arms:*[11] The student draws and writes key words for his or her own coat of arms that include the most significant event in life, the greatest achievement, how he or she would want to be remembered, and so forth.

Students respond to various activities in many ways. There are exercises that involve ranking, sorting, completion of sentences, composition writing, role playing, formal discussions, public interviews, and checklists. The ultimate purpose is the same: to allow students to become actively involved in determining their past, present, and future values.

REINFORCEMENT, PHYSICAL INTERVENTION, AND ISOLATION

It should be obvious that teacher behaviors that shape and control students are antithetical to values clarification and are not to be used.

WHAT HAPPENED TO SIMMIE?

The reader may feel that he or she has been left hanging on the outcome of values clarification for Simmie. Did Simmie become more in control and less erratic in her school behavior? Did she decide to become an actress and to work hard for it? Or, did she change her values and become content with improving her present homelife? Well, as the television "soap opera" announcer tells the waiting audience, "Tune in tomorrow for these answers and more." We, as teachers, will not find immediate and dramatic changes in our students. Values take a long time to change, and we should not look for results until after continuing such techniques over a lengthy period.

This may seem awfully long to wait, but the values clarificationists point out that if teachers expect academic skills to be attained slowly, then so should they expect social skills to be learned slowly. A student undergoes literally hundreds of reading activities before being expected to read. A student similarly needs numerous values activities before being able to think and behave in ways that are different. Returning to Simmie, we will have to wait before seeing what changes have resulted.

SUMMARY

Briefly we can summarize teacher behaviors related to values clarification on the Teacher Behavior Continuum in Figure 5–1.

The teacher should a) avoid *directive statements* that judge, influence, and impose teacher values and b) avoid all teacher control in the forms of *reinforcement, physical intervention,* and *isolation.* The teacher overtly should 1) look and listen for *(silently looking on)* value indicators from the student. The teacher should 2) listen carefully, paraphrasing or repeating the student's thoughts *(nondirective statements).* After listening, if the student is receptive, the teacher can 3) ask *questions* that probe the seven elements of a true value. The exposure and modeling of alternative values are brought about by the teacher's using 4) formal group exercises.

NOTES

1. Louis E. Raths, Merrill Harmin, and Sidney B. Simon, *Values and Teaching* (Columbus: Charles E. Merrill Publishing, 1966), p. 30.

Silently Looking On	Nondirective Statements	Questions	Directive Statements	Modeling	Reinforcement	Physical Intervention and Isolation
(1) Look for value indicators—attitudes, aspirations, purposes, interest, activities	(2) Active Listening, paraphase student's thoughts	(3) Probe for true value —choose freely? —choose from alternatives? —choose thoughtfully & reflectively? —prizing & cherishing? —affirming? —acting? —repeating?	(a) Avoid judging, influencing, or imposing teacher values.	(4) Group exercises; i.e., —ranking —sorting —role playing —discussing dilemmas	(b) Avoid	

Ct   cT

Valuing Model

Authors: Louis E. Raths, Sidney Simon, Robert Hawley, and others

(numbers) overt behaviors
(letters) covert behaviors

FIGURE 5–1. Teacher Behavior Continuum (TBC)

2. Raths, Harmin, and Simon, *Values and Teaching*, p. 4.

3. Raths, Harmin, and Simon, *Values and Teaching*, p. 7.

4. Raths, Harmin, and Simon, *Values and Teaching*, p. 46.

5. Raths, Harmin, and Simon, *Values and Teaching*, pp. 65–79.

6. Raths, Harmin, and Simon, *Values and Teaching*, p. 63.

7. Sidney B. Simon, Leland W. Howe, and Howard Kirschenbaum, *Values Clarification: A Handbook of Practical Strategies for Teachers and Students* (New York: Hart Publishing, 1972), pp. 58–75.

8. Simon, Howe, and Kirschenbaum, *Values Clarification: A Handbook of Practical Strategies for Teachers and Students*, p. 246.

9. Simon, Howe, and Kirschenbaum, *Values Clarification*, p. 329.

10. Robert C. Hawley, *Value Exploration Through Role Playing* (New York: Hart Publishing, 1975), p. 93.

11. Sidney B. Simon, Robert C. Hawley, and David D. Britton, *Composition for Personal Growth: Values Clarification Through Writing* (Hart Publishing, 1973), p. 58.

REFERENCES

Harmin, M. *What I've Learned about Values Eduction*. Bloomington, Indiana: Phi Delta Kappa Educational Foundation, 1977.

Harmin, M., & Saville, S. *A Peaceable Classroom: Activities to Calm and Free Student Energies*. Minneapolis: Winston Press, 1977.

Hawley, Robert C. *Value Exploration through Role Playing*. New York: Hart Publishing, 1975.

Presno, V. and Presno, C. *The Value Realms: Activities for Helping Students Develop Values*. New York, Teachers College Press, 1980.

Raths, Louis E., Harmin, Merrill, and Simon, Sidney B. *Values and Teaching*, p. 30. Columbus: Charles E. Merrill Publishing, 1966.

Simon, Sidney B., Hawley, Robert C., and Britton, David D. *Composition for Personal Growth: Values Clarification Through Writing*. New York: Hart Publishing, 1973.

Simon, Sidney B., Howe, Leland W., and Kirschenbaum, Howard. *Values Clarification: A Handbook of Practical Strategies for Teachers and Students*, rev. ed. New York: Hart Publishing, 1978.

For additional materials and workshops offered, write to the Adirondack Mountain Humanistic Education Center, Upper Jay, New York 12987.

INSTRUCTIONAL MEDIA

The following materials are available from:

> Media Five
> 3211 Cahuenga Boulevard, West
> Los Angeles, California 90068

Discussion and demonstration of the development and meaning as well as strategies of values clarification. Shows how teachers are making values strategies a regular part of the school day.

Values Clarification in the Classroom

Sidney Simon

> 30 minutes; color. Rental fee $100 (Leader's manual with 25 teacher packets for in-service workshops).
>
> *Provides background for utilizing the values-clarification approach in the classroom.*

Beginning Values Clarification

Sidney Simon

> 30 minutes; color. Rental fee $100 (Leader's manual with 25 teacher packets for in-service workshop materials).
>
> *Provides background for the values clarification approach in the classroom.*

The New Focus on Values and Morality

> 29 minutes; color. Sale price $395; rental fee $45 per week.
>
> *Introduces ideas, people, and practices in the morals/values area. Visits to elementary and secondary classes where strategies are in use.*

Values, Identity, Responsibility

29 minutes; color. Sale price $395; rental fee $45 per week.

Underlines the importance of communication in a child's affective development. Identity and responsibility are seen as the keys to deal effectively with student concerns and values issues.

Teaching Morals and Values

Madeline Hunter

29 minutes; color. Sale price $395; rental fee $45 per week.

Illustrates a staff seminar on the teacher's role in the area of values and morality.

Beginning Values Clarification

Louis Raths

29 minutes; color. Sale price $395; rental fee $45 per week.

A primer on values-clarification covering three levels of education: facts, concepts, and values. Raths provides an explanation of the genesis of values clarification; Sidney Simon, Merrill Harmin, and Howard Kirschenbaum discuss and demonstrate classroom techniques.

Values Clarification in the Classroom

29 minutes; color. Sale price $395; rental fee $45 per week.

Demonstrates values clarification teaching styles by Merrill Harmin. Description of theory-to-practice aspects of values clarification by Raths with others explaining how to raise issues, stimulate thinking, and be nonjudgmental.

Finding Values Through Simulation Games

29 minutes; color.

Depicts a twelfth-grade class playing the simulation game, "Star Power." Garry Shirts, the game creator, points out the values discoveries and discusses the use of simulation games for values development from the fourth grade on.

6

The Social Discipline Model of Rudolf Dreikurs

It is the first day of winter semester and Mr. Garcia is casually observing his new class of students entering the room for third-period chemistry class. He finds nothing particularly distinctive about this new group until Ronald appears. This student is dressed in faded blue jeans that are covered with sign patches expounding such messages as "Luv," "Keep on Trucking," and "Far out." Even more noticeable are the two patches running across the seat of the pants with the words "Screw You" on one hip pocket, and "Mother F___ker" on the other. The rest of Ronald's attire includes a T-shirt and a western-style hat pulled down over his eyes. In order for him to see while walking, he has to lead with his chin and look out over his nose.

Mr. Garcia gradually loses sight of Ronald as he visually skims the remaining members of the classroom, but suddenly he hears a girl's scream, another student's laugh, and the classroom quiet. Everyone's attention focuses on Ronald, who is slouched down in his seat with his hat pulled over his face. The class glances from the teacher to Ronald and back to the teacher. Seeing that neither the teacher nor Ronald is going to make any further move, the class returns to their chatting. A few minutes later Mr. Garcia begins reading through the class roster, calling each student's name and receiving in return a proper acknowledgment such as "I'm here." When he calls out "Ronald Foster" the response is, "OK, keep cool, teacher-o!" which breaks up the class with laughter. Mr. Garcia ignores this response, finishes calling the roll, and finally introduces himself and the content of the course. He turns his back to the class and begins to write the name of the textbook across the chalkboard. Before he can finish, the same girlish scream is heard, but this

84

time with such intensity that it signals something more serious. The girl seated in front of Ronald jumps to her feet, crosses her arms across her chest, and runs frantically to the classroom door. As she passes before Mr. Garcia and the front of the class, everyone can see that her bra is open in the back. A few nervous giggles come from the class, and now all eyes focus on Ronald and then, unfortunately, *back to Mr. Garcia.*

Mr. Garcia is quite obviously "on the spot." It is the beginning of the semester, he faces a troublesome male student, a distraught female student, and a class of thirty-one teenagers waiting to see what will transpire. What specific steps should he take to defuse this situation, get the class back on track, help the girl, and eventually aid Ronald in improving his behavior? What would you do? We will explain Rudolf Dreikurs's techniques as we apply them to Mr. Garcia's treatment of Ronald. As the explanation unfolds, the reader will see a particular application of teacher treatment to the category of student misbehavior that Ronald fits as well as Dreikurs's applications to three other common categories of misbehavior, as identified by him.

DREIKURS AND ALFRED ADLER'S SOCIAL THEORY

Dreikurs's writings flow out of the work of the noted social psychologist Alfred Adler. Adler believed that the central motivation of all humans is to belong to and be accepted by others. Man is foremost a social animal. Books written by Dreikurs and his various associates (*Children: The Challenge, Logical Consequences, Encouraging Children to Learn, Psychology in the Classroom*, and *Discipline Without Tears*) all have a common bond with Adler. This bond is that all behavior, including misbehavior, is orderly, purposeful, and directed towards achieving social recognition.[1] Each action taken by such students as Ronald Foster is goal-directed. The "inner" goal results in the "outward" behavior. The teacher must have a student like Ronald recognize his "inner" goal and then help the student to change to the more appropriate goal of learning how to belong with others. This is the rationale for placing Dreikurs with the Confrontation-Contractors. He believes in an underlying cause for misbehavior (similar to the Relationship-Listeners), yet he believes that its correction is the result of a teacher actively showing a student how to belong.

When a student is unsuccessful in obtaining social acceptance (sometimes as early as his or her infant or toddler years at home), a pattern of misbehavior begins. He or she is left with the recourse of trying to fulfill inner needs by annoying, destructive, hostile, or helpless behavior. If we, as teachers, can help misbehaving students understand their mistaken, faulty goals and provide them with avenues for group acceptance, then such students will rationally change their own behaviors. These subconscious goals that motivate misbehavior are 1)*Attention Getting*, 2) *Power and Control*, 3) *Revenge*, and 4) *Helplessness*.[2]

1. *Attention Getting:* This is evident when a student is constantly looking to belong and be recognized in the class. Instead of receiving such recognition through productive work, often a student will resort to acting in ways that demand incessant praise or criticism. Both praise and criticism of an incessant nature are equally undesirable.

2. *Power and Control:* This is a goal for a student who feels inferior, who feels unable to measure up to the expectations of others or of self. It makes no difference whether the student is actually handicapped in some way or has only a false perception of being inferior. In either case, the youngster will try to remedy this perception of inferiority by trying to get his or her own way, by being the boss, by forcing himself or herself onto others, or by bragging or clowning.

3. *Revenge:* This is a goal for the student who feels unable to gain attention or power. This student sees himself or herself as having unequal status because of what others have done to him or her. This student places the blame for his or her plight on those outside. The student feels hurt by others and compensates by following the injuncion of an "eye for an eye." In other words, "If I'm hurting, then I have the right to make others hurt." The student goes beyond the desire for attention and power, beyond the desire to win. He or she resorts to achieving status, not by merely winning over others, but by beating others with maliciousness and humiliation.

4. *Helplessness or Inadequacy:* The student operating with this goal is the most pathetic. He or she has given up on the possibility of being a member of or of gaining any status in the group. This student not only feels uncared for, unequal, and wrongfully treated but also feels incapable of doing anything (either constructively or destructively) about it. The student has accepted the feeling of being a nobody and no longer cares what happens.

With this beginning understanding of Dreikurs, let us move to the Teacher Behavior Continuum with Mr. Garcia and Ronald Foster.

DREIKURS'S METHODS AND THE TEACHER BEHAVIOR CONTINUUM

To begin, the teacher must determine which of the four faulty goals is motivating the student. This determination is basically a four-step process, as follows:

1. The teacher observes and collects information about the student in situations involving peers and family.
2. Once the teacher has gathered information about the student, he or she can then hypothesize or guess which of the underlying goals is held by the student.
3. This goal can be verified by the teacher by reflecting on what feelings arise within the teacher as a result of the student's behavior.
4. Final verification is achieved by confronting the student with a series of four questions and looking for the student's recognition reflex.

In carrying out this procedure, the teacher moves through *Silently Looking On, Questions, Directive Statements*, and back to *Questions*.

Silently Looking On

Mr. Garcia, in the immediate situation with thirty-one pairs of eyes peering at him, disinvolves himself emotionally from Ronald's behavior. He has noted the first impression of rudeness, braggadocio, and flashiness that Ronald has created. Mr. Garcia makes a mental note to himself to search for more information by looking at school records, talking to former teachers, and possibly making a home visit. For now, though, with limited information, he suspects that Ronald's goal may be attention getting, power, or revenge. It certainly is not helplessness!

It is important to remain calm during the beginning encounter with a student operating under any of the faulty goals, and not to give the student what he or she seeks. For example, the worst thing Mr. Garcia could do would be to call out loudly and angrily to Ronald. To do so would give Ronald the attention he seeks (attention getting), or it would accelerate the battle of who will win out (power), or it would drive Ronald into physically lashing out (revenge).

Mr. Garcia can remain calm because he knows rationally that Ronald's behavior is not directed at him personally but is simply the student's previously learned mode of responding in groups. Of course, a quite human reaction from a teacher would be to explode, but his urge must be held in check. Examining this emotional urge or feeling toward the student will be most helpful in narrowing down and identifying the student's goal.

Questions (covert)

Now Mr. Garcia can capitalize on the inner emotions that Ronald's behavior has evoked. Dreikurs suggests that teachers covertly ask themselves four questions related to the goals.[3]

1. Do I feel annoyed? If so, the teacher may have reason to suspect *Attention Getting* as a goal.
2. Do I feel beaten or intimidated? If so, he or she may have reason to suspect *Power* as a goal.
3. Do I feel wronged or hurt? If so, he or she may have reason to suspect *Revenge* as a goal.
4. Do I feel incapable of reaching the child in any way? If so, he or she may have reason to suspect *Helplessness* as the goal. Mr. Garcia analyzes his feelings as "annoyed," to say the least, and even slightly intimidated, which suggests that Ronald's goal was attention getting or power.

If the teacher had given free rein to his first impulses, let us see what Ronald's probable responses would have been. If Mr. Garcia had yelled at him, Ronald might have responded with, "That's cool, daddy-o. Don't get all upset; you are losing your head over nothing." In other words, if Ronald's goal was power, he would have won at that point. He would have "shown up" Mr. Garcia in front of the class as a teacher who becomes easily flustered while he, a seventeen-year-old student, was more of a man, with calm and collected reactions. If Ronald's goal was to get attention, he would have responded in a different way. Mr. Garcia's yells might have caused Ronald to put his head down sheepishly and grin to himself. The rest of the class would be observing Ronald, and as soon as Mr. Garcia turned away, Ronald's head would be back up, face smiling, and looking around to make sure that everyone had seen him. In both cases, Mr. Garcia's primary reaction would have done little to prevent numerous future occurrences. Mr. Garcia knows he can't play into the student's scheme and is ready now to take specific action. He makes a guess that *attention getting* is Ronald's primary goal.

Directive Statements

The previous reflective and covert behaviors of *silently looking on* and *questions* were primarily enacted to gather information, to narrow down and identify the student's possible goal, and to make a tentative plan for action. A teacher trained in Dreikurs's approach would take only a split second from first witnessing the girl running out of the classroom to begin action with Ronald.

Having identified attention getting as Ronald's underlying goal, Mr. Garcia acts in a way that deprives Ronald of the attention related to his misbehavior. Mr. Garcia turns to the girl and quietly tells her to come back in the classroom when she is ready and to take another seat away from Ronald.

He then turns to the class and states,"Class, I would like to introduce you to some of the laboratory equipment you will be using this year. In a few minutes I would like you to break up into groups of four people and gather around the lab tables at the back of the room. When you get settled, open to the first page of your lab manual, where you will find pictures of the various kinds of equipment. As a group, see if you can first learn the equipment names, then I will join each group briefly to demonstrate how to use some of the more dangerous equipment, such as the Bunsen burner. OK, class, find your groups of four and move to your tables." Turning to Ronald, he adds, "Oh, Ronald Foster, your behavior has told me that you are not ready to work with others. I want you to remain in your seat. When you think you can join a group without being disruptive, you may do so."

Having attended to the class, Mr. Garcia gives Ronald a *directive statement*. He has told Ronald that he can join the group if and when he is ready to contribute in an appropriate way. This is an example of a teacher applying *logical consequences*, rather than punishment. (We will explain this difference more fully in the section on reinforcement. For now, let us say that Mr. Garcia has employed the loss of the student's right to engage in an activity as a result of behavior that would be counterproductive to accomplishing that activity as a logical consequence.) Before Mr. Garcia can conclude definitely that attention getting is Ronald's goal and then continue with a long-range plan based on that goal identification, he needs further verification. He can achieve this by returning to overt questioning with Ronald.

Questions (overt)

Ronald has stayed by himself, slouched down with his hat over his face for nearly half the period. This is a further sign that Mr. Garcia has correctly identified Ronald's goal. If Ronald had wanted power, he would have continued to defy the teacher's rules. If Ronald had wanted revenge, he would have physically retaliated against the girl or teacher.

Mr. Garcia eyes Ronald slowly getting out of his seat and moving towards the lab table. There is only one spot open in the groups of four, and he heads towards that spot. When this group of three notices that he is ready to join them, one of the girls at the table (the very one that Ronald bothered) begins to complain and shout, "No, no, you don't! You're not joining our table, turkey." Ronald then turns to another nearby group and is greeted with, "You're not coming into our group. There is dangerous stuff here—you'll get us killed!" With a parting shot, "You're all a bunch of jerks," Ronald returns to his desk. Mr. Garcia moves towards him, takes a seat nearby, and in a voice that cannot be heard by anyone else begins to question Ronald.

Teacher: "Do you know why you acted like you did this morning?" *(confronting)*

Ronald: (Simply shrugs his shoulders)

Teacher: "I have some ideas. Would you like to know?"

Ronald: (Gives a yes nod)

Teacher: "Could you want special attention?" *(verifying)*

Ronald: For the first time his eyes look directly at Mr. Garcia, and he gives a slight smile. *(recognition reflex)*

During a discussion in a calm setting, Dreikurs proposes that the teacher do as Mr. Garcia has done.[4] The teacher should ask the student if he or she is interested in knowing why he or she behaves as he or she does. If the student does not resist, the teacher asks four sequential questions. Dreikurs listed them as:

(Attention)	1. Could it be that you want special attention?
(Power)	2. Could it be that you want our own way and hope to be boss?
(Revenge)	3. Could it be that you want to hurt others as much as you feel hurt by them?
(Helplessness)	4. Could it be that you want to be left alone?[5]

After the teacher asks each of these questions, he or she looks *(silently looking on)* for behavioral verification. If the student smiles, laughs, looks up suddenly, moves his or her shoulders, or shows other signs of response to the implied goal, then the teacher has conclusive evidence that his or her hypothesis is correct and treatment can proceed. The teacher formulates a plan and returns to appropriate *directive statements*.

Directive Statements

Now that Ronald has given the "recognition reflex" to question number one, Mr. Garcia can be confident that *attention* is his goal. Mr. Garcia's task now becomes one of finding ways for Ronald to receive attention through constructive social behavior. In other words, he needs to give Ronald the attention that he craves. Following are descriptions of treatment for each of the four goals that correspond with Dreikurs's prescriptive chart for teachers.[6]

Attention: A student who seeks attention should not receive it when he or she acts up. To give attention to the student for inappropriate behavior would be playing into the student's plan and would not help the student to learn how to behave productively in the group. Instead, the teacher might do some of the following:

- Tell the student that he or she will be talked to three times each morning. The teacher then initiates conversation with the student at three times that are divorced from any misbehavior.
- Set aside a period of time when the student will be listened to by everyone in the class. He or she may tell a story, a joke, or share something at a designated time each day.

Power: A student who wishes to possess power should not be able to engage the teacher in a struggle. The teacher who falls for this "bait" and gets pulled into the battle is merely continuing the excitement and challenge for the student. The student becomes increasingly bolder and pleased with trying to test the teacher. The teacher should attempt to remove the issue of power altogether and force the student to look for some other goal for behaving. Some examples of a teacher disengaging from a power struggle would be:

- When the student defies the teacher, the teacher merely says, "I cannot force you to do this. If you will not work on your paper, then choose to do something else that is quiet. Later, you can tell me when you will get your work done (at recess, at home, in the morning, and so forth)."
- Give the student power by allowing him or her to be lunch monitor, take messages to the office, collect homework, take attendance, be group leader, and the like.

Revenge: In this case, the teacher is dealing with a more difficult task. A student who feels hurt and wishes to retaliate must be handled in a caring, affectionate manner. It is probable that this student appears unloving and uncaring, and is very hard to "warm up to." But this is exactly what the student needs, to feel cared for. The teacher might show such care by:

- Saying, when the student attempts to hurt someone else, "I cannot let you hurt anyone, and I don't want to see you get hurt. I care for you and want to help you. How can I help you solve this problem?"
- Having special moments with the student. Take him or her out to lunch or to an after-school event, or even a visit to your home. Have frequent private, friendly conversations. Be sure to greet the student with a smile and a cheerful "hello" each day.

Helplessness: The student who shows inadequacy or helplessness is the most discouraged. He or she has lost all initiative of ever trying to belong to the group. The teacher must exercise great patience and attempt to show the child that he or she is capable. Some practices that might help a helpless student would be:

- To allow the student to bring in a favorite project or hobby from home that he or she can work on in school (building miniature cars, embroidery, coin collections, and the like).
- To bring in a project for the child to do in school from which he or she will experience success and be able to show the rest of the class his or her achievement (a walkie-talkie kit, painting by numbers, building a stereo component, learning Morse code, and so on).
- To respond to a despairing student, who throws his or her papers, pencils, or books, by saying, "You are trying hard and it is difficult to learn to write (spell, divide, compose, and so forth). I know that you are going to improve and learn. Let's pick up these papers and try again."

Let us see how Mr. Garcia takes the general guidelines for the attention-getting student and develops a unique treatment for Ronald.

After questioning the student, Mr. Garcia continues his conversation. He discovers that during the summer Ronald works on a ranch in Montana (the reason for the cowboy hat). One of his hobbies over the past three years has been collecting belt buckles. His collection currently contains over two hundred different types, one of which he is wearing. Mr. Garcia asks him if he knows what metal is in the belt buckle. Ronald does not know.

Mr. Garcia capitalizes on Ronald's interest in buckles by telling him that during this semester the class will be learning a great deal about various metals. He further tells Ronald that, after he learns to use the equipment safely and understands the general principles of chemistry, he can melt, combine, and cast metals to make his own belt buckle. Ronald might also learn how to control various acids and then burn designs into the metal. In fact, to help interest the other students in the chemistry of metals, Ronald is told he may bring his buckle collection in to share with the class. As can be seen, Mr. Garcia is finding a socially acceptable way for Ronald to receive attention.

Ronald is obviously interested, but he jars Mr. Garcia back to the immediate situation with a sarcastic, "Well, teach, this sounds groovy but there's one big problem. I can't do all these neat things without equipment, and no one wants me in their group. What do you suggest? Maybe you'll buy me my own laboratory?" Mr. Garcia, as a Dreikurs teacher, knows that he must capitalize on using the group of students as a *model* to help Ronald to adjust.

Modeling

Mr. Garcia informs Ronald that at the end of class today, and on every Friday, there will be a short class council meeting to discuss problems that are of concern to the members of the class. He adds that Ronald could bring up his problem at that time and see what he and the class might work out.

Dreikurs believes that Western schools and classrooms, as part of a democratic society, need to be models or laboratories of that society.[7] In other words, students need to practice democratic principles in school in order to learn how to contribute later to society as a whole. The central process for carrying out this modeling of democracy is the use of the class meeting, which Mr. Garcia refers to as the class council. Regular meetings should be held to discuss everyday occurrences as well as long-range policies. We will see in the next chapter how a fellow Confronting-Contractor, William Glasser, has further refined and elaborated on this concept of classroom meetings.

Meetings can be conducted informally without a designated leader, or formally with a rotating president, recorder, and treasurer. Voting should be avoided as it has a tendency to alienate the minority. Instead, decisions should be made through arriving at a consensus of all members. When many people agree with a decision, peer pressure tends to influence the one or two "holdouts" and thus make the decision unanimous. (We see this at political party conventions. After a hard battle among several candidates, one individual finally emerges a winner and all opposition evaporates. A united party once again emerges.) Let's see how Mr. Garcia capitalizes on the group process.

Mr. Garcia calls the class back to their seats and tells them that, in his classes, he always has a class council meeting on Fridays for the last twenty minutes of the period. However, since this is the first week of a new semester and they have a lot of problems to work out, they will have a meeting every day this week, beginning today. The class is then encouraged to begin an open general discussion. One or two students bring up different problems pertaining to missing lab equipment, how they are going to be graded, and whether the lab could be open during their free period after lunch. Finally, Ronald raises his hand, and everyone turns to look at him. "I have no equipment, and I'm in no group." The girl whom he previously embarrassed shouts, "Serves you right." Mr. Garcia interjects, "What Ronald has done is in the past. What can we do about his not having a group to join?" The class begins in earnest to discuss the issue. Most students express the feeling that if Ronald has no equipment then he cannot pass the course and that would be unfair. Some members ask the three-member group if they would let Ronald into their group. Again, the girl that had been embarrassed states, "No way! He will bug us and keep us from our work. Those chemicals are dangerous!" However, the other two members of the group say that they would be willing to work with him on a trial basis. Finally, after much discussion, it is decided that the girl will change places with a student in another group and Ronald would now have three people with whom he could work at the laboratory table. Ronald appears greatly relieved to hear this decision.

Up to this point, everything seems to have been resolved. But what happens if Ronald continues to misbehave? What recourse does the teacher or class have? We need to look at Dreikurs's interpretation of *logical consequences* to answer these questions.

Reinforcement

Dreikurs does not believe in the use of punishment, negative reinforcement, or praise (positive reinforcement). Instead he substitutes *natural/logical consequences* and the process of *encouragement*. Let us explain each as it applies to Ronald.

> *Natural/Logical Consequences:*   If Ronald should create a commotion after becoming accepted in the group, he could be disciplined as a result of some of the following logical consequences:
> Generally,
>
> • Have the group of three decide what should be done with Ronald.
> • Have Ronald work alone and have him use the laboratory equipment on his own time (at lunch, study hall, after school).
> • Bring Ronald's misbehavior back to the entire class in a classroom meeting to decide on future consequences.
>
> Specifically,
>
> • If Ronald has been causing a disturbance by poking students with a pencil, take away all of his pencils and tell Ronald that whenever he needs to write he'll have to come to the teacher's desk to ask for a pencil.

- If Ronald has been constantly moving out of his chair and distracting others, tell Ronald that he does not seem to need a chair and take it away from him. Let him stand until he requests to have it back and agrees to stay in it.

A *natural* consequence is defined as that which happens as a result of one's behavior. If a student is rushing to get into line and trips and falls, we call this a natural consequence. On the other hand, if a student is rushing and pushing others in order to be first in line and is removed by the teacher to a place at the end of the line, then this would be identified as a *logical* consequence. In other words, a natural consequence is an inevitable occurrence that happens by itself, while a logical consequence is arranged but directly related to the preceding behavior. Dreikurs believes that, in a democratic society and in a democratic classroom, students must be responsible for how they behave. There is no room for autocratic punishment, as such punishment further alienates and discourages a child. Extensive punishment serves as a force to drive a student toward the goal of revenge. Punishment is not seen as being logically related to a student's behavior. It is inflicted as a reaction to personal dissatisfaction felt by the teacher. Punishment says to the student, "You had better behave or I (the teacher) will make life miserable for you." If the student does "knuckle under," it is because of the power of the teacher and not because the student has learned how to be a proactive member of the group. If one accepts Dreikurs's definition of human behavior as a purposeful attempt to belong, then a teacher who uses punishment blocks a student's purpose. Punishment "plays back" into the student's misdirected goals. It gives attention, enhances the power struggle, stimulates further revenge, and keeps the helpless child in his or her place.

Additionally, Dreikurs rather pragmatically points out that, in today's age of equal rights and militancy, students are not easily coerced by the use of authoritarian power. Not only does punishment thwart a student's ambition, but it simply does not work.[8] Let us further explore the operational distinction between punishment and natural/logical consequences. Sending a student home with a note, keeping him or her after school, paddling, scolding, ridiculing, or standing the student in a corner are all forms of physical or psychological punishment. The teacher's actions are aimed at hurting the child or making him or her feel badly. Punishment is the teacher's vengeance for a committed crime. On the other hand, students who clean up the mess they created, who are put at the end of the line for shoving, who miss recess because of tardiness with their assigned work, or who are barred from using certain materials until they choose to use them properly are all actually involved in the effects of logical consequences. Logical consequences are not always easy to tailor **to** every disruptive action. However, it is the teacher's task to arrange the situation that follows the disruption in a way that the student can see a relationship between the consequences and his or her behavior. (This is a further break from the Relationship-Listener position, particularly Gordon's, who would criticize logical consequences as being false, contrived, and manipulative.)

Finally, it is important to note the differences in a teacher's attitude and manner in the application of logical consequences as opposed to the act of punishment. Two teachers might arrive at the same solution for a problem caused by a child's behavior, but one will be an example of logical consequences and the other will be an example of punishment. Sounds confusing, but it really isn't! During quiet work time, Sue Ann continually pokes Ernie with a pencil. One teacher, "Mr. Matter-of-Fact," tells Sue Ann, "Sue Ann, if you continue to poke Ernie then you will have to give me all your pencils. I'll give them back to you at recess when the rest of the class is outdoors. Then you can finish your work without bothering anyone." The other teacher, "Mr. How-Dare-You," says, "Sue Ann, I have told you a thousand times not to do that. Can't you understand anything? If I catch you once more I'll take all your pencils away and you'll stay in at recess. Maybe being alone is the only way that you can work!" Mr. Matter-of-Fact has calmly told the student to use the pencil correctly or give it up. Mr. How-Dare-You acts as though he has been personally affronted and that Sue Ann's misbehavior is a direct challenge to his authority. He tries to hammer her down by scolding, questioning her competence, and challenging her. The same outcome has occurred, the student has had the pencil confiscated, but Mr. Matter-of-Fact has used logical consequences and Mr. How-Dare-You has applied punishment.

Encouragement: At the same time that the class and Mr. Garcia are applying logical consequences to Ronald's behavior, Mr. Garcia is also using the encouragement process. Mr. Garcia asks Ronald to keep inventory of all laboratory equipment and to prepare an order of new supplies for the class. He makes sure that Ronald brings in his belt buckle collection. Mr. Garcia also makes a mental note to greet Ronald warmly each day.

The encouragement process is an attitude taken with a misbehaving student that results in a climate of respect and optimism.[9] One must remember that a student whose goal is attention feels stifled by authority, and may retreat to the even more destructive goal of *power*. When that goal is "beaten down" by an overbearing, punitive teacher, the student may then resort to the goal of *revenge* to retaliate. When revenge is crushed by even more coercive means, we may finally have the most pathetic result, a student who has simply given up and has internalized the goal of *helplessness*. This lowering of goals is the result of a student becoming further discouraged. Not only does the student retreat further back into gloom and despair, but so does the teacher. The vicious cycle compounds the problem.

The role of the teacher is to stop this dissipation of hope by using encouragement. This is accomplished by such teacher-actions as:

- *Emphasizing improvement rather than a perfect product.*
- *Criticizing the student's actions, but not the student;* i.e., "I like you but I don't like to hear you shouting."
- *Keeping the student in a group with other students who are willing to help.* Determine those peers who are most accepting and tolerant of the student in question. Seat the student with them and arrange for him or her to work with them in groups. Find a companion or friend for the student.
- *Refraining from having the student compete against others.* Do not compare the student to others ("Why can't you behave like Rufus?") or constantly single out for praise others who outperform the youngster. De-emphasize grades; try to grade the student on effort, not his or her rank in relation to others. Avoid contests for the best-behaved student or citizen of the week, where the student has little chance of winning.

Dreikurs believes that the provision of positive reinforcement is generally not a desirable method. Encouragement is much broader than the Rules/Rewarders-Punishers' use of verbal praise, material or situational rewards as conditioning to achieve appropriate behavior. In 1963, Dinkmeyer and Dreikurs wrote:

> Unfortunately, even the well meaning and sincere educator may often fail to convey much needed encouragement if he tries to express his approval through praise. . . . Praise may have a discouraging effect in the long run, since the child may depend on it constantly and never be quite sure whether he will merit another expression of special approval and get it.[10]

Dinkmeyer and Dreikurs are not saying that praise should be totally avoided, but what they are suggesting is that too much praise makes a child dependent on the teacher. The student who is "won over" by the teacher to work quietly due to the teacher's praise ("Oh look at Hillary! What a fine student to be working so quietly! I am so proud that you're being so quiet.") has not learned social behavior. Instead of learning how to act out of consideration for others, the child instead is learning how to act for purposes of receiving the teacher's special compliments and dispensations. In other words, the child behaves well, but for all the wrong reasons. If the teacher is removed from the scene, the child's behavior will deteriorate. The child needs to internalize the correct motivation for being well behaved (acting as a productive member of the group), in order for it to be lasting.

In addition, the child who sees himself or herself as a failure and is motivated by *revenge* or *helplessness* will tend to disbelieve the authenticity of the teacher's words. A child who refuses to work and "gives up" on carrying out any order may have reason to speculate on why the teacher makes such an effort to praise him or her ("Oh, Sam, look what a good job you did! You make me so pleased when you hang your coat up!" Or, "Margie, it's great the way that you answered that question!"). The student will in effect believe that the teacher is overcompensating and that he or she is being singled out because he or she is indeed inferior. The child may think, "Why make such a big deal about hanging my coat up or answering a simple question? The teacher must think I'm a real nincompoop (idiot, jerk, bozo, and so on)." Thus the opposite effect of what the teacher intended will result, a further sign that reaffirms the child's inferiority. In this vein of thought, Dreikurs and Grey wrote that there is a fundamental difference between the act of reward and the act of encouragement. Few realize that, at times, success can be very discouraging. The child may conclude that, although success was achieved once, it could not happen again. The student's recent "success" may become a threat to his or her future ability to succeed. But what is worse, such an event often conveys to the child the assumption, which actually is shared by most of his or her teachers and fellow students, that he or she is worthwhile only when he or she is successful.[11]

What we have, then, is the premise that praise or other forms of reward seem to heighten a child's anxiety always to have to "measure up." It puts constraints on a child who feels such pressure. He or she feels comfortable only when being successful. The discomfort with being unsuccessful discourages a child further from feelings of being accepted and of being an acceptable person. He or she feels accepted only when successful, but not when something less than success occurs as a result of efforts expended. The child who needs to learn to be a member must learn to accept his or her individual self as being a person capable of both success and failure but, despite outcomes, who is still worthy of being loved and accepted by others.

A child who is always dependent on being rewarded for what he or she does is in a bind when it comes to taking a risk. The child who is learning how to belong must be encouraged to try new ways of behaving. The student who learns that it is safe and rewarding to be meek and passive will not easily venture into the unknown by being assertive and active. He or she won't venture into untried areas. This is the danger of having "success-proof" programs or "praise-laden" teachers.

The teacher must not stress the concept of success but, instead, promote a climate of always accepting the student as worthwhile. This happens when a teacher uses encouragement rather than such reinforcement as praise.

Following are two contrasting lists that give examples of praise versus encouragement. Praise focuses on the teacher being pleased by the child and on the child achieving a completed product. Conversely, encouragement focuses on the student and on the process of the student trying.

Praise	*Encouragement*
1. "I (teacher) like what you have done."	1. "You're trying harder."
2. "Great job! What a smart person."	2. "You must be happy with (playing that game, being with others, and so on)."
3. "You get a star (token, free time) for doing that."	3. "It must be a good feeling to know you're doing well."
4. "I'm going to tell everyone how proud I am of you."	4. "You have every reason to be proud."

Physical Intervention and Isolation

Forms of teacher intervention such as paddling or shaking a student would be rejected by Dreikurs. Such treatment would be seen as a form of punishment that would drive a student further away from social cooperation. Pain experienced as a natural consequence (without the possibility of serious harm) could be allowed. Some examples of this might be the student who rushes to be first in line and in his or her haste falls and is bruised, or the student who repeatedly provokes the classroom gerbil and is bitten. On the other hand, there are some natural consequences that can eventuate when a student precariously tilts back in his or her chair, or when a "ninety-pound weakling" begins to taunt and enrage a two-hundred-and-fifty-pound high-school football tackle. These could be dangerous consequences, and the teacher would be wise to prevent them from occurring. It is important to note that a teacher should carefully judge the natural consequence before deciding to act or not to act in a given situation.

The use of isolation must also be judiciously used by the teacher. Dreikurs advocates the use of isolation only as a logical consequence. We saw that Ronald was isolated temporarily by Mr. Garcia when his behavior was immediately disruptive of others. However, Ronald was given the opportunity to join the group once he decided that he wished to belong.

It is obvious that if being part of a group is the ultimate goal for all individuals, then each person needs to learn to relate successfully to others. One only learns such relationships by practicing appropriate behaviors with others. One does not learn cooperation by being lectured to or having to sit by oneself. For these reasons, instead of relying on isolation, the teacher is required to look constantly for ways to encourage attachments between the offending child and other members of the class.

SUMMARY

We have positioned Dreikurs as the initial example of Confronting-Contracting for three reasons. First, closely aligned with the Relationship-Listeners, he has an optimistic belief in the child's rational capacities. Second, unlike the Relationship-Listeners, he believes that such a development must occur in a social milieu where adults or peers need to intervene and redirect the child's misplaced goals. Third, Dreikurs instructs the teacher to use specific actions to redirect the child's misdirected goal. The use of such actions is much more assertive than the Relationship-Listeners' non-judgmental approaches. Dreikurs has the teacher use strategies that personally combat the child's game and aim consciously to pull the group to his or her side. The teacher then arranges *logical consequences* for the offending student to experience. Dreikurs believes that every student can attain his or her place in life but needs the active help of the adult. His approaches therefore are more intrusive than the Relationship-Listeners', but could hardly be described as the shaping mechanisms of the Rules/Rewarders-Punishers.

Looking at Figure 6–1, we can now identify the covert and overt behaviors of a teacher using this model. The teacher begins by covertly observing and collecting information about the student by a) *silently looking on*. This is followed by the teacher's analysis of his or her own feelings toward the student's behavior by b) asking him- or herself such *questions* as, "Do I feel . . . annoyed (reflecting the student's goal of Attention Getting); beaten (the goal of Power); hurt (the goal of Revenge); or incapable (the goal of Helplessness)." The teacher can then make an immediate guess at the student's goal and respond with 1) an appropriate *directive statement* that

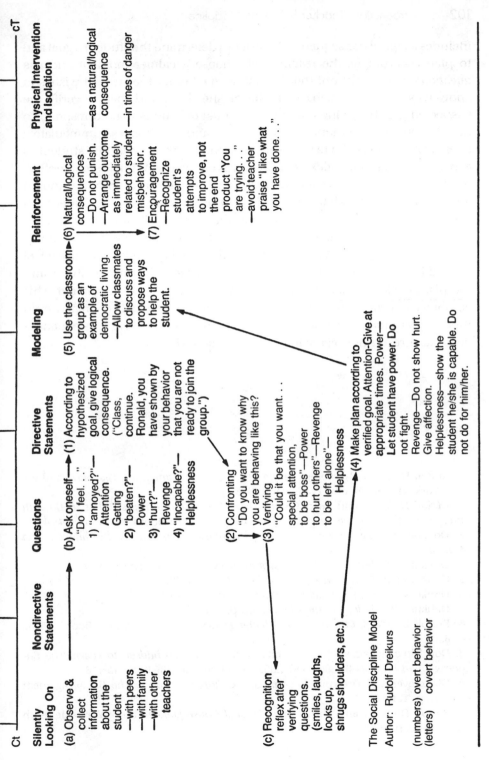

FIGURE 6-1. Teacher Behavior Continuum (TBC)

The following text appears within the figure:

cT

Physical Intervention and Isolation —as a natural/logical consequence —in times of danger

Reinforcement
(6) Natural/logical consequences —Do not punish. —Arrange outcome as immediately related to student misbehavior.
(7) Encouragement —Recognize student's attempts to improve, not the end product "You are trying. . ." —avoid teacher praise "I like what you have done. . ."

Modeling
(5) Use the classroom group as an example of democratic living. —Allow classmates to discuss and propose ways to help the student.

Directive Statements
(1) According to hypothesized goal, give logical consequence. ("Class, continue. Ronald, you have shown by your behavior that you are not ready to join the group.")
Confronting "Do you want to know why you are behaving like this?
(2) Verifying "Could it be that you want. . . special attention, to be boss"—Power to hurt others"—Revenge to be left alone"— Helplessness
(4) Make plan according to verified goal. Attention-Give at appropriate times. Power—Let student have power. Do not fight. Revenge—Do not show hurt. Give affection. Helplessness—show the student he/she is capable. Do not do for him/her.

Questions
(b) Ask oneself "Do I feel. . ."
1) "annoyed?"—Attention Getting
2) "beaten?"—Power
3) "hurt?"—Revenge
4) "Incapable?"—Helplessness
(3)
(c) Recognition reflex after verifying questions. (smiles, laughs, looks up, shrugs shoulders, etc.)

Nondirective Statements

Silently Looking On
(a) Observe & collect information about the student —with peers —with family —with other teachers

The Social Discipline Model
Author: Rudolf Dreikurs

(numbers) overt behavior
(letters) covert behavior

Ct

101

includes a logical consequence. In order to determine the student's goal and to plan accordingly, the teacher will choose a calmer moment and use *questions* that 2) confront the student as to whether the student wishes to know why he or she behaves as he or she does, and then 3) verify the suspected goal by asking the four sequential questions that correspond to the elements of attention, power, revenge, and helplessness. Immediately after each question, the teacher will be *silently looking on* for the student to exhibit a "recognition reflex" identifying his or her goal. With the goal verified, the teacher can 4) initiate a long-range plan by conferring with the student and describing, through the use of *directive statements*, how the student can successfully have his or her needs met through socially appropriate ways. The classroom group can serve as a *model* of democratic living by 5) proposing ways to help the student. Finally, the teacher builds the use of 6) natural/logical consequences for those misbehaviors that may continue into the plan, while simultaneously using the process of encouragement. This combined approach prevents the student from becoming discouraged, even though there may be future instances when natural/logical consequences occur as a result of socially inappropriate behavior.

NOTES

1. Rudolf Dreikurs, *Psychology in the Classroom: A Manual for Teachers*, 2nd ed. (New York: Harper & Row, Publishers, 1968), pp. 16–17.

2. Rudolf Dreikurs and Pearl Cassel, *Discipline Without Tears: What to Do with Children Who Misbehave*, rev. ed. (New York: Hawthorn Books, 1972), pp. 34–41.

3. Dreikurs and Cassel, *Discipline Without Tears: What to Do with Children Who Misbehave*, p. 41.

4. Dreikurs, *Psychology in the Classroom: A Manual for Teachers*, p. 55.

5. Dreikurs and Cassel, *Discipline Without Tears*, p. 42.

6. Dreikurs and Cassel, *Discipline Without Tears*, p. 44.

7. Dreikurs, *Psychology in the Classroom*, pp. 71–73.

8. Rudolf Dreikurs, *Children: The Challenge* (New York: Hawthorn Books, 1964), p. 76.

9. Don Dinkmeyer and Rudolf Dreikurs, *Encouraging Children to Learn: The Encouragement Process* (Englewood Cliffs: Prentice-Hall, 1963) pp. 45–56.

10. Dinkmeyer and Dreikurs, *Encouraging Children to Learn: The Encouragement Process*, p. 121.

11. Rudolf Dreikurs and Loren Grey, *Logical Consequences* (New York: Meredith Press, 1968), p. 157.

REFERENCES

Dinkmeyer, Don, and Dreikurs, Rudolf, *Encouraging Children to Learn: The Encouragement Process*. Englewood Cliffs: Prenctice-Hall, 1963.

Dreikurs, Rudolf. *Children: The Challenge*. New York: Hawthorn Books, 1964.

Dreikurs, Rudolf. *Psychology in the Classroom: A Manual for Teachers*. 2nd ed. New York: Harper & Row, Publishers, 1968.

Dreikurs, Rudolf, and Cassel, Pearl. *Discipline Without Tears: What to Do with Children Who Misbehave*, rev. ed. New York: Hawthorn Books, 1972.

Dreikurs, Rudolf, and Grey, Loren. *Logical Consequences*. New York: Meredith Press, 1968.

INSTRUCTIONAL MEDIA

Films

The following materials are available from:

American Personnel and Guidance Association
1107 New Hampshire Avenue
Washington, D.C. 20009

Individual Psychology in Counseling and Education, Part I.
Rudolf Dreikurs

35 Minutes; color.

Examines the background and basic concepts of individual psychology and emphasizes that the term "individual" stands for uniqueness of the individual as well as for his or her individuality. Provides an overview of Alfred Adler's concepts; discusses the role of emotions, and relationship of emotions to personal intentions; and presents the optimism of the Adlerian position, specifically that it sees in every human being the immediate potential for being different

Individual Psychology in Counseling and Education, Part II

35 minutes; color. Sale price $250; rental fee $25 per day of use.

Explores some of Adler's major contributions on the concept of holism, the use of early recollections, and the idea of social interest or the feeling of belonging.

He compares individual psychology with other theoretical approaches, and stresses educating teachers, counselors, and parents in personality development and understanding children.

Individual Psychology: A Demonstration with a Parent, a Teacher and a Child, Parts I and II.
Dreikurs

70 minutes (two reels); color. Sale price $400; rental fee $40 per day of use.

Demonstrates, through interviews with a "problem" child, his mother, and his teacher, how individual psychology can be applied to normal situations in counseling and education. Then the psychologist sums up what he sought to accomplish and what the central points were in the demonstration.

Filmstrips

The following instructional materials are from:

Association for Counseling and Development
5999 Stevenson Avenue
Alexandria, VA 22304

Coping With Kids
Thomas J. Sweeney

This award-winning series was produced by the Ohio University College of Education and the Telecommunications Center as a ten-film series (adapted from videotape) to cover behavior problems often encountered by parents and teachers. Utilizing a variety of demonstration and interview techniques, Thomas J. Sweeney provides a systematic training sequence to use in discipline and guidance, based on the individual-centered psychology of Alfred Adler as taught by Rudolf Dreikurs. The films help teach how to understand the goals of misbehavior; the use of natural and logical consequences, methods of encouragement including sex education, classroom meetings and study-consultation groups. Both the series and individual programs have proven effective as training tools.

Adults 0, Children 1
30 minutes, 16 mm, color and sound. Sale price $345; rental fee per day of use $35.

This film helps adults understand why they sometimes feel defeated by youth rebellion. Parents and teachers share their experiences in attempting to guide young people. Manford Sonstegard explains the Adlerian view on why social equality is essential regardless of age, sex or race. (order no. 75101C)

Dennis The Menace Is Afraid
30 minutes, 16 mm, color and sound. Sale price $345; rental fee per day of use $35.

Sweeney and Manford Sonstegard explain that young people who persistently use self-defeating behaviors are revealing the extent of their personal discouragement. Neither by giving in nor punishing do we truly help them. Common errors in discipline and a review of the major concepts and methods of this approach conclude this film. (order no. 75110C)

Making Sense Out of Nonsense

30 minutes, 16 mm, color and sound. Sale price $345; rental fee per day of use $35.

Sweeney gives a summary of pertinent Adlerian assumptions related to child guidance. All behavior is purposive and directed toward making one's place in the family, school and life. The influence of one's family position (e.g., oldest) is explained. Lack of confidence in facing life's tasks is seen as the root problem in misbehavior. How emotions are tools to help or hinder us is revealed. (order no. 75102C)

Misbehavior: What You Could Have Done But Didn't

30 minutes, 16 mm, color and sound. Sale price $345; rental fee per day of use $35.

The film identifies the four goals of disruptive behavior engaged in by the discouraged child: (1) attention seeking; (2) power; (3) revenge; (4) inadequacy. Adults who recognize these goals are taught how they can "do the unexpected" and help redirect the discouraged child's behavior. (order no. 75103C)

Out of the Mouths of Babes and Other People, Too

30 minutes, 16 mm, color and sound. Sale price $345; rental fee per day of use $35.

Brenda Davis is interviewed concerning her approach to teaching teachers how to conduct classroom meetings. Drawing on the works of both Rudolf Dreikurs and William Glasser, Davis outlines three types of meetings and common rules, techniques and problems which relate to this very useful method of helping young people think and behave responsibly. (order no. 75109C)

Rules Are For Everyone

30 minutes, 16 mm, color and sound. Sale price $345; rental fee per day of use $35.

Explains the Adlerian value of natural and logical consequences to responsible behavior. Both uses and precautions are illustrated from common life experiences of adults and young people. An essential component to this approach, consequences free adults from self-defeating thoughts and behavior which further inhibit cooperative behavior by young people. (order no. 75104C)

Twice Upon a Time, or Helping You Helps Me

30 minutes, 16 mm, color and sound. Sale price $345; rental fee per day of use $35.

Since a basic Adlerian concept is that people are social beings with socially goal-directed behavior, parent-teacher discussion groups and consulting groups are a natural way to explore his theories and methods. This film focuses on the advantages of problem solving through these groups. (order no. 75108C)

When Winning Means No One Loses

30 minutes, 16 mm, color and sound. Sale price $345; rental fee per day of use $35.

The four steps to social-conflict resolution are illustrated through a family interview and a brief discussion with elementary school children. The counselor's role as consultant is modeled. Establishing mutual respect, pinpointing the real issue, finding a new agreement, and involving everyone are shown. (order no. 75105C)

When a Word Is Worth a Thousand Pictures

30 minutes, 16 mm, color and sound. Sale price $345; rental fee per day of use $35.

Encouragement has a special meaning and significance to helping prevent and correct misbehavior. Both verbal and nonverbal methods are presented within a context that reveals how we often discourage children with rewards, punishment, and praise. (order no. 75106C)

7

The Reality Model
of William Glasser

"Then after Billy Hunt pushed you off the monkey bars, all WHAT broke loose?"
Cartoon by Ford Button

Sara sits nervously waiting in the administration office of the middle school. She shuffles her feet, keeps her head down, and turns away from anyone who might enter the room. Mrs. Washington, her eighth-grade teacher, has sent her with a note to see the principal.

The moment arrives when the secretary beckons to Sara, indicating that the principal is ready to see her now. The secretary swings open the door to the inner office, and Sara slowly shuffles into the room. Keeping her eyes averted, she hands the principal the note. Ms. Powers reads it through carefully, pauses, and then says to Sara, "Mrs. Washington would like to meet with us before we decide about what should be done about your behavior. Recess is in a few minutes, so we will wait. Please go back to the other room and wait."

The note from Mrs. Washington read:

Dear Ms. Powers

As you know, Sara has a tendency not to hear directions that she does not want to follow. Last week we made a plan where she agreed to respond to all my directions (put away personal belongings, stop talking, line up, and so on) within fifteen seconds. Each day that she complied I agreed to let her have the *privilege* of reading her favorite *Movie Glamour* magazine. However she also agreed that if she did not comply then she would have to do extra school work during the period allocated for her "privilege" time.

Well, today, Sara continued talking and wisecracking while I was trying to get class started. I told her three times to stop, yet she just pretended not to hear. I told her that she was responsible for her behavior and therefore would have to take the agreed-upon consequences of extra work. Well, when the last ten minutes of class came, she took out her movie magazines and refused to do the work that we had agreed upon. I told her that if she broke her commitment she would have to go to the principal's office.

I would appreciate your not discussing anything with Sara until I get there. Let's continue with Glasser's approach of "starting fresh" and drawing up another *contract* with which all three of us can agree. I'll be there after class at 10:45.

Mrs. Washington

Both the principal and teacher are well versed in William Glasser's approach to discipline. Upon Mrs. Washington's arrival, she and Sara move into Ms. Power's office. They seat themselves in a semicircle, facing each other.

Ms. Powers begins, "Sara, what happened? What were you doing to be sent to me?"

Sara says, "The other kids were bothering me. I could not hear the teacher."

Ms. Powers replies, "No, Sara, I didn't ask that. I want to know about what you were doing. How is your behavior in class helping you?"

Sara stares back and says, "I guess my not listening doesn't help me much."

Ms. Powers continues to press. She asks, "What rules are you breaking?"

Sara mumbles, "Oh, I'm supposed to listen to the teacher and put away my stuff and stop talking when she tells me to. But really, Gloria was making me talk."

Ms. Powers disregards Sara's last comment and says, "What are you going to do about *your* behavior? Mrs. Washington and I want to help you to enjoy school, and we will work with you, but *you* are going to have to make another plan to improve yourself. It has to be a plan with which we all can be comfortable. Do you have some ideas?"

Sara replies, "Yeah, I'll do the same plan I had before about the magazines."

Mrs. Washington enters the conversation. Addressing Sara, she says, "We have already tried that plan and you did not do what you agreed to do when we made that contract. We could try again but I want you to think it out so that the next time it will work. Ms. Powers should be part of the new contract."

Sara speaks, "You all decide. That'll be all right with me."

Ms. Powers interjects. "No. Sara, we are not going to be responsible for your behavior; only you can be responsible. We'll help you after you've decided what your plan will be. You are to stay in the in-school isolation room until you've made your plan. See me when you've decided that you have a plan that works."

Sara spends the remainder of the day in a comfortable but small room, isolated at the end of the corridor. At the end of the day she tells Ms. Powers and Mrs. Washington that she has a plan written out for them. They all read it and, after a little help with the wording, finally agree upon the following:

Sara's Plan   Thursday, February 17

I, Sara Orton, agree to listen to the teacher's directions and to do what she says.

If the teacher, Mrs. Washington, does not have to repeat her directions to me for an entire day, then I can have the privilege of being named the "Office Helper" and going to Ms. Powers' office to answer the school phone during the next lunch time.

If the teacher only has to repeat directions to me twice during the day, then I can have the privilege of ten free minutes to read my magazines, but I can't hold the job of "Office Helper."

If the teacher has to repeat directions to me more than twice, then no magazines and no phone.

I agree to carry out this plan for one week and report to Ms. Powers next Friday on how I'm doing.

Signed   Witnessed by

Sara Orton   Mrs. Washington

                                                              Ms. Powers

GLASSER AND REALITY THERAPY

What the preceding case has illustrated are some of the steps of "reality therapy," as espoused by William Glasser. Glasser is a psychiatrist who was trained in and later broke from Freudian psychoanalysis. He believed that the traditional clinical approach of working with disturbed patients was seriously deficient. He believed that Freudian and play therapy encouraged dependence. He believed that the approach of allowing a person to give free vent to his or her emotions and to dissect and analyze his or her personal history, with the psychoanalyst then giving interpretations and labels to the individual's inner conflicts, was an inefficient one and did not help patients live in the real world. He believed that individuals who were escaping reality by behaving in inappropriate ways did not need to find a rationale and defense for their illogical behavior. Instead, people must be helped to acknowledge their behavior as being irresponsible and then to take action to make it more logical and productive. As a psychiatrist, Glasser does not believe in working with the unconscious, or of being nonjudgmentally accepting (such as the Relationship-Listeners believe) of a person's action. His statement, stripped to its essentials, is that human beings must live in a world of other human beings. Each individual must satisfy his or her own needs in a way that does not infringe upon another's.[1] He clearly states that individuals are each responsible for their own actions and, regardless of how disturbed or dependent they claim to be, people must bear the consequences for their own behavior and make a commitment to act in a responsible manner toward others.

This might read as a rather harsh manner of treating inappropriate behavior, but Glasser's work and writings are not cold and dictatorial. Rather, the reverse is true. He has applied his psychiatric concepts of reality therapy to work with delinquent girls (as cited in *Reality Therapy*) and to work with children in public schools (as cited in *Schools Without Failure*). In both settings, he is found to be one who practices and advocates for others a personal and caring relationship with misbehaving students. He sees the establishment of care and warmth as a necessary human prerequisite for an individual who hopes to begin to come to grips with the sometimes awesome responsibility of being planner, manager, and executor of one's own actions.

GLASSER'S METHODS AND THE TEACHER BEHAVIOR CONTINUUM

Silently Looking On

Silently looking on is not in the Glasser model as a specific overt step by a teacher in working with a child, as it is with the Relationship-Listeners.

Rather, Glasser asks the teacher to assess the situation covertly. This is a three-part process. As the teacher, one needs to:

1. Reflect on your past behavior with this student.
2. Start with a fresh approach. (If your actions haven't been successful in the past, why think that they will work in the future?)
3. Expect a better tomorrow. (Since the past has not been effective, the teacher can be optimistic. After all, the situation can hardly get much worse!)

Nondirective Statements

Again, Glasser is too much of a Confronting-Contracting believer to use this central behavior of the Relationship-Listeners. He does not agree with empathetic, all-supportive acceptance of the child. He makes this quite apparent when he discusses one of his first cases as an intern with an emotionally disturbed young boy. After weeks of using play-therapy steps of visually looking on and nondirective statements, he became increasingly frustrated with the child's continuing egocentric and destructive behavior. Finally he wrote:

> I began a kind of Reality Therapy. I told him (the child) to shut up and for once in his life to listen to what someone had to say. I informed him that the play was over, and that we would sit and talk in an adult fashion, or if we walked we would walk as adults. I explained clearly that I would not tolerate any running away or even any impolite behavior while we were walking. He would have to be courteous and try to converse with me when I talked to him. He was to tell me everything he did and I would help him decide whether it was right or wrong.[2]

Directive Statements

As is evident in the previous quote, Glasser believes in defining clear boundaries of acceptable behavior. Further, he suggests that the teacher's role is to enforce and encounter, with *directive statements* or commands, the student who transgresses. When a child steps out of line, the teacher confronts the student and tells the student to stop transgressing. Examples of such directive statements might include:

- "Johnny, put that ruler down and get back to work."
- "Felix, if you are going to talk you must first raise your hand."

- "Selena, this is quiet reading time, so open your book and begin reading."
- "Antonio, give me that slingshot. A slingshot is not to be used around people or animals that can be hurt by it."
- "Johanna, keep your hands off that mural! It was just painted and must dry."

The teacher does not berate the student with such warnings as "Don't you dare do that again," or insults like, "You are acting like a little baby!" or such negative speculations as, "There must be something wrong with you to act that way." Instead, Glasser wishes the teacher to express directly the misbehavior and then to follow with a description of an appropriate behavior. The issue at stake is the student's *irresponsible* behavior. Therefore, the teacher needs to tell the student in effect to stop the wrong, irresponsible behavior and to act correctly and responsibly. If this does not achieve results, then the teacher is to follow such directive statements with questions.

Questions

The teacher frames *questions* for the student to make the child think rationally about his or her actions and eventually verbalize concerning these irresponsible behaviors. The teacher might confront the offending child at the time of disruption with a question such as, "What are you doing?"

The teacher is not interested in excuses or reasons; he or she simply wants the child to verbalize what is happening. The teacher is not to ask the student *why* he or she is doing something. A "why" question simply gives the student the opportunity to disown the behavior with such excuses as "Oh, I was mad (tired, or hungry)," "He made me do it," "They're always picking on me," and so on.

We saw how Ms. Powers avoided a "why" question, yet Sara still wanted to rationalize her behavior with "But Gloria made me . . ." Ms. Powers would not accept such excuses. The confronting adult attempts to keep the student's discussion of the problem within the present, in order to get the issue of misbehavior out on the table, and then presses for a plan to be made.

After the question "What are you doing?" the teacher asks the child to tell in what ways this behavior fulfills the child's needs. For example: *"How does (spitting, fighting, coming in late, and so forth) help you?"*

The student is thus asked to think of the consequences of his or her own actions. Usually the student will not be able to give a ready answer. The last objective of the teacher is to press for a plan or contract and commitment by the student by asking, *"What are you going to do about your behavior?"* or *"What is your plan going to be so that you don't break that rule again?"* These questions are crucial to reality therapy because they force responsibility back on the student. Many students get into a "cat-and-mouse" game with their teachers by constantly challenging the teacher to do something. By turning this challenge for action back to the student, there is no game left to play. Now the student's irresponsible actions will be dealt with according to the student's own plan. They will not be dealt with according to the dictates of an adult who has been forced to play supervisor. It is not the teacher who is responsible for the child's behavior, but the child who is responsible for that behavior. This does not mean that the teacher is passive in the student/teacher interaction; rather, the teacher becomes an active partner with the student in making a plan and then provides the student with the help necessary to implement the plan, which reflects the student's own feelings and thoughts.

Modeling

Glasser does not address this behavior as a specific step in working with a disruptive child. He would, however, surely agree that a teacher should set an example of being responsible to others and of being committed to carry out any stated pledge to students.

Reinforcement

Reinforcement is not advocated by Glasser in terms of schedules and concrete rewards, as seen by the Rules/Rewards-Punishment advocates. Yet he does agree with the use of reinforcement as it applies to the loss of privileges for breaking one's plan or contract. In this respect, he and Dreikurs are in agreement. A student needs to have logical consequences follow his or her behavior, whether that behavior be positive or negative. The student is encouraged to decide what those privileges or negative results should be.

It is not for the teacher to impose his or her praise or punishment because, in so doing, the teacher lets the student off the hook. Rather, the student must accept the natural repercussions of the misbehavior and should not be shielded from them. If the student does not respond to the question, "What are you going to do about it?" then the teacher can help by suggesting a plan that the student can agree to, or by sending the student away until he or she comes up with an acceptable alternative plan. Once a plan is agreed upon, Glasser goes so far as to tell the teacher to *have the student sign a written pledge to honor his or her plan.*[3] *The student agrees in writing to lose the privileges if he or she should falter and break the agreement. Commitment* is Glasser's key word!

For example, a student named Hector had agreed to a plan with his teacher that he would not fight during the morning recess. Hector knew and agreed to the terms of the plan which meant that to fight would mean the loss of recess. If partaking in recess was, in fact, more reinforcing to Hector than the pleasure of fighting, then in time the teacher would expect that the loss of that privilege would rationally alter the student's behavior. Hector would be expected eventually to realize that his physical aggression was not helping him enjoy his prized outdoor activity, and that to fight would mean that he had broken his commitment. The message became simply, "If you really like to go outdoors, then behave in ways that will make going outdoors a certainty."

Of course, the reader might wonder how this strategy, which appears so foolproof in theory, would work with the student who could care less about recess or who never thinks about any of his or her actions in terms of the consequences they might have. Glasser would admit that the student who could care less will be a more difficult case to treat.[4] It is obvious that, to a student such as this, being able to play outdoors at recess is not sufficiently motivating. The student would rather fight and stay in than not fight and stay outdoors. So what do we do? The answer, which might well appear somewhat simplistic, is merely to find some other activity or situation that is more valued by the child than fighting. Some alternatives for younger children might be suggested by the teacher:

- awarding the job of classroom helper.
- granting free time for personal projects.
- permitting the child to work with the school custodian.
- allowing time to listen to records.
- making the child the "official" messenger to the school office for the day or week.

Some possibilities for older students might be the teacher granting permission for:

- free time for personal projects.
- listening to popular records.
- reading popular movie or sports magazines.

- playing a game (electric football, hockey, chess).
- watching television.

If it is determined that the student cannot engage in any activity that is more personally reinforcing than his or her misbehavior, then the problem falls into one of two categories. Either the classroom situation is in need of being drastically overhauled, or the student is beyond the help of the school.[5] In other words, if the child is experiencing no success and finds no relevance in what he or she is doing, then the teacher must stand back and assess the entire classroom curriculum and organization.

Glasser believes that misbehavior of most students results from the failure of teacher and schools to fulfill their needs. He believes that students want to experience success, they want to have feelings of self-worth, and they want to learn. In too many situations, students are obstructed by such practices as:

- grades that label a few as successful and many as failures.
- constant teacher lectures to be sat through passively.
- reading materials that are geared for the average student and are thus too hard for the slower ones and too easy for brighter students.
- classroom topics or subjects that are irrelevant to the students.
- too much memorizing and recitation of facts instead of discussions and experiments.

With such conditions, it is a wonder that more students don't misbehave. School for students in such classes is simply an unhappy, unsuccessful, irrelevant, and boring place to be. On the other hand, if the classroom is an exciting place for all but one student, and the teacher cannot find (after numerous times) any activities that interest this misbehaving child, then the teacher has further ground to suspect that the child's problems are beyond the scope of the immediate classroom. Such a student might need to be referred for outside psychological or social help.

There are some students who simply are unaware of consequences, and dealing with these youngsters is an easier matter. A student perhaps has always exploded with rage whenever his or her "feathers have been ruffled." The aftereffect of this temper may never have been consciously processed by the student. As this student is still liable for his or her actions, regardless of the internal degree of cognizance, it is therefore the teacher's role to:

a) raise the child's level of awareness by pointing out the immediate behavior and consequences.

b) commit the student to creating a signed plan.

c) enforce the natural consequence of loss of privileges if the plan is violated.

For example, it might take months of repetitive loss of recess before a child such as Hector (in the earlier illustration) becomes aware of what his behavior is doing to him. In time, with consistent application, the lesson cannot help but be learned. Glasser suggests that the teacher begin anew by (1) reflecting on past behavior, (2) starting fresh, and (3) expecting a better tomorrow. The student is given as many chances as have been agreed upon with the teacher.

Physical Intervention and Isolation

Physical Intervention: Glasser is not a believer in the teacher's use of physical control. He is certainly not an advocate of paddling or spanking. He has even more concern with the psychological damage that adults do to children by using humiliation and ridicule. He does not believe that any form of punishment, whether physical or psychological, is appropriate. He does not justify his position on moral grounds, but on the grounds that punishment simply is not effective. To paraphrase a statement he made to a group of school teachers and administrators, he said:

> If punishment really worked we should have no delinquents or criminals. After all, as children, most of today's convicts have been punished and abused frequently. If punishment worked then we should now have a perfect society. We obviously don't and we obviously need to look for other methods."[7]

Isolation: Glasser sees the use of isolation, not for the purposes of punishing a student, but instead, for providing a place for the student to sit quietly and think about a plan for re-entering the classroom milieu. When a student persists in breaking his or her commitment, or refuses to make one, then the student is removed to a place so that he or she can begin again. The first step of isolation takes place "in class." Glasser calls this "off to the castle." The student should be able to observe or listen to what is going on, but his or her placement should not interfere with the classroom routine. In the elementary school, such a place is easily made in the classroom; in the junior high or secondary school, such a place, if not available within the room, can be set up in close proximity (i.e., the hall). The student is told to stay in the designated area until he or she has made a plan to insure a successful return to the group. This plan, again, has to be agreeable to both student and teacher. If the student bothers others while in the isolation area or persists in acting out after returning to the classroom, then the teacher could move to the second step of isolation, which leads *away from the classroom to an "in-school" suspension room.*

The teacher would need to have the principal's and faculty's support to free the necessary space for such a purpose. If an extra room is not available, a large storage area or a seldom-used office would be suitable. The environment should provide a relaxing place that is physically apart from the busy school activities. Movement to this area means that the student is being treated in a realistic manner. Until he or she takes the responsibility to plan and implement acceptable behavior in the classroom, he or she cannot participate in such activities. Glasser would suggest that, after all, this is the basis for societal enforcement of reasonable law and order. If you break the rules, then you are removed from the larger society. During the periods of in-school suspension, the principal or guidance counselor will need to be involved, but the parents will not. The teacher need not be concerned with the student's past, home life, or what his or her parents can do about the student's behavior. The teacher is only concerned with what can be done within the context of school. Not until the teacher has to resort to out-of-school isolation is it essential to involve the parents. This does not mean that the teacher must keep parents ignorant of their child's behavior. However, it does mean that the teacher should not look to the child's home as a source for help. The student's problem is in school, and it is the school's responsibility to handle it.

The child needs to learn to live appropriately in a classroom and to deal with the immediate consequences of his or her behavior in that room. Therefore, sending warning notes home or asking parents to punish the child would make the parents responsible for a problem that is not theirs. In effect, making the parents accountable to "shape up" their youngster removes that responsibility from the school and, more importantly, from the child.

The next form of isolation is suspending the student from school. If the student cannot show minimal control in an in-school suspension, then out of the school he or she goes. The student can return when a plan is made.

Throughout each form of isolation (in-class, in-school, out-of-school), the teacher remains a helping person, one who is not afraid to tell the student where he or she has transgressed, one who is willing to ask pointed questions as to what the student is doing, and one who will encourage the student to commit himself or herself to a plan. The teacher never lets the child get away with breaking his or her commitment and the teacher never lets the student shift responsibility for his or her behavior to others. At the same time, the teacher is not a mechanistic enforcer of law and order. The teacher constantly tells the student, "I want to help you to become more in control of your own actions. I will talk, listen, give opinions and offer advice, but at the end it is you who have to make the decision and commitment. I cannot and will not do that for you." So, as can be seen, the teacher becomes personally involved with his or her student. The teacher cares, and that caring is clearly shown by the teacher never allowing the child to transcend the boundaries of the commitment that the child has made. The teacher remains as one who will enforce reality behavior and the student remains as one who must learn the meaning of that reality.

In fully explaining the mechanism of isolation, let us refer to our previous teacher behaviors of *questions* and *directive statements*. These teacher behaviors do not stop when isolation begins. Rather, the teacher continues to ask the student through each stage of isolation to reply to such questions as, "What are you doing?" "What rules are you breaking?" "In what ways is this behavior helping you?" "What are you going to do about it?" and "What is your plan?" The teacher also tells the student directly what his or her transgressions are and what the consequences of these behaviors are. Any interaction with the student should contain such direct confronting statements as, "Stop doing that!" "The rule is. . . ," "You are breaking the rules and therefore cannot be part of the group," "You cannot have back your privilege (or return to the group) until you tell me your plan," and "Don't give me any excuses, tell me what you did!" Therefore, questions and directive statements are interspersed throughout the process of isolation and are essential in aiding the child to become aware of his or her actions, the consequences involved, and the responsibilities that need to be met. Glasser also points out that there may well be a few students who will actually need to be referred to an outside agency, such as a treatment center for delinquent children, when they engage in types of criminal behavior and none of the previous steps have met with any success.

THE CLASSROOM MEETING

It would be a disservice to the reader to omit one of the major formats for applying the teacher behaviors of reality therapy. What Glasser is perhaps best known for among school practitioners is the classroom meeting.[8] This practice of holding regular meetings provides a structure for dealing with both an individual student's problems as well as for revising the overall organization and curriculum of the class. The teacher meets with the entire class on a regular basis. They always sit in a circle facing each other, usually on a rug, sometimes in chairs. The teacher stresses to the class that during this meeting there are no wrong answers, and that each child should feel free to express his or her ideas, opinions, and feelings. The teacher is expected to express his or her ideas, opinions, and feelings in the same manner. The students are told that they are to talk about the present and the future, not to dwell in the past. The teacher further adds that students are not "to put down" or use insulting terms when speaking to or about others.

Since there are no "wrong" answers, every child in the meeting has the opportunity to be successful. A child need not fear being corrected for what he or she says. The teacher (silently looking on) encourages everyone, with nods and words of approval, to speak, but does not force anyone who resists. The teacher may ask a student for his or her ideas, and if no reply is forthcoming, may say (nondirective statement) something like, "Well, you think about it and let me know if you come up with an idea that you would like to discuss. I'd like to hear it."

Glasser speaks of three types of meetings: 1) open-ended, 2) educational/diagnostic, and 3) problem-solving. Open-ended meetings are held for students to create their own fantasies and to explore imaginary problems; for example, "What would we do if we were stranded on the moon?" The educational/diagnostic meeting is one where the teacher discusses a curriculum topic in order to find out what students already know about it, what they don't know, and what further interests they might have (i.e., What is pollution? Where does it come from? Why is it a problem?). The teacher then uses that information to make curriculum decisions as to what aspects of the topic would be most essential to cover and what activities would be most relevant to the students. The third type of meeting is the problem-solving one, whereby the class focuses on a real problem that affects all of them. They clarify the problem, add information, propose alternative solutions, and finally commit themselves to a plan of action. Examples of such general problems might be:

- How the playground balls are to be distributed at recess.
- What to do about missing items in the class.
- How to cut down on asking the teacher questions when he or she is busy.
- What to do about name calling among the students.
- What to do about the length of time it takes to get the whole class settled before starting the next lesson.
- What to do about graffiti and littering problems in the restrooms.

Specific problems concerning individual students are also a topic for problem-solving meetings. The use of this kind of meeting as a vehicle for working with student misbehavior is an application that we would now like to discuss. Behaviors by an individual that would be relevant as topics for a classroom meeting might include:

- A student who "hogs" the playground equipment (balls, bats, frisbees, and the like).
- A student who physically pushes other students around.
- A student who constantly distracts others from working (by making loud noises, talking, and so forth).
- A student who takes items from others.
- A student who plays cruel "tricks" on others (locks children into closets, writes on others' homework, and so on).
- A student who tries to be boss all the time, who is always telling others what to do but will not accept any criticism of self.

As we have seen, integral to Glasser's approach is for a student to be made aware of and become responsible for the consequences of his or her actions. When a student has behaved in ways that are constantly disruptive to the majority of other students, and the problem has escalated from one that is solely between student and teacher, then Glasser believes that the student needs to be confronted and helped by the entire class. Therefore, the problem-solving classroom meeting is held, and the misbehaving student hears what others think of his or her behavior.

The teacher holds a firm rein on this type of meeting to insure that it does not become a name-calling free-for-all. The teacher explains the reason for the meeting, such as wanting to discuss a student who has been destroying other children's property. The teacher then suggests that, as a group, perhaps the class can help the student to act more appropriately.

1. The teacher asks each student to express openly what this student has recently done to interfere with him or her personally. The students are asked to tell that student, face-to-face, what those behaviors are and what effects they have had on them (emotionally and/or physically).
2. After all have had their chance to speak (including the teacher), the misbehaving student is given an opportunity to explain what others have done to interfere with him or her.

At this juncture, the meeting swiftly swings from "getting all the cards out on the table" to doing something constructive with the information that has been gleaned.

3. The teacher suggests that the class and the offending child may be able to offer some possible solutions to the problem, ones which would be agreeable to all. The teacher listens to all ideas and then asks the group to narrow down the alternative plans and ideas that were offered.

4. Finally, the child is asked to select a plan and commit himself or herself to it. At the same time, the members of the class (including the teacher) commit themselves to carrying out any actions that will help the child in implementing his or her plan.

The conclusion of such a meeting is the achievement of an agreed-upon, manageable plan. The participants leave the meeting with a feeling of positive action.

The reader should notice that the *teacher's role in such a classroom meeting is identical to the role required in dealing with a child on a one-to-one basis*. The same techniques of *"what" questions* and *direct statements* are used to keep the discussion on target and within the boundaries of rules. All verbalizations are designed to help the class and child come to grips with the reality of behavior and for them to "get on" with a course of action. The offending child is kept in the "straitjacket" of responsibility, and, after a *plan* is agreed upon, the teacher remains as the enforcer of *logical consequences*. Breaking of such a commitment could result in the student being led through the three levels of isolation.

To many teachers, the use of a classroom meeting for the confrontation of a child by his or her peers seems to be a harsh approach. Many would feel that, for some children, there is the danger of emotional harm and the reinforcement of a child's negative self-concept in such a confrontation. Glasser is careful to point out that such a meeting needs to be carefully guided by the teacher to avoid any such destructive outcome.[9] The teacher needs to move the discussion carefully from the phase of eliciting peer perceptions to that of developing helpful solutions. The classroom meeting is purposefully used to show the offending child that he or she cannot act in an egocentric vacuum of being oblivious to the effects of his or her behavior on others. If the teacher shields the disruptive child from feedback from peers, then that child has little opportunity to explore the reasons for cooperative behavior. If the child is really bothering his or her peers, as well as the teacher, then the student needs to know this directly by those affected. If the student is to live with others, then there is nothing more realistic than for others to inform the student when his or her actions are transgressing on their rights. The meeting is not designed, or held, to blame or punish the child, but to *find solutions* that will help the child.

SUMMARY

In the book, *Schools Without Failure*, Glasser goes beyond the specifics of working with disruptive, "unrealistic" students and addresses what he considers to be the major source of inappropriate behavior. In doing so, he speaks of covert behaviors that the teacher might use with such students. Students, as all humans, wish to fulfill their needs, and misbehavior can be explained as a person's unsuccessful attempt to succeed in these efforts. Glasser sees schools as institutions that breed failure and irrelevancy.[10] Most misbehaving students do not feel successful in school. They are not involved in what they learn, and therefore they erect a shield of defiance, apathy, and unconcern to protect them from the further hurt of inadequacy. Consequently, when a misbehaving student is expected to give up privileges (or successful experiences) as a result of wrong action, the student has none to give up and the defiant behavior continues. So, in these situations, Glasser tells the teacher to be covert about *silently looking on* with the student while:

a) observing the student and the situation.
b) assessing what the teacher himself or herself is currently doing and what success the student is having.
c) if necessary, starting fresh by reversing classroom organization and/or activities.

Only at this point, if failure continues, does the teacher begin the process of overt behaviors.

The central technique for the teacher to use is an approach that confronts the student and makes him or her responsible for his or her own behavior. A student, upon transgressing rules, is:

1. Confronted and told to stop. *(directive statements)*
2. Asked "What" questions. *(questions)*
3. Pressed for a plan and commitment. *(directive statements)*
4. Faced with logical consequences that have been agreed upon. *(reinforcement)*

Silently Looking On	Nondirective Statements	Questions	Directive Statements	Modeling	Reinforcement	Physical Intervention and Isolation
a) Observe —the student —the situation b) Assess —what the teacher is currently doing —what success the student is having c) Classroom reorganization and activities d) Move to overt behaviors —if step c does not work —if present teacher behaviors are unproductive		(2) "What" questions: "What are you doing?" "What are the rules?" "In what ways is your behavior helping you?" "What is your plan?"	**(1) Confront transgressor. "Stop that, the rule is . . ." (3) Press for a plan. "You must make a plan; I will help but you are responsible."		(4) Reap the consequences of plan	(5) "Off to the castle" (classroom isolation) repeat 1, 2, 3, 4, (6) Off to the office (with principal doing 1, 2, 3, 4) (7) Removal from school; repeat 1, 2, 3, 4, 5, 6. (8) Referral to outside agency

**Steps 1-4 can be carried out in class meetings.

The Reality Model
Author: William Glasser

(numbers) overt behavior
(letters) covert behavior

FIGURE 7–1. Teacher Behavior Continuum (TBC)

5. Faced with failure to carry out commitment and plan—which results in class *isolation* ("off to the castle")—where steps 1, 2, 3, and 4 are repeated.

6. In the case of continual failure, placed in in-school *isolation* (principal's office or school isolation room), where principal repeats steps 1, 2, 3, 4, and 5.

7. If he or she persists in continual failure, placed in outside-of-school *isolation* (sent home); when the student returns, the teacher and principal repeat steps 1, 2, 3, 4, 5, and 6.

8. Referred to an outside agency if the previously cited steps fail.

William Glasser is a Confronter-Contractor. He believes in the capability of each individual to be responsible, but he tempers that optimism with the need for an individual to learn the moral or acceptable boundaries necessary to live successfully in society. As he wrote:

> All students must be accepted as potentially capable, not as handicapped by their environment.[11] They do not decide, however, whether or not rules, once established, should be enforced. They may choose to disobey the rules; this choice is open to all. But they then have to accept the consequences of their choice.[12]

NOTES

1. William Glasser, *Reality Therapy: A New Approach to Psychiatry* (New York: Harper & Row Publishers, 1975), p. 13.

2. Glasser, *Reality Therapy: A New Approach to Psychiatry*, p. 170.

3. William Glasser, *Schools Without Failure* (New York: Harper & Row Publishers, 1969), p. 126.

4. William Glasser, "Disorders in Our Schools: Causes and Remedies," *Phi Delta Kappan*, January 1978, p. 331.

5. William Glasser, *Glasser's Approach to Discipline* (pamphlet published by Educator Training Center, Los Angeles, California), step 10, pp. 8–9.

6. Glasser, *Glasser's Approach to Discipline*, step 7, p. 6.

7. Glasser's presentation to the School Council of Ohio Study Group, (Delaware, Ohio: December 6, 1976).

8. Glasser, *Schools Without Failure*, chapters 10 and 11.

9. Glasser, *Schools Without Failure*, p. 129.

10. Glasser, *Schools Without Failure*, chapter 3.

11. Glasser, *Schools Without Failure*, p. 199.

12. Glasser, *Schools Without Failure*, p. 200.

REFERENCES

Glasser, William. "Disorders in Our Schools: Causes and Remedies." *Phi Delta Kappan*. January 1978.

Glasser, William. *Glasser's Approach to Discipline*. Los Angeles: Educator Training Center.

Glasser, William. *Reality Therapy: A New Approach to Psychiatry*. New York: Harper & Row Publishers, 1975.

Glasser, William. *Schools Without Failure*. New York: Harper & Row Publishers, 1969.

For additional information contact the Educator Training Center, 2140 West Olympic Boulevard, Suite 518, Los Angeles, California 90006; (213) 386-2511.

INSTRUCTIONAL MEDIA

Filmstrips

The following materials are available from:

Media Five
3211 Cahuenga Boulevard, West
Los Angeles, California 90068

Glasser's Ten Steps to Discipline
William Glasser

Two filmstrips with two cassettes with teacher's guide; color. Purchase price $45.

Presents an illustration of the ten-step approach to all disciplinary problems, no matter how severe, with classroom scenes.

The following materials are available from:

Social Studies School Service
10,000 Culver Boulevard, Dept. E3
P.O. Box 802
Culver City, California 90320

Five Steps to Conflict Resolution
William Glasser

Two filmstrips with two cassettes with teacher guide; color. Purchase price $50.

A five-step approach for solving classroom, schoolwide, and community-related conflict is introduced by Dr. William Glasser. Situations such as student fights, teacher-administration conflicts, policymaking confrontations, and personality conflicts are examined, with methods for achieving positive results. Glasser's five steps—stating the problem, identifying who's involved, helping the parties involved to devise a solution, making a commitment to work at the solution, and establishing a time frame and follow-up—are applied in various group and individual situations. MDF110C-E3

Films

The following materials are available from:

Media Five
3211 Cahuenga Boulevard, West
Los Angeles, California 90068

Documentary film of teachers successfully using concepts developed by Glasser to achieve effective school discipline. Explains the five-part approach to discipline and the seven steps of reality therapy.

Dealing with Discipline Problems

29 minutes; color. Sale price $375; rental fee $45 per week.

Teachers supply the commentary on what they are doing and why, often suggesting alternative ways of dealing with real-life situations. Filmed on location at model schools-without-failure, revealing how teachers apply success concepts of reality therapy in everyday practice.

The Reality of Success

28 minutes; color. Sale price $395; rental fee $40 per week.

The film provides a background on reality therapy, helping problem students to achieve self-motivated, productive behavior. Pinpoints the value and importance of maintaining good personal relationships, dealing in the present, and getting the troubled child to make a value judgment and plan his or her improvement.

Glasser on Discipline
William Glasser

> 28 minutes; color. Sale price $395; rental fee $45 per week.
>
> *Details a successful approach to an old problem: school discipline. Glasser outlines five basic elements for achieving effective discipline in school.*

Roles and Goals in High School
William Glasser

> 29 minutes; color. Sale price $395; rental fee $45 per week.
>
> *Illustrates the relevance of Glasser's Identity Society and School-without-Failure concepts in the high school milieu. Includes role play with teachers and use of reality therapy to handle discipline problems.*

The Glasser Up-Date
William Glasser

> 30 minutes; color. Sale price $750. Four programs on ¾" video cassettes, with two programs per cassette.
>
> 1. *Basics for School and Life—Examines how to gain the strength needed to strive toward success.*
> 2. *The Problems of Weakness—Discusses the "acting out" and other weakness symptoms resulting in school disciplinary problems. Details the causes of student weakness that result in alcohol and drug abuse.*
> 3. *Eight Steps to Success—Provides the revised and updated approach to applying Reality Therapy to help students move toward personal responsibility and success in school.*
> 4. *Ten Steps to Discipline—Emphasis on stopping undesirable behavior, discouraging its reoccurrence, and working toward more responsible behavior with the ten-step discliplinary approach.*

Reality Therapy in High School
William Glasser

> 29 minutes; color. Sale price $395; rental fee $45 per week.
>
> *Authentic situations describing how to use reality therapy, and how it resulted in an over 80 percent drop in disciplinary problems the first year. Examines the effects of reality therapy on the total school climate.*

What Is Discipline, Anyway?
William Glasser

> 30 minutes; color. (Leader's manual with 25 teacher packets—in-service work-shop materials). Rental fee $100.

> *A look at discipline, differentiating it from punishment. Demonstrates alternative methods of achieving discipline.*

A Success-Oriented Classroom

> 28 minutes; color. Sale price $375; rental fee $40 per week.

> *A documentary film showing students working alone and with others on mini-contracts. Discussion of techniques and suggestions for guiding and checking student progress.*

8

The Behavior
Modification
Model

It's early morning and the kindergarten children are entering the classroom. Almost all the children enter through the door next to the cloakroom, where they hang their coats and hats and then move into the classroom to begin working on coloring projects at their desks. However, there is one child, Jerry, who does not follow this pattern. Instead, he enters class through the outside hallway door and begins to wander about the room, still wearing his coat. Mr. Sills, the kindergarten teacher, surveys the scene and goes immediately to the first two children who have taken their seats. Standing near the children, Mr. Sills states in a clear, audible voice, "Judy and Robert, I'm so glad to see that you have remembered our classroom rules of coming in through the cloakroom, hanging up your coats, and then beginning to work at your seat. I have a special treat for the two of you. You may help me pass out our "snack" today *and* you may have the extra two cookies I have brought!"

The teacher then turns to the remainder of the students who have also followed the correct entrance pattern. He says, "Each of you who has remembered the classroom rules about 'coming in' will receive one paper punch on your 'play' cards, so that you may earn points to choose the toys you would like to play with during free play period." Jerry glances quickly at the other children, back to the teacher and, seeing what is transpiring, retreats out the hall classroom door and reenters through the correct cloakroom door, hangs up his clothing, and goes quickly to his seat.

Mr. Sills resisted the tendency to single out Jerry to reprimand him for failing to obey "classroom rules." It would have been easy for him to command. "Go out and come inside like everyone else, Jerry! You know better

129

than this!" Mr. Sills is a teacher who believes in the idea of controlling a child's behavior through the use of incentives and working within a behavior modification framework. A discussion of such techniques often elicits strong opinions. There seems to be little middle ground. There are those who swear by behavior modification as the only realistic way of teaching children how to behave properly. There are others who feel that such practices are rigid, inhumane, and that they stifle the "spirit" or creativity of children. Although all of our other cited authors and models have their critics and proponents, none seem to have the "lightning rod" effect of attracting heated debate as the behaviorists have with their philosophy. In this chapter, we will explore the writings of those who advocate behavior modification being used in the positive sense of providing rewards and other positive reinforcements. In the next chapter, we will look at well-known advocates of behavior modification who additionally emphasize the use of punishment and other negative reinforcements as practices in shaping behavior. Their stance adds fuel to an already volatile argument.

THE BEHAVIORAL POSITION

Behavior modification techniques with humans came out of the experimental work of Pavlov with his famous (or infamous) salivating dogs. He found he could condition dogs to salivate by ringing a bell when they were about to be fed. During the process of repeated feedings, Pavlov eventually was able to substitute the bell for the food as the *stimulus* for the *response* of salivating. In other words, when the bell rang, even with the absence of food, the dogs got their digestive juices in gear. This admittedly is a somewhat fractured version of Pavlov's experiments, which the reader can pursue for greater accuracy and amplification in any introductory psychology text. The point Pavlov was making was that animal behavior could be explained in terms of stimulus and response. An animal's actions could be traced to an occurrence in the outer environment.

B. F. Skinner, the experimental psychologist, philosopher, and Utopian visionary, is the now recognized leader of the behaviorist movement. He, more than any other, has taken the stimulus-response theory of Pavlov, verified it with other animals (pigeons and mice), and has applied it to the human condition. In essence, a human is no different from any other animal. All human behavior can be explained as responses to environmental stimuli. There is no inner rational person. Any student who behaves rationally does so because of adults who have rewarded correct rational behavior and ignored (or punished) irrational action.

Using Skinner's work as a base, there is a host of writers, psychologists, and educators who have attempted to translate those behavioral principles for teachers to use in classrooms with children who misbehave. It is difficult to pick out one writer who is clearly identified as *the* behavior modification person for teachers. As a result we have drawn from the writings of some of the more popular ones—Axelrod,[1] Bandura,[2] Homme,[3] Madsen and Madsen,[4] Blackham and Silberman,[5] and Walker[6]—to show how these principles work. These writers share a common belief that a student's misbehavior can be changed and reshaped in a socially acceptable manner by directly changing the student's environment. The behaviorist accepts the premise that students are motivated by the factor that all people will attempt to avoid experiences and stimuli that are not pleasing and will seek experiences that are pleasing and rewarding.

In discussing motivation and school discipline, Madsen and Madsen stated:

> Particular patterns of responses are learned from the external world (external stimuli). If a student is "motivated," it is because he has learned to associate certain behaviors with certain outcomes. Motivation does not exist in a vacuum; it is a way of behaving. If the teacher wants a student to behave in a certain way, the teacher must structure the student's external world (i.e., control his environment) to insure the desired outcome. The disciplined child is a child who (1) has learned to behave socially in appropriate ways, and (2) evidences proper patterns of responses to academic work. If either one of these two general categories of behavior is absent, we usually say the child "has a problem."[7]

Based on this position, behaviorists would not engage in trying to do detective work to learn what might be the earlier origins of the child's problems. Their position is that the labeling of children as coming from a deprived family background, having a poor early academic background, having been an abused child, or the many other descriptors that suggest to us what has happened to the child gives little or no help to the classroom teacher who needs to deal, daily, with this same child's "acting out" behaviors. For the same reasons, it is useless to discuss a child's "inner feelings" or to expect the child to find his or her own solution. Rather, the teacher must ascertain what is happening in the classroom environment to perpetuate the child's behavior and in turn what can be changed in the environment "to reverse the tide."

Before we begin using the Teacher Behavior Continuum as our common construct in explaining particular teacher practices of the Behaviorists, the reader needs to reorient somewhat. *Because the concept of reinforcement is so powerful and influential, all the other categories (silently looking on, nondirective statements, questions, and so on) are advocated as practices only*

FIGURE 8-1. Teacher Behavior Continuum (TBC)

when they are a form of reinforcement. In other words, the behaviorists explain that all these practices emanate from the right-hand side of our continuum. This is illustrated in Figure 8–1.

THE BASICS OF REINFORCEMENT

According to Blackham and Silberman, there are three categories of positive reinforcement, as follows

1. *Token Reinforcement:*   A tangible item to be bestowed after desirable student behavior. The token has value in that it can be exchanged for materials or a reinforcing event.
2. *Social Reinforcement:*   The use of teacher attention, approval, and praise after desirable student behavior.
3. *Primary Reinforcement:*   A tangible item that satisfies a biologically based need. The use of sweets, popcorn, cereal, or something similar after appropriate behavior.

Reinforcers can be generally categorized as positive or negative. The rewarding of approved behavior with something desired by the student, such as extra recess, candy, praise, smiles, or special privileges, is an example of positive reinforcement. The above three categories of token, social, and primary are positive reinforcers.

When rewards are dispensed following a behavior, that particular behavior will increase its rate of occurrence. Negative reinforcers are those happenings or events that a student does not desire. For example, the teacher tells the student, "if you finish your assignment without me reminding you, you'll have no homework." In the case of negative reinforcer, the undesirable event (homework) is in place but is removed when the student demonstrates appropriate behavior. In other words, the lessening of an undesirable event or activity can be something that is desired. The student will tend to behave in ways to reduce discomfort. Again, just as with positive reinforcement, we get an increase in the desired behavior (seated and working) with the contingency that a negative reinforcer (homework) will be lessened. Reinforcers will vary in their degree of desirability from student to student. What we as adults assume will be unpleasant for students may not be at all. Some students do not mind staying after school, being sent to the principal's office, doing extra homework, and the like. The reader who wonders how the teacher will be able to identify valid reinforcers for individual children can refer to Chapter 6 on reality therapy and read Glasser's discussion of privileges.

Punishment often is confused with negative reinforcers, although experts in behavior modification usually do not advocate its use. Punishment is not a negative reinforcer! Punishment, if successful, decreases inappropriate behavior but does not increase appropriate behavior. One problem with punishments is that they often do not work in the long run, even though in the short run, they appear to be decreasing misbehavior. Punishments are undesirable events given to a student as a result of misbehavior, ranging from scolding, frowning, yelling, extra work, making the student stand in front of the room, to inflicting physical pain.

One of the reasons that punishment often does not work is that students perceive the punishment act as a positive reinforcer in that they gain peer approval. Punishment does not show the student what he or she should do. For example, if the teacher shouts at Judy to stop talking (punishment) and Judy stops for a short period of time, the teacher will, when Judy begins talking again, repeat this behavior thinking that the punishment worked before and will work again. Judy might become less sensitive to the teacher's reprimand, requiring the teacher to shout louder. The effect is one of a vicious cycle. The teacher yells, Judy gets noisier, the teacher gets noisier, and then the entire class is affected. This inverse effect might also be seen when some speeding motorists have to pay fines. They, in turn, might not see the fine as a reason to stop their speeding. Instead, they simply become more skilled at evading the police by watching for them more closely, by purchasing a CB radio, or by buying a radar detector. In this case, the punishment resulted in an increased number of drivers who were in less jeopardy of being caught. A child must learn how to behave, rather than how not to behave. This learning takes place only when appropriate behavior is positively reinforced.

Reinforcement is based on the premise that a teacher may observe and record behavior of students and the elements in their surrounding circumstances. It is presupposed that the specific behavior is heavily influenced by the events that follow the specific act. For example, if we want kindergarten children to enter the classroom in a certain way, to hang up their clothing properly, and to begin to work quietly at their seats, we follow those behaviors with such positive consequences as "You get one punch on your play card which will permit you to choose the play toys or activities you prefer at 'free play' period." Thus, a "contingency" is created, which can be defined as those consequences that the student faces as a result of his or her behavior. When we order or arrange these "contingencies" (also called "rewards") and the desired behavior increases, for example, more children enter the classroom more often in a "correct" manner, we can claim we have shaped or conditioned the students to behave in that way.

The behavioral technique, unlike our previous models, lends itself to being more exactly controlled and scientifically validated as to cause and effect. This is done by recording observable behavior of students through a process of (1) baseline measures, (2) reinforcement, (3) reversal, and (4) postcheck data.

Let's see how this procedure works. The teacher wants to use operant-conditioning techniques to get his or her fourth-grade students to remain in their seats during work periods. There is a particular problem with three boys who continually wander around the room, and whose behavior has been most distracting. The teacher begins by simply counting the number of students out of their seats during three-minute intervals over a fifteen-minute period during normal work time for five days. The teacher counts fifteen to eighteen times per day and has a baseline score for "out-of-seat behavior" during a *baseline* stage. Having done this, the teacher prepares to enter the *reinforcement* stage. This stage begins when the teacher gives each student a score card with the numbers 1 to 25 on it. The students are told that periodically a number will be punched on their card when the teacher sees that they are staying in their seats during work time. Each completely punched card can be redeemed for a prize (ruler, pencil, eraser, candy bar). For the next five days the plan is carried out, with the teacher making a point to punch the cards of other students when the three troublesome youngsters are wandering around, or to punch troublesome children's cards whenever they do sit for a length of time. After a period of applying the reinforcement, the teacher records a second score for "out-of-seat" behavior over the same three-minute interval for a fifteen-minute period. This score is plotted on a chart (see Figure 8–2) to permit a comparison to be made.

Since the teacher is experimenting and does not know for certain that it is the reinforcement (punches on the play card) that is making the difference on the second score, the teacher now moves to a third stage called *reversal*. During this period, the teacher withdraws the reinforcement (punch cards and prizes) and takes a new score for "out-of-seat" behavior. If the score during the *stage of reversal* rises dramatically, the teacher can be certain that his or her reinforcements are having an effect and, now, can reapply the reinforcement in the second experimental or *reinforcement* stage. If, again, the *"out-of-seat"* behavioral score drops, there is additional evidence that the contingency or reinforcement is effective. After a sufficient period of time, the reinforcement can gradually be dropped and a postcheck score taken to see if the behavior is lasting and having a long-term effect.

FIGURE 8–2. Out-of-Seat Behavior

With this rudimentary understanding of reinforcement and the scientific stages of validating cause and effect, we will return to the categories of the Teacher Behavior Continuum as practices of reinforcement. We will move through each category and, when encountering the reinforcement category, we will extend the operability of schedules and different plans for shaping behavior.

TEACHER BEHAVIOR CONTINUUM AND BEHAVIOR MODIFICATION

Silently Looking On

This generally unintrusive practice of the Relationship-Listeners is a bold practice for the Rules/Rewarders-Punishers. Most teachers know that there are different ways to observe children. There are looks that convey kindness and there are looks that could destroy a concrete building. The teacher can use these different ways of observing children as positive and negative reinforcers. Examples of some positive reinforcing looks occur when the teacher:

- smiles
- nods, showing approval
- gives gestures of satisfaction (the "V" sign for victory or the "OK" sign for acceptance)

Some negative reinforcing looks can be described as:

- raised eyebrows
- scowl or frown
- rolling the eyes
- shaking the head
- staring menacingly

It may be of interest to a teacher who is experiencing difficulty with a particular child to judge privately (or have an outsider record a sample of time) how many times and types of *silently looking on* reinforcers he or she uses. The teacher may find that he or she is using negative looks at a ratio of ten to one over positive looks. With these data, the teacher may change the ratio to one of ten positive looks to one negative and use the four-stage experimental approach (baseline, reinforcement, reversal, and postcheck) to see what results may occur.

Once again, we must caution that reinforcers differ for individual students. A teacher working with a small group of children may suddenly stop writing an assignment on the chalkboard to look at Tommy who is crawling under his desk (looking for the pencil that he "accidentally" dropped). A few minutes later the same teacher again gives hostile attention to Tommy, who is now rummaging through his desk, followed by noisily sharpening his pencil, or "borrowing" a piece of paper from an unsuspecting neighbor. If the teacher were to take a baseline recording of the child's disruptive behavior and his or her reactive "silently looking on," the teacher might be surprised to discover that he or she was reinforcing these student behaviors with frowns, scowls, and stares. The teacher then might reverse the process and refuse to "look on" at the student's behavior, but instead only acknowledge Tommy by "silently looking" at him when he was working properly. Only when the teacher caught Tommy being good would his behavior be reinforced with the teacher's visual presence. For Tommy, any type of teacher attention was a positive reinforcement of his preceding behavior. By ignoring the incorrect behavior, the teacher was practicing what psychologists call *extinction*. By removing the reinforcement, Tommy will find his incorrect behavior useless, and therefore he will gradually decrease his practice of it.

The usual practice is for the teacher to ignore a student's misbehavior in conjunction with the awarding of approving looks for correct behavior. The beginning of this procedure is tough on teachers because the student's inappropriate behavior usually *rises* dramatically when it is first ignored. It is as though the child gets frantic, not believing that he or she can't get the teacher's attention as he or she has always been able to do in the past. As a result, the student "shoots the works" and goes through his or her entire previously successful repertoire. A teacher who can "grit out" this initial stage and continue to ignore the child will find his or her patience rewarded. Obviously, the exhibition of some extreme behaviors such as the student who attacks others physically, damages property, or inflicts self-mutilation will prevent a teacher from practicing extinction.

Nondirective Statements, Questions, and Directive Statements

The use of language is valuable both as an important reinforcer as well as a tool for setting up reinforcement plans. Upon detection of a student's mis-behavior, the teacher might use quick, direct statements that tell the student to stop. One of our experiences with a student teacher made us more aware of the power of words. This student teacher was having difficulty trying to get Bubba in her fifth-grade class to listen to her. The school psychologist, who was working with the same youngster, sat in on her class. After the class the psychologist gave the teacher a simple analysis of the situation. The teacher had a quiet, soft voice. Whenever she told the offending student to do something, her voice would become high pitched and sound nonassertive. She would also follow up her pleas with a rhetorical question or explanation. She would ask her students to line up and direct a plea to her "problem" student by saying, "Bubba, it's time to get in line. OK? As soon as you do, we can all get going." The school psychologist advised her to go home and practice (using a tape recorder) giving assertive, direct commands in a low voice. Later, in a similar situation, she would be able to look directly at Bubba, make sure that eye contact was established, and then say in a low, clear voice, "Bubba, get in line!"

This change of voice and abbreviation of words worked more success-fully than the teacher's earlier attempts with Bubba. Her whining voice, defensive questions, and explanations were a positive reinforcement for the student. He liked what his behavior was doing to her. When she took the offensive and showed control and authority, the language was no longer positively reinforcing to Bubba. Therefore we can see that *how words are said* and *what words are chosen* can be examined by a teacher as a practice to be considered for its reinforcing value.

Let us take a look at language as positive and as punitive. Positive language builds upon the social behavior expected of the student; punitive language puts the student down without telling him/her what to do.

Questions—positive

- "Lucy, I'd like to help you. Do you need my help?"
- "Melinda, you're usually so happy. What's wrong?"
- "Melanie, did you start that fight? You're so honest that I know you'll tell me the truth. Did you?"

Questions—punitive

- "Barbara, can't you do anything right?"
- "Stephanie, what is wrong now?"
- "Veronica, how many times do I need to tell you?"

Directive statements—positive

- "George, you're a smart boy. Use the tools properly."
- "Gus, show me how well you know how to listen."
- "Hector, let's keep cool. You're too good a kid to get into trouble fighting."

Directive statements—punitive

- "Charles, you act like a baby. This is what you do."
- "Pete, I get so mad at you when you behave like that."
- "Fred, I'm so disappointed in you."

Most of the behavior modification advocates urge teachers to use language as a positive reinforcer of appropriate behavior and to avoid language as punishment. We have already seen how punitive language is often interpreted by students as being better than no reinforcement (or attention) at all. A teacher should be aware of the kind and amount of language that he or she uses with a particular student. It is clear that that ratio should favor the positive over the punitive.

Language is also advocated as an information-gathering and explanatory device for setting up individual reinforcement programs with children. The teacher should state directly to the student, "If you do X, then you can do, or get, Y." (If you do your homework, then you can go out to recess.) It might be necessary to interview students to determine what they value so that you would know what to offer as a strong reward. One junior high school or middle school was having trouble getting students into the classroom immediately after changing classes. It was discovered after interviewing that the students really wanted most of all to be able to go across the street to a local fast-food restaurant during lunch period and to have a school dance on Fridays. The school, therefore, used "going across the street for lunch" and "Friday dances" as reinforcers or contingencies to get students to class on time.

In discussing language, we have deliberately neglected nondirective statements. We have shown how questions and directive statements are important for conditioning behavior. Nondirective statements have little reinforcing value. For a teacher to repeat a student's statement, "So you are mad at Sara for swearing at you," does nothing to correct the behavior. Therefore, behavior modification proponents have little use for such a teacher practice.

Modeling

The use of modeling is an important concept in the behavioral model, and it can be especially helpful for providing disruptive children with an example to imitate. There are three kinds of modeling: (1) modeling of peers, (2) modeling of fictitious or idealized characters, and (3) modeling of an important adult. We will discuss each of them in turn.

To illustrate the modeling of peers, we see a kindergarten teacher seated before a semicircle of students. She wants to begin reading a story, but the children are shouting and inattentive. The teacher looks directly at Darlene, who is attentive and waiting patiently for the story to begin. The teacher states, "Darlene, I can tell by your behavior that you are ready for a story. You may be first in line for recess today. Now, I'm going to see who else is ready for the story and I will pick someone to be second." With statements like these repeated over following days, we will discover the students quickly becoming attentive. After a while, the teacher may simply need to say, "I see by Johnny's behavior that he is ready for a story." This teacher has put together modeling with the use of verbal statements as reinforcers to obtain the desired student behavior. Other examples of peer modeling can be seen in such school activities as appointing certain well-behaved students to be the class leader, or the use of school honor societies and award days. These students are held up as models to be emulated by others. When they get special rewards such as plaques, their names and pictures in the local newspaper, or recognition from teachers or administrators, other students may aspire to be like them. (There is always the danger that too much recognition of a particular few will cause envy and hostility. It is best to make such recogition attainable for all.)

The second form of modeling is that of fictitious or idealized characters. It comes as no surprise to teachers who have first-hand experience with students acting like Batman, Muhammed Ali, or Wonder Woman. Today, the characters in TV series, children's books, or films can have a powerful effect for reinforcing both positive and negative social behavior in students. The effectiveness of such modeling can be seen in recent studies (showing the relationship between how much time children view television and the increase in violence among school-age children.)[9] In Chapter 6, which is devoted to Dreikurs, we have already mentioned how he uses storybooks and certain storybook characters as examples of behavior that students should follow. The same can be said for the use of television and film stories in the school.

The last form of modeling is that of an adult who is important to a child. In many cases a teacher fits this description (particularly with young children). According to Albert Bandura,[10] who has done the most extensive research in this area, a child will imitate those adults whom he or she would aspire to be like. Such an innocuous statement places a heavy burden on the teacher. *A teacher has to behave in the same manner as what he or she desires from a student.* Let us show how this works:

- A student who screams and is countered by a screaming teacher will continue to scream.
- A physically aggressive student who is disciplined by a physically aggressive teacher will continue to be physically aggressive.
- A perpetually tardy student corrected by a perpetually tardy teacher will continue to be perpetually tardy.

The behaviorists' explanation for all forms of modeling is that the student observes and emulates behavior that is rewarded. It may be a storybook character who acquires many friends, a cultural folk hero who rises from poverty to fame, or a teacher who has status, authority, and wealth (if they only knew!). Observing this rewarded behavior stimulates a response to imitate. Such a theory makes it quite clear, for example, how a child's life in the ghetto can be turned around by having contact with a famous civil rights leader or a highly regarded teacher.

Reinforcement

Putting together the knowledge about the three kinds of reinforcement (token, social, and primary) and the scientific method of validation (baseline, reinforcement, reversal, and postcheck), with the use of language, the teacher can create a contingency management plan for individual children.

After the teacher determines the appropriate reinforcer, Homme[11] proposes the following steps:

1. Give immediate rewards for short, correct behavior (i.e., coming into the room and sitting attentively for the class to begin).
2. Keep the rewards based on small steps of correct behavior (i.e., coming into the room quietly, sitting down, looking up).
3. Reward the correct behavior frequently (i.e., every five minutes that the student stays in his seat).
4. Reward the accomplishment, not the obedience (i.e., "If you stay in your seat quietly, you will be rewarded by . . . ," not, "If you do what I say, I will give you . . .").
5. Reward after the performance. Do not let the student determine the sequence (i.e., not the child saying, "I want to play ball another five minutes, then I'll get to work and be quiet"; rather the teacher saying, "You work and be quiet and then you'll have five extra minutes at recess to play").

Homme refers to his system as contingency contracting, whereby the teacher lays out the bargain plan. "If you (the student) come into the room each day quietly, I'll give you a token. After you've earned ten tokens, you can redeem them for less homework (a magazine, time to play a game, and so on)." Homme goes on to explain that the contract must be fair, clearly understood, honest, positive (what the student will earn, not what he will be deprived of), and lastly systematic. The key to contracting is that the child gains a sense of accomplishment and satisfaction (rewards) for correct behavior.*

The reader at this point might be thinking, "How, in my busy and full classroom, can I find the time to be constantly reinforcing one child?" The answer is that the teacher will need to spend a lot of time at first, but then can plan a schedule of reinforcement that is less frequent. There are two basic

---

*There have been some recent innovations in behavior modification that should be watched closely to see what impact they will have in the school. An example is Workman (1982) who advocates students developing their own behavior-modification contract. In the future, we may have more "hybrid" approaches.

schedules, the *fixed interval* and the *ratio interval*. In the beginning of the contingency plan, the teacher might use the fixed interval plan, where the child receives a token every morning that he or she is on time and is sitting in his or her seat. After a period of time the teacher might go to a ratio interval, where the student will be given two tokens for behaving properly on "surprise days." The teacher needs to plan privately what days they will occur (Monday and Wednesday one week, Tuesday, Wednesday, and Friday the next). In this way, the child has the incentive to continue behaving each day, not knowing when the "surprise day" will be. The teacher is still dispensing the same ration of tokens, ten for ten days, but less often. There may be occasions when a teacher wishes to "shoot the works" and reinforce daily (or the same time each day), as well as use "surprise days." In this case we have a combination of fixed and ratio intervals. In all cases the point is the same, reward frequently at first and then once the proper behavior is occurring, taper off the frequency.

Another aid in saving time and frustration for teachers is the process of *shaping*. Basically, this is the breaking down of gross misbehavior into simple successive behaviors. The teacher then works on reinforcing behavior priority number one before thinking about number two, three, four, and so on. To be honest, as we all know, there are children who are considered general, all-around nuisances. Not only are they tardy, but they swear, bully, neglect homework, steal, lie, and defy their teachers. According to the tenets of shaping, one key behavior needs to be worked on at a time. Therefore, if the teacher feels that "Dennis the Menace" would be making some progress if he could get through the first five minutes of homeroom attendance taking without fighting, then a contingency plan would begin there. (This doesn't help for the remaining six hours and twenty-five minutes, but it's a start.) After success is evident, then the teacher can move to Dennis's lack of attention during reading period, and so on.

Another example of shaping is the case of the teacher who believes that if Carol would work on, and complete, her math assignments that both her math abilities and her grades would improve. However, Carol only comes to school one or two days out of the week, and when she is there, she fights with other students, verbally offends the teachers, and will not remain in her seat, much less attempt to do the math assignments. Her teacher wishes to obtain the "terminal result" of getting Carol to do her math work. In Carol's case, therefore, the teacher initially needed her to simply come to school on a regular basis. Contingencies were set up and a reward was given for attendance. Once at school, the teacher then rewarded Carol for being simply near her desk even though she was still not seated. Finally, with Carol seated, the teacher began reinforcing the child when she picked up her pencil or had her materials at hand. The next step was to get her to finish one problem that the teacher knew she could do. This accomplishment was followed by the teacher gradually increasing the number and difficulty of tasks. Through this "shaping" process, Carol eventually performed the terminal behavior of doing her math assignments. Teachers who seem to have trouble with reinforcement techniques are those who move too fast and do not break the shaping tasks down into small, manageable behaviors that will lead to the final objective.

Physical Intervention and Isolation

As stated earlier, the behaviorists suggest that there are times when children find misbehavior is more reinforcing (in terms of peer and teacher attention) than proper behavior. Also, it is obviously impossible to begin reinforcing appropriate behavior with desirable teacher rewards until a child exhibits some suitable activity. Mentioned before were the types of destructive behavior that a teacher cannot ignore. For all these reasons, there are times when a teacher is called upon to intervene physically by removing the student from the classroom setting and isolating him or her in a space lacking any reinforcing support. This is generally called a "*time out*" area. The "time out" area might be an isolated seat in the back of the classroom, the hallway, an isolated supply room, or even the principal's office where the child will be out of the view of his or her peers. In order for the "time out" intervention to be successful, the new environment must not be reinforcing for the child. If the student who is isolated doesn't want to be in the classroom with peers in the first place, the isolation becomes desirable and therefore reinforcing. He or she will continue to act out to get "timed out." The next important consideration is that the area should be nearly void of all stimuli. If a student is sent to a room with toys or interesting magazines to read, or the school secretary chats with the student, then these objects or activities become reinforcing for the student and the "time out" area loses its effectiveness. Generally, the specified period that the student has to stay in the "time out" area should be established when the physical intervention occurs. Some kindergarten teachers may set a five-minute egg timer, while older children can be told the exact time period they will be isolated.

Another form of physical intervention within a behavioral modification framework is the use of *saturation*. There are certain behaviors that students first engage in, such as spitting or striking out, which are sporadic and appear difficult to eliminate with negative or positive reinforcers. The teacher can use saturation techniques to deal with these behaviors. Let's use the example of spitting. The teacher takes the saliva-expelling student to the bathroom and gives him or her several glasses of water. The child is required to spit until the supply of water is exhausted. Saturation can also be used by having an aggressive student repeatedly hit a pillow or inflated doll until he or she is tired. At first these actions are a delight to the child, but by the time the student has finished, he or she has the feeling that, "I never want to spit (or strike) again."

Isolation and saturation are not used as forms of punishment. Punishment is one person inflicting pain or discomfort on another. Isolation is used as a neutralizing action, while saturation is simply a forced repetition of the child's previous wrongful act. The repetition should become tiring, but the activity itself will not cause harm to the child. All the writers cited in this chapter resist the use of punitive physical intervention and isolation. They do not advocate punishment or forcing a student to sit in a hostile environment. In the next chapter, we will see how some fellow behaviorists depart from this position and advocate punishment as essential and effective in promoting good behavior.

SUMMARY

The behavior-modification writers cite the need for teachers to set easily understood standards of behavior. Their basic premise is that all children will learn to abide by these standards if they receive proper reinforcement. *Whenever possible, inappropriate behavior should be ignored and acceptable behavior rewarded.* If these means fail, then the teacher must resort to isolation and saturation but must stay away from punishment. The approach should be positive, and a teacher needs to check the quantity of positive reinforcement that is being dispensed.

Using the Teacher Behavior Continuum, we can identify the general categories of teacher behavior and covert behaviors offered in the behavior-modification model.

The teacher begins by covertly observing and counting the number of behaviors exhibited by the student(s) over an established time period to establish a *baseline*. Later, similar data are collected in *experimental* phases where reinforcement is applied, and then again when such reinforcements are withdrawn in *reversal* and *postcheck* phases.

The teacher may also use nonverbal behavior as positive and negative reinforcement, or refrain from "silently looking on" in the form of *extinction*. Depending on how it is expressed, the use of language can clearly serve as a

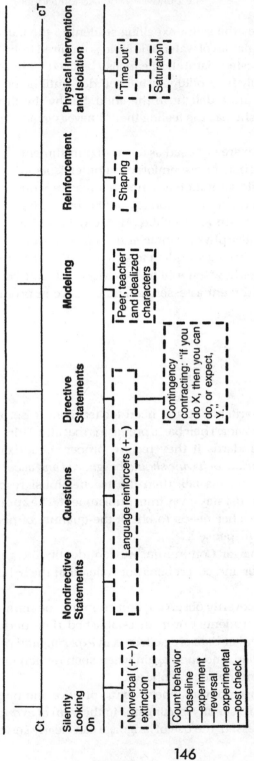

The Behavior Modification Model

Authors: Axelrod,
Madsen and Madsen,
Homme, and others

☐ covert behavior
⋮ ⋮ general category of behaviors

FIGURE 8–3. Teacher Behavior Continuum (TBC)

negative or positive reinforcement. Through directive statements we may establish *contingency contracts*, where a student agrees to work for some reward. Many behaviors can be learned or taught to students, directly or indirectly, through peers, teachers, and idealized characters, all of whom serve as models to imitate. Many behavioral changes can also be established through *"shaping,"* where the teacher reinforces a series of small behaviors that gradually moves the student towards the desired terminal behavior. The final tools in behavior modification are the use of *"time out,"* where the student is isolated from a reinforcing situation and then returns, usually with the establishment of a *contingency contract*, and the use of *saturation*, where we require the student to repeat an undesirable behavior until it becomes tiring and thus serves as a negative reinforcer.

NOTES

1. Saul Axelrod, *Behavior Modification for the Classroom Teacher* 2nd ed. (New York: McGraw-Hill, 1983).
2. Albert Bandura, *Principles of Behavior Modification* (New York: Holt Rinehart & Winston, 1965).
3. LLoyd Homme, *How to Use Contingency Contracting in the Classroom* (Champaign, Illinois: Research Press, 1970).
4. Charles H. Madsen and Clifford K. Madsen, *Teaching Discipline: Behavioral Principles Towards a Positive Approach* 2nd ed. (Boston: Allyn and Bacon, 1974).
5. Garth Blackham and Adolph Silberman, *Modification of Child and Adolescent Behavior* (Belmont, California: Wadsworth Publishing Company, 1975).
6. James E. Walker and Thomas M. Shea, *Behavior Modification: A Practical Approach for Educators* (St. Louis: C. V. Mosby, 1976).
7. Madsen and Madsen, *Teaching Discipline: Behavioral Principles Towards a Positive Approach*, p. 7.
8. Blackham and Silberman, *Modification of Child and Adolescent Behavior*, pp. 144–51.
9. Charles Wolfgang, "It's O.K. I'm Bionic!" *Phi Delta Kappan*, 59 (1978):10.
10. Albert Bandura, *Social Learning Theory* (Englewood Cliffs, New Jersey: Prentice-Hall, 1977), pp. 39–48.
11. Homme, *How to Use Contingency Contracting in the Classroom*, pp. 18–19.

REFERENCES

Axelrod, Saul. *Behavior Modification for the Classroom Teacher* 2nd ed. New York: McGraw-Hill, 1983.

Axelrod, S. and Apsche, J., eds. *The Effects of Punishment on Human Behavior*. New York: Academic Press, 1983.

Blackham, Garth, and Silberman, Adolph. *Modification of Child and Adolescent Behavior*. Belmont, California: Wadsworth Publishing, 1975.

Bandura, Albert. *Principles of Behavior Modification*. New York: Holt Rinehart & Winston, 1969.

Bandura, Albert. *Social Learning Theory*. Englewood Cliffs, New Jersey: Prentice-Hall, 1977.

Hessman, Therese. *Creating Learning Environments—The Behavioral Approach to Education*. Boston: Allyn and Bacon, 1977.

Madsen, Charles H., and Madsen, Clifford K. *Teaching Discipline: Behavioral Principles Towards a Positive Approach*. Boston: Allyn and Bacon, 1970.

Homme, Lloyd. *How to Use Contingency Contracting in the Classroom*. Champaign, Illinois: Research Press, 1970.

Skinner, B. F. *Skinner for the Classroom: Selected Papers*. Champaign, Illinois: Research Press, 1982.

Workman, E. A. *Teaching Behavioral Self-Control to Students*. Austin, Texas: Pro-Ed., 1982.

INSTRUCTIONAL MEDIA

Films

The following material is available from:

> University of California Extension Media Center
> 2223 Fulton Street
> Berkeley, California 94720

Behavior Modification in the Classroom

> 24 minutes; color. Sale price $300; rental fee $22.
>
> *Demonstrates teachers using positive reinforcement techniques to modify the behavior of students whose performances suffer because of their distracting behavior or daydreaming.*

The following material is available from:

> Prentice-Hall, Inc.
> Sylvan Avenue
> Englewood Cliffs, New Jersey 07632

Behavior Modification—Teaching Language to Psychotic Children

> 43 minutes; color. Sale price $600; rental fee $55 per day.
>
> *Examines the steps involved in teaching psychotic children the func-tional use of*

speech and discusses the need for correction of self-stimulation and destructive behavior before learning can begin. Describes how instruction may proceed through reward and punishment techniques in the imitation of sounds, labeling of objects, discrimination among alternatives, recall of experiences, and the development of a degree of spontaneity.

The following films are available from:

American Association for Counseling and Development
599 Stevenson Avenue
Alexandria, VA 22304

Observing and Recording Behavior
17 minutes, 16 mm, color and sound. Sale price $275; rental fee per day of use $30.

The counselor helps a teacher learn how to observe and record so that she can tell if a student is changing his behavior in response to her efforts. (order no. 77543C)

B. F. Skinner on Education (Part I)
25 minutes, 16 mm, color and sound. Sale price $300; rental fee per day of use $30.

Explores such important issues as: how Skinner's concepts on freedom and control are related to the classroom experience . . . what values are implicit in his technology of a behavioral change . . . given the current status of our educational system, how and where the process of effecting change will begin. (order no. 77522C)

B. F. Skinner on Education (Part II)
25 minutes, 16 mm, color and sound. Sale price $300; rental fee per day of use $30.

Continues the exploration of such important issues as: What the implications are for our educational system of the increased leisure time provided by the techno-logical society and whether schools should help develop people who will be deeply concerned about the welfare of their fellow man. (order no. 77523C)

9

The Assertiveness
Model of Lee and
Marlene Canter

Mr. Blum tells his eighth-grade industrial arts class to quiet down. He notices that Carl is talking loudly to another student, in apparent disregard of his instructions.

Mr. Blum: "Carl, I want you to be quiet now."
Carl: "What's the big deal? I'll be quiet but what's the big deal?"

Carl does quiet down but for only a moment. When his voice is heard again, Mr. Blum moves over to the chalkboard where Carl's name has already been written and places a check by it. The rest of the class hushes and Carl sees his name and one check on the board.

Mr. Blum: "Carl, I'm not going to allow you to talk and disrupt me and the class. You know the rules. If you talk again, then you will have chosen to go to the principal's office."
Carl: "This project is boring—can I do something else?"
Mr. Blum: "No, Carl, this is the project assigned, and if you talk again then you've chosen to go to the principal's office.

Carl turns away, is quiet for five minutes, but then once again his voice is heard arguing loudly with another student. Mr. Blum walks to the chalkboard puts a second check by Carl's name and turns to him.

Mr. Blum: "Carl, you know the rule for misbehavior. Your name is on the board, and two checks means that you are out of the class. You've

"Mrs. Eggleston has been quite successful with reluctant readers.
Cartoon by Ford Button

chosen to go to the principal's office—take this note with you."

Carl: "I'm not going, this is such a stupid class!"

Mr. Blum: "I'm sorry you feel that way, but you've chosen to go to the principal's office and you will go."

Carl remains in his seat not moving. Mr. Blum sends another student to the principal's office with a message for assistance. Quickly the assistant principal and another teacher arrive; they move towards Carl. Carl gets up and is led away. He knows that he will spend the next two industrial-art periods in the school's isolation room.

The above incident is an example of a teacher practicing assertive discipline. The teacher has determined his own rights to teach, has developed a clear punishment system, and will not back down when a student violates a rule. The teacher is not concerned with Relationship-Listening or Confronting-Contracting approaches with the student. Instead, the assertive teacher clearly is aligned with the Rules/Rewards-Punishment approach to discipline. The teacher holds maximum control while the student has minimum control over correction when discipline problems occur. Shortly, we will discuss the range of Rules/Rewards-Punishments that an assertive teacher can use, but first let's review the assertiveness model.

THE ASSERTIVENESS MODEL

The assertiveness-model approach to discipline has been popularized by Lee Canter and Marlene Canter in their book entitled *Assertive Discipline*. After the book was published in 1976, Lee and Marlene Canter and their associates began conducting discipline workshops, primarily on the west coast of the United States. Since then, the assertive discipline approach has been disseminated across the United States by additional consultants, videotapes, and workbooks. It is rare to find a locality in the United States where the assertive discipline approach is not known.

The Canters' approach to discipline is derived from the application of assertion or assertiveness training to various forms of human conflict. Such books as *Stand Up, Speak Out, Talk Back* (Alberti and Eamons, 1975) and *When I Say No I Feel Guilty* (Smith, 1975) are examples of the human conflict literature that were forerunners to the Canters' approach.

Assertiveness training is based on the premise that humans can respond to conflict in one of three ways; nonassertively, hostilely, and assertively. For example, if an employer at the last minute asks his or her employee to stay after work to do an extra assignment and the employee already has family commitments, the employee can respond in one of three ways.

The first way is *nonassertively*, by not telling the employer of one's previous commitments and instead passively complying; i.e., "OK, boss, I don't mind staying after work."

The second is the *hostile* way, by telling the employer in a vindictive and emotional tone what he or she thinks of such a request such as, "You may be my boss but I don't care! That's the most inconsiderate request I've ever heard! Don't you have any feeling for others?"

The third is the *assertive* way, by telling the employer in a calm but serious manner of the previous commitment and suggesting a solution that is within an employee's rights; i.e., "I'm sorry, but I have family obligations after work. If it is a real emergency, I could arrange to start work early tomorrow morning, let's say at 7:00 a.m. But I would want to finish work at 3:00 p.m. instead of the usual 5:00 p.m."

The assertive person states what his or her reasonable rights are without being obnoxious, aggressive, vengeful, apologetic, or "wishy-washy." As the assertiveness writers state, every person has the perfect right to express his or her own needs and desires.

In the teaching context, examples of nonassertive, hostile, and assertive responses can be found in the beginning conflict that Mr. Blum was having with Carl who was continuing to talk in class.

A *nonassertive* response would be for Mr. Blum to plead, "Carl, could you please be more quiet?" or just meekly ignore Carl's loud and incessant talk.

A *hostile* response would be for Mr. Blum to yell, "Carl, shut your mouth! You're the most juvenile, inconsiderate student I've ever had! I've had it with you!"

An *assertive* response would be what we've already seen Mr. Blum do. He walks to the board, checks Carl's name and says, "Carl, I want you to be quiet. I'm not going to allow you to talk and disrupt me and the class. You know the rules; if you talk again, then you will have chosen to go to the principal's office."

The Canters and their associates have applied assertiveness training to the teaching context by stating that you as a teacher have the following rights:

1. The right to establish a classroom structure and routine that provides the optimal learning environment in light of your own strengths and weaknesses.
2. The right to determine and request appropriate behavior from the students which meets your needs and encourages the positive social and educational development of the child.
3. The right to ask for help from parents, the principal, etc., when you need assistance with a child.[1]

The Canters believe that teachers must attend to their own needs and not become confused by other approaches to discipline (such as the supportiveness model of Thomas Gordon or the reality model of William Glasser) which they believe attend more to student than teacher needs. The assertiveness model of discipline is therefore a systematic combination of verbal assertiveness training combined with teachers using the everyday rewards and punishments that they have at hand. Let us turn to the Teacher Behavior Continuum and see how a teacher would apply the assertive model to his or her classroom.

Ct ——— cT

Silently Looking On	Nondirective Statements	Questions	Directive Statements	Modeling	Reinforcement	Physical Intervention and Isolation
(a) Establish discipline plan —teacher needs —class rules (b) Consistency —avoid road-blocks (c) Mental rehearsal	(3) Hints (verbal limit 1) "Class, we should be reading it."	(4) Disguised directive statement (verbal limit) (2) "Would you return to reading. . .?"	(1) Disclose the plans (2) Verbal limit setting (5) "I" statement (verbal limit) 3) "I want you to stop talking now. . ." (6) Demands (verbal limit) 4) "Be quiet now or you'll choose to. . ." (7) Broken record "Be quiet now or choose. . ." "Be quiet now or choose. . ."	(8) Composed, stern, and steady gaze	(9) Follow-through punishment	(10) Systematic exclusion using principal using other teachers —using principal —using parents

Rewards

The Assertiveness Model
Authors: Lee and Marlene Canter

(numbers) overt behavior
(letters) covert behavior

154

THE ASSERTIVENESS MODEL AND THE TEACHER BEHAVIOR CONTINUUM

Silently Looking On

Critical to the success of an assertive approach is for the teacher first to establish covertly *a discipline plan* for his or her students. The teacher makes such a classroom plan based on his or her own desires and limits of tolerance towards student behavior. The plan includes relatively few *classroom rules*, no more than five, that are clearly stated. The teacher then thinks through *consistent actions* that will be taken toward students who break the rules, and also actions toward students who obey the rules. The teacher writes the plan out, shares it with his or her principal for approval, and has it filed in the principal's office.

An example of such a plan for a teacher that has a low tolerance for noise and activity might be as follows:

Rules:

1. Absolutely no talking during lessons.
2. Whispering only at break times.
3. Students must stay in their seats during classtime unless teacher permission has been given.
4. Do not touch other people or their property.
5. Follow teacher orders immediately.

Notice that the rules are specific; i.e., "do not touch other people," and not global such as "be considerate." The student is to know exactly what the teacher means by each rule without having to make his or her own interpretation. Next, the action plan for violations as well as the action plan for compliance are clearly stated. Such an action plan might be as follows:

Violations

1. First violation, name on board.
2. Second violation, check next to name and ten-minute detention.
3. Third violation, second check next to name and note sent to parent.
4. Fourth violation, third check and isolation in principal's office.

Compliance

1. Each student who is not reprimanded during the day earns one point.
2. Thirty points earns a free cheeseburger at "Fast Food Sam's" or an entire free period to play video games on the microcomputer.

The options that a teacher has in developing his or her plan will vary according to his or her own needs and the agreement of the school principal. The teacher must be able to carry out each consequence for a violation or compliance in a direct and quick manner. Therefore, it is essential that the school principal agrees with and supports the teacher's plan. Other consequences for violations and compliance will be explained as we continue through the behavior continuum.

It is important to note that the Canters urge a teacher to treat students alike and not be confused by what they refer to as *roadblocks*. Roadblocks are thoughts teachers have that students can't behave because of factors beyond the teacher's control, ranging from emotional illness to hyperactivity to family conditions to socioeconomic background. Such a defeatist attitude becomes a self-fulfilling prophecy. If the teacher excuses the student from being able to follow his or her rules, then he or she is accepting a discipline problem that will probably affect the entire class for the entire year. Instead a teacher should expect the same standards from all students, and the teacher should expect to succeed. He or she may have to call in the help of other resources of parents, counselors, juvenile authorities, and administrators, but that is the teacher's right to do so. The teacher has the right to teach and for students to behave.

Finally, the last course of action under silently looking on, taken by the teacher before going into overt action, is mental rehearsal. The teacher should rehearse explaining to a student his or her rights, the classroom rules, and violation and compliance actions. The teacher also should rehearse what he or she will do when students begin to violate the rules. The rehearsal can be simply going through the plan in one's head or actually acting out what one will do and say. This rehearsal is done for purposes of being assured, assertive, and confident when facing students. Students then will know that the teacher has "his or her act together" and means business.

Directive Statements

Following the mental rehearsal, the teacher moves into overt action, *disclosing* the plan. He or she might insure that the students comprehend the plan by passing out written copies of it and asking students to sign the copy indicating their understanding. The teacher can file the signed copy and no longer have to accept a misbehaving student's explanation that "I didn't know or understand the rules." Now when a student misbehaves the teacher can resort to four verbal limit-setting behaviors that can be used before initiating negative consequences.

Nondirective Statements

The first verbal limit on a student's misbehavior is a teacher hint whereby the teacher directs a message to the entire class. For example, Carl may be talking and the teacher says "Class, we should all be reading Chapter Twelve." This nondirective hint attempts to alert the individual student to the task at hand without singling him or her out.

Questions

If the hint has not worked, then the teacher can ask a question which is, in reality, a slightly *disguised directive statement*. For example, the teacher can ask students who are still talking, "Would you get back to reading the chapter now?" The message being sent is not really "Would you?" but "stop talking"; however, the teacher has softened the command by putting it in the form of a question. The disguised directive statement is used to avoid unnecessary confrontation.

Directive Statements

Verbal limit 3 is used when the teacher feels ready to confront the student with his or her expectation. The Canters label a confronting statement as an *"I" message* (not to be confused with Gordon's "I" message, which consists of teacher's feelings, student behavior, and effect on teacher). The Canters' "I" message is simply a teacher statement of what he or she wants from the student; i.e., "I want you to stop talking, open to Chapter Twelve, and begin to read."

If the student still does not comply, then the teacher uses verbal limit 4, *demands*, which are promises (not threats) of what will happen to the student if he or she does not immediately behave correctly. A threat can often be construed as an "I dare you" statement. A teacher can threaten a student by saying "If you keep it up, I'll make life so miserable for you you'll stay after school for a month!", but often the threat is not realistic and the student knows it. Therefore, the student can back the teacher down by continuing to misbehave. Is the teacher really going to stay after school with the student every day for a month? The Canters warn the teacher not to use a demand unless he or she is prepared to enforce it.[3] A reasonable demand would be "Carl, be quiet and read now or you'll choose to stay after school." A demand is given as a choice so that the student knows his or her options; if students continue to misbehave, then they have in effect chosen to face the consequences of their actions.

Repeating the demand is another technique that the teacher is encouraged to use. Often students will attempt to argue away a teacher's demand by giving excuses. If the teacher is to be effective, he or she sticks with the demand and refuses to negotiate with the student. This use of repetition is called the "broken-record method."

Mr. Blum: (After hints, questions, and "I" messages to Carl) "Carl, either be quiet, or you are choosing to stay after school for ten minutes."

Carl: "Why pick on me? Sara was talking too, didn't you see her?"

Mr. Blum: "You will either be quiet or choose to stay after school for ten minutes."

Carl: "I wasn't talking that much—Sara was talking more than me! I can't stay after today; I'm supposed to meet my father. . ."

Mr. Blum: "You've now chosen to stay after school for ten minutes. Either be quiet or you'll now be choosing to stay for twenty minutes."

Carl: (Stops talking to the other student and opens his book.)

The broken-record method keeps the focus on the student's behavior and personal choice. The student eventually sees that the teacher will carry out the promise and further talking will add to the student's trouble. The Canters caution the teacher to use the broken-record method only when the student has no valid response. For example, if a boy had cut himself and was trying to explain to the teacher why he was yelling, the broken record would be not only inappropriate but an insensitive response to a student who needed help.

Modeling

When the teacher speaks to a student, he or she should physically model assertive behavior. His or her voice should be low and composed. The teacher should directly face the misbehaving student, use hand gestures to make a point, refer to the student by name, and keep his or her gaze steady. The gravity of the matter can be further conveyed by a light touch on the student's shoulder while talking. (Again, common sense is advised for the teacher; staring at or touching some students might ignite an explosive situation.) The teacher's tone, posture, and facial expression should convey an appearance of firm resolve, demonstrating that the teacher will not back down nor will he or she become emotionally upset.

Reinforcement

As part of a teacher's discipline plan, *punishments* should follow teacher demands. The Canters advocate that the teacher choose punishments that a student does not like but that are not physically or psychologically harmful.[4] These punishments should be given to students as choices: they either behave correctly or they are choosing to be punished. Punishments suggested are depriving a student of an activity he or she enjoys, such as free time, recess, classroom responsibilities, movies, a field trip, or physical education. Other forms of punishment would be remaining after school, going to the principal's office, sending a note home, asking parents to restrict the student by such means as isolation to his or her room, taking away the use of TV, or loss of use of the car.

It is clear that the Canters' follow-through actions are not the logical/ natural consequences of Gordon or Dreikurs or the negative reinforcers of the behaviorists but are actually punishments. On the other hand, *rewards* for the class or for students who do behave are similar to the positive reinforcers of the behaviorists. Students are to be rewarded and various reinforcement systems by which students can earn a prize or privilege are suggested. For example, the teacher can use a marble system to reward the entire class. When the class is behaving, the teacher drops a marble into a fishbowl. Marbles can accumulate in the bowl for an individual or class reward. For example, a class that totals a certain amount of marbles or fills the bowl might earn a movie, party, field trip, grab bag, a raffle lunch at the local fast-food restaurant, or attendance at a sports/entertainment event. A token coupon system also may be used to reward individual students. A certain number of coupons could be redeemed at a lottery for records, magazines, coupons, or tickets. The teacher is asked to plan a daily system for rewarding students that includes positive notes and calls to parents as well as token systems earning awards and privileges.

Physical Intervention and Isolation

The most severe punishment used is *systematic exclusion*. Students who repeatedly do not behave are isolated in different contexts. First, they can be isolated to another classroom (worked out previously among teachers) where they are unfamiliar with the other students and teacher. Canter believes that placing a student in an unfamiliar room is a more effective isolation than isolation within a student's own classroom or in the hall. Second, a student can be isolated to the home by having the parents come to school and remove the student for an agreed-upon length of time. It is important that teacher and parent agree to how the student is to be punished when the student is taken home. The parent might restrict the student from the use of the phone, the auto, or a night out and have the student complete school work that he or she would have done in class.

A teacher using the assertiveness model has the right to ask for the parent's (and principal's) assistance with a particularly troublesome student. When meeting with parents to develop a systematic exclusion plan, the teacher should be prepared for parent denial. The Canters believe that the teacher can deal with parents who do not accept that their child misbehaves by taking careful notes on the misbehavior and even tape recording particular student incidents that can be played back to the parent. The teacher should be prepared to use the broken-record method with parents when they attempt to excuse their child's behavior.

Mr. Blum: "Carl refused to stop talking when I spoke to him yesterday. I told him that he had a choice of being quiet or staying after school. He continued to talk and he stayed after. If he continues to talk when I tell him to stop he will receive three checks. I want three checks to mean that you will come and pick him up."

Parent: "Carl's not a bad boy; maybe he didn't hear you."

Mr. Blum: "Carl's not a bad boy, but if he continues to talk and receives three checks, I'd like you to come and pick him up."

Parent: "Sometimes Carl doesn't listen to me either. Maybe if you were sterner. . . ."

Mr. Blum: "Carl will know that we are serious if you agree to pick him up when he receives three checks."

Parent: "I'm so busy at home. . . ."

Mr. Blum: "Will you pick him up if I call?"

DISCUSSION OF THE ASSERTIVENESS MODEL

The popularity of the assertiveness model can be attributed to the concrete guidance that it provides for teachers. Canter and Associates have developed packets of materials on this technique (see reference section) for classroom teachers that include bulletin boards, memos, worksheets of class rules, procedures, rewards, punishments, and forms for parent conferences.

The assertiveness model departs from the behaviorist model by its emphasis on teacher rights to enforce standards and a teacher's right to punish students. In some ways, the assertiveness model draws together typical types of punishments that teachers already use with students into a consistent, operational system. It allows for little negotiation or discussion with students and does little to help a student understand and control his or her own behavior. The Canters have cautioned teachers that assertive discipline should be viewed as a beginning model for teachers needing to establish control in their classrooms.[5] After students know the rules and have learned to comply with them, the Canters urge teachers to use the more democratic and student-centered approaches of the Confronting-Contracting models of Dreikurs and Glasser and the Relationship-Listening models of Gordon, Harris, and Raths.

SUMMARY

The premise of the assertiveness model is the right of a teacher to teach and the right of a teacher to expect students to obey. An assertive teacher clearly conveys his or her rules and actions for compliance and noncompliance. The assertive teacher does not back down. He or she covertly makes a discipline plan for all students and rehearses (silently looking on). The assertive teacher explains the plan and verbally warns students of their limits (directive statement). He or she gives hints (nondirective statements), disguised statements (questions), and "I" statements (directive statements) before confronting the student with a demand either to behave or choose to be punished (directive statements). If the student argues, the teacher repeats the demand as if it were a broken record (directive statements). To enforce his or her demands, punishment such as withholding privileges, in-class isolation, staying after school, a visit to the principal, and notes home are used (reinforcement). Rewards for appropriate behavior are given through a token system whereby students can earn free time, trips. games, and entertainment as well as receive positive notes and rewards (reinforcement). Severe and reoccurring violations are handled by systematic exclusion of the student to another classroom, the principal, or to the student's home.

NOTES

1. Lee Canter and Marlene Canter. *Assertive Discipline: A Take-Charge Approach for Today's Educator*. (Seal Beach, California: Canter and Associates, 1976.) p. 2.
2. Canter, *Assertive Discipline*, p. 72.
3. Canter, *Assertive Discipline*, p. 92.
4. Canter, *Assertive Discipline*, p. 95.
5. Lee Canter, *Assertive Discipline*. Presentation to the Annual Conference of the Association of Supervision and Curriculum Development, Anaheim, California, March, 1981.

REFERENCES

Alberti, R. E. and Emmons, M. L. *Stand Up, Speak Out, Talk Back*. New York: Pocket Books 1975.
Alberti, R. E. *Your Perfect Right: A Guide to Assertive Living*. San Luis Obispo. California: Impact Publishers, 1982.
Canter, L. and Canter, M. *Assertive Discipline: A Take-Charge Approach for Today's Educator*. Seal Beach, California: Canter and Associates, 1976.
Silberman, M., and Wheelan, S. *How to Discipline Without Feeling Guilty: Assertive Relationships with Children*. New York: Hawthorn Books, 1980.
Smith, M. J. *When I Say No, I Feel Guilty: How to Cope—Using the Skills of Systematic Assertive Therapy*. New York: Dial Press, 1975.
Zuker, E. *Mastering Assertiveness Skills: Power and Positive Influence at Work*. New York: American Management Associations, 1983.

INSTRUCTIONAL MEDIA

For additional information on assertive discipline contact Canter and Associates, P.O. Box 64517, Los Angeles, California 90064, (213) 395-3221.
The following materials can be ordered from:

Social Studies School Service
10,000 Culver Boulevard
Dept. E3, P.O. Box 802
Culver City, CA 90230

Filmstrips

Assertive Discipline in Action
> 2 color filmstrips, 2 cassettes, guide. $50.
> *Lee Canter, author of Assertive Discipline, explains and demonstrates his "take charge" approach to achieving discipline in the classroom. His four-part systematic approach enables teachers to set firm, consistent limits while recognizing the students' needs for warmth and positive support. Elementary and junior high classroom scenes illustrate this approach, while teachers and a principal explain how the program works and why it has proven successful. Media Five. MDF111C-E3*

Assertive Discipline in the Classroom
> 2 color filmstrips, 2 cassettes, guide. $50.
> *Lee Canter, author of Assertive Discipline, combines an animated and sometimes humorous presentation with role playing to illustrate his effective "no-nonsense" approach to discipline. His comments go straight to the heart of many teachers' feelings about the difficulty of and the need for maintaining an effective classroom learning environment. The strategies are easily understood and applied. Media Five. MDF021-E3*

Guides and Workbooks

Assertive Discipline: A Take Charge Approach for Today's Educator
> CAN100-E3   Assertive Discipline: Basic Guidebook $6.95.
> CAN101-E3   Assertive Discipline: Workbook and Reproducibles $6.95.
> CAN102-E3   Assertive Discipline: Follow-Up Guidebook $6.95.
> *By Lee and Marlene Canter. The goals of this classroom-tested program are: 1) to deal with student behavior problems in a confident, take-charge manner, 2) to establish firm, consistent limits for all students, and 3) to foster a positive educational environment for all. The guide describes in detail the techniques of this competency-based program for grades K–12. In addition, the complete program includes a set of reproducible worksheets and guidelines for use with teacher groups. Finally, a new follow-up guidebook contains additional "hands-on" materials, including discipline plans for individual classrooms, positive reinforcement ideas, and guidelines for discipline plan analysis. Canter and Associates.*

10

The Behaviorism/ Punishment Model of Engelmann and Dobson

Ms. Sieckle was writing the spelling words for the day on the chalkboard with her back turned to her class of third graders. Sitting near the front of the class, Mary Jane Fischer began to make circles with her fingers. She circled her head and then pointed her finger at the teacher's back. The class began to giggle. Ms. Sieckle turned around and faced the class. She spoke sternly, "Let's stop this talking this minute. I have two more words to write down and then we'll begin our spelling lesson."

Mary Jane, who had quickly put her hand down when the teacher turned toward the class, was just as quick to resume her gesturing now that Ms. Sieckle was back at work at the board. Her circular hand motions concluding with the pointing figure was an "in" symbol meaning that the person pointed at was crazy, "cuckoo," or "off his or her rocker." The students could no longer contain their giggles, and unrestrained laughter erupted.

Ms. Sieckle quickly turned, and this time caught Mary Jane in the midst of her antics. She said, "Mary Jane, you stop that this very minute. Do you understand me?" Mary Jane bowed her head and with a sheepish grin mumbled, "Yes, Ma'am." The class was quiet again, but with their attention riveted on Mary Jane. They knew there would be more. Mary Jane would surely have the last word. Sure enough, as soon as Ms. Sieckle turned her back to the class again, Mary Jane's hand went into motion. This time she augmented her circular motions by sticking her tongue out and making faces.

Ms. Sieckle, knowing that Mary Jane was a child who constantly challenged authority, was expecting more defiant behavior. Midway through writing the last spelling word, she spun around and caught Mary Jane with tongue distended, face grimacing, and finger waving. She spoke, "Mary Jane, I

"Actually, it's a rather old form of behavior modification therapy."

Raymond E. Vogler, from *Phi Delta Kappan*

told you to stop and you continue to misbehave. I've warned you and now you'll have to be punished." As the teacher spoke, she walked over, grabbed Mary Jane firmly by the arm, and pulled her out into the hall. Closing the classroom door behind them, the teacher spanked Mary Jane hard on the buttocks. Mary Jane felt the pain and began to cry.

After the crying subsided, Ms. Sieckle put her arm around the girl. Quietly, she spoke to the child. "Mary Jane, you can be a very good girl when you want to be. I do not like to punish you, but if you do not do as you're told, you will be punished again. I will not put up with you trying to be the boss. I am in charge in this classroom, not you. Let's see if you can do better." With that last statement, Ms. Sieckle hugged Mary Jane and they both returned to the classroom.

The use of corporal punishment in school is one of the most controversial issues debated between and among educators, psychologists, and parents. In some school districts, as well as in some states, it is absolutely impermissible; in others it is an accepted means of discipline. Any book that purports to contain the major popular approaches dealing with children and the issue of discipline would be remiss if it did not discuss the rationale and practices of those authors who espouse physical punishment as an effective and essential method of controlling children's classroom behavior.

We realize there are some readers who object to this method so strongly that they are about to close this book. There are other readers who are saying, "Well, it's about time we got into the real way of dealing with disruptive behavior." To both kinds of readers we say, "Let's read and think about this chapter carefully." We must not take such a prejudicial stand that our minds are closed to the arguments and evidence pertaining to both sides of this issue. The reader who firmly believes in such an approach has already read through six previous chapters devoted to those authors who believe that physical intervention is morally wrong and/or ineffective. Therefore, it would appear only fair that the reader who is firmly against physical intervention should give at least equal attention to this chapter.

Both Siegfried Engelmann (in his books, *Teaching Disadvantaged Children in the Preschool* and *Preventing Failure in the Primary Grades*) and James Dobson (in his books, *Dare to Discipline* and *Hide or Seek*) have positioned themselves firmly as advocates of corporal punishment. They reserve such punishment primarily for young children. (Dobson approves of its use until the ages of 8 to 10; Engelmann, through the primary grades.) Engelmann admits such a position is not popular. He and Carl Bereiter say:

> The writers are quite aware that their suggestions about behavior and especially about punishment, represent an unpopular viewpoint. They were tempted, in fact, to do what some others probably do when offering suggestions about handling behavior problems; say what is more popular, even if it is not what they think . . . the test of whether an adult means what he says is to ignore him and see whether punishment follows.[1]

James Dobson has evidence to indicate that such a position is not so unpopular. His book, *Dare to Discipline*, a clear challenge to teachers and parents to use firm punishment, has sold over 500,000 copies. He sees the reasoned use of physical punishment as essential to rearing children effectively. He wrote:

How can we teach constructive attitudes to a generation of young people which is no longer listening to our advice? We can't. We must direct our attention toward the next generation of Americans—the children who are still pliable to guidance and training. Not only must we reinstate discipline at home (the first obligation) but the authority of the school must also be reconstructed. Parents have the primary responsibility in both objectives, since the school is largely responsive to their wishes. They should let the teachers and administrators know that they favor reasonable control in the classroom, even if it requires an occasional application of corporal punishment.[2]

THE RATIONALE FOR PHYSICAL INTERVENTION

Engelmann and Dobson justify the use of physical punishment according to the need for children to learn standards of behavior. Engelmann is concerned with those "disadvantaged" students whom he feels have been deprived of the early learning experiences that are common to middle-class youngsters. This deprivation of early home preparation for school results in children from low economic and minority cultures being behind at the beginning of school and falling further behind throughout their school experiences. The focus of his books is not on a child's social-emotional welfare but on ways to accelerate learning. He wants to prevent failure of disadvantaged youngsters by having them undergo direct, repetitive, and sequential instruction in basic skills. He sees such structured instruction as their only hope of "making it" in later society. Many educators take issue with Engelmann's stance, particularly in regard to his definition of "disadvantaged." Such a debate, although important and of interest to many, is not germane to this book. What we are concerned with is, "Why does Engelmann believe in physical punishment?" The answer is that his instructional system is predicated on efficiency. The teacher needs the disadvantaged children to cram in as much instruction in the shortest time possible in order for them to catch up with their middle-class counterparts. A student's misbehavior impinges upon his or her own time as well as the class's instructional time. To use the methods of the Relationship-Listeners advocates or the Confronting-Contracting writers consumes more of that precious time in dialogue, conferences, and the like. The student(s) and teacher could be using that time for academic learning; therefore, dealing with disruptive behavior should be quick and to the point. If a child is doing something wrong, he or she is not learning; thus, the teacher needs to stop the misbehavior and get back to instruction. The quickest way to stop severe misbehavior is physically to punish the child.

Dobson has a different rationale for the use of corporal punishment. Unlike Engelmann, he is concerned primarily with the child's overall social and moral development. Where he is in disagreement with most other writers is that he sees the child as "going to hell" without firmly imposed boundaries. The words "going to hell" are not used in jest. Dobson is a firmly religious person who believes that Christian principles, as he interprets them, should be the guiding rules for working with children. He does not have an optimistic faith in the child's own capacities for solving problems. The varying degrees of reason that the Relationship-Listeners and the Confronting-Contractors credit the growing child with is absent in Dobson's writings. Dobson takes clear issue with those who do give such credit. In regard to child rearing, he wrote:

> This mother had read that a child will eventually respond to patience and tolerance, ruling out the need for discipline. She had been told to encourage the child's rebellion because it offered a valuable release of hostility. She attempted to implement the recommendation of the experts who suggested that she verbalize the child's feelings in a moment of conflict: "You want the water but you're angry because I brought it too late";...."You wish you could flush Mommie down the toilet." She had been taught that conflicts between parent and child were to be perceived as inevitable misunderstandings or differences in viewpoint. Unfortunately, Mrs. Nichols and her advisors were wrong.[3]

Instead, Dobson sees the need for adults to make very clear moral, ethical, and behavioral rules for children, and when those boundaries are violated, the offending youngsters are to be disciplined. In writing how children should be raised according to God's values, Dobson stated:

> Fortunately, the Bible provides the Key to God's value system for mankind, and in my judgment, it is composed of six all-important principles. They are: (1) devotion to God; (2) love for mankind; (3) respect for authority; (4) obedience to divine commandments; (5) self-discipline and self-control and (6) humbleness of spirit ... when applied, they encourage a child to *seek* out the opportunities in this world rather than forcing him to *hide* in lonely isolation.[4]

Dobson, a former educator who is now a psychologist, does not separate his psychological views from his religious ones. They are integral to each other. Many of us do the same. Although we know that public schools are legally bound to avoid religious teaching, we as individuals cannot make that kind of separation. The ways that we believe and act in our professional lives have to be influenced by our personal, philosophical, and religious beliefs. In Dobson's writings we see a clear rationale for intervening and shaping a child's behavior in order to adhere to his (Dobson's) established religious standards.

Engelmann and Dobson both use the need to attain standards as the justification for teaching the practice of bold intervention. Yet each man's standards differ from the other's quite markedly. Engelmann's is a standard of efficiency and academic attainment; Dobson's is a standard of religious values.

Before we explore their concrete teacher applications through our Teacher Behavior Continuum, a few more words about these two corporal punishment advocates are necessary. *Neither Engelmann nor Dobson advocates the unrestrained, unplanned use of corporal punishment.* They are not advocating physical violence or abuse. *They are not "mean" people who want to see children beaten.* Whenever they speak of physical punishment it is only in regard to specific situations and to using it with restraint.

Dobson in particular makes a plea that his advocacy not be taken as an excuse for excess. In an interesting aside, he notes how the use of controlled physical punishment by adults might actually protect the child from extremes in this area. His argument goes like this: A teacher (or parent) is having a hectic day and has developed a splitting headache. One child is being particularly bothersome, and the teacher tells the child," Look, I am tired, have a headache, and want you to keep quiet. Take out a book and read silently." If the child refuses and continues to be too loud, the teacher can act in one of two ways: The teacher who does not believe in corporal punishment can, with mounting frustration, continue to tell or ask the child to be quiet. Eventually faced with repeated refusals by the child to calm down, the teacher might explode and irrationally shake or slam the child and inflict real harm. After such an explosion, not only will the teacher feel remorse and shame, but he or she could be vulnerable to legal action. On the other hand, if the teacher believes in corporal punishment, then, after the first instance of refusal, he or she might slap the child's backside and the child quiets down. Thus, with the consistent administration of expected and restrained physical punishment, the matter is over. So Dobson's rationale makes for an interesting twist. According to him, reasonable corporal punishment will prevent possible physical harm of an excessive nature.[5]

THE TEACHER BEHAVIOR CONTINUUM WITH PUNISHMENT

Silently Looking On

Engelmann and Dobson use silently looking on as an information-gathering device. They want the teacher to record the circumstances surrounding a child's misbehavior. What is it about the environment that is affecting the student's actions? In most instances, it will be found that the child is receiving a higher payoff in receiving the class's or teacher's attention than if he or she were acting appropriately. This information will serve as the basis for later reversing the payoff for the child.

The teacher does not simply stand back and observe a child when misbehavior is noted. Rather, he or she should step in immediately with directive statements to the child.

(*Note:* Neither Englemann nor Dobson makes any mention of *non-directive statements*, and neither author is concerned with *questions* as a teacher practice.)

Directive Statements

This is the beginning of Engelmann and Dobson's Rules/Rewards-Punishment program. Both feel that the teacher should "lay the law down" at the outset of the school year. The teacher should make perfectly clear how students will be expected to behave. At the beginning of the year, the teacher should go over the rules every day and have the students repeat them. For example, some rules might be:

- There is to be quiet during work time.
- Raise your hand and stay in your seat when you want to speak.
- Line up and stay in line when we walk into and out of the classroom.

The teacher, when presenting the rules, should be businesslike, serious, and firm. The rules are not to be changed or discussed; they simply are the laws to be followed. At the same time, the teacher should make clear that those who follow the rules will be better off than those who do not. In fact, children should be told that those who do not follow the rules can expect to be dealt with severely. Dobson cited an appropriate teacher discourse as follows:

> This is going to be a good year and I'm glad you are my students. I want you to know that each one of you is important to me. I hope you will feel free to ask your questions, and enjoy learning in this class; . . . But there's one thing you should know: if you choose to challenge me I have one thousand ways to make you miserable. If you don't believe me, you just let me know and we'll start with number one.[6]

Obviously the teacher should be prepared to back up a statement of this nature. The first time a child misbehaves, he or she should sternly be told to cease. Both Engelmann and Dobson believe firmly in the power of positive reinforcement, but they acknowledge it contains an inherent deficiency. The child who chronically misbehaves provides little opportunity to be reinforced positively for appropriate behavior. It follows that the teacher must coerce the student into making an appropriate response in order to dispense the reward. Only then does a child have an opportunity to see what behaviors have the greatest payoff. Engelmann wrote that the teacher needs to take "the bull by the horns":

> For the serious behavior problem, begin with commands that can be enforced. . . . Start with a set of simple commands, such as "stand up" and "sit down." If the child does not stand up on command, forcefully stand him up. From time to time remind him, "When I say 'stand up,' you stand up." If he manages to make the other members of the group laugh, ignore their responses. If he turns his head away or tries to communicate with other members of the group, forcefully turn his head back. Do not repeat commands. Say, "stand up," count to three to yourself, and forcefully stand the child up.[7]

Modeling

The manner in which a teacher behaves has a powerful effect on his or her students. Teachers who remain businesslike and serious will convey an attitude that they mean what they say. There are more informal times (at recess, lunch, or on the playground) when teachers might loosen up and be more relaxed with students. However, when it comes to teaching and learning, there is work to be done, and the adults in charge need to set that tone.

Dobson takes issue with those who claim that a teacher who uses corporal punishment is serving as a model of physical violence whom students will emulate. He says such an argument is fallacious. A restrained use of corporal punishment does the opposite. The child who goes around smashing things or hitting people must learn that uncontrolled violence is unacceptable. The teacher who uses the paddle or hand on the child's derriere is showing the child that if one goes about being destructive then one can expect to be hurt. Dobson uses the example of a child yanking the dog's tail. The child has every right to be bitten and to learn something about dogs' tails from that moment on. There are "painful consequences of acting selfishly, rebelliously, and aggressively."

The teacher, then, is a model of one who is wiser and more experienced than the student. It is his or her job to circumscribe boundaries of acceptable behavior. When a student transgresses, the teacher is to enforce the consequences, even those that are painful. This does not mean that the teacher is not loving or affectionate. He or she is. The teacher shows genuine love, respect, and understanding for students. Part of this caring attitude is displayed when a teacher takes the time and responsibility to enforce boundaries of behavior.

Reinforcement

Dobson and Engelmann are advocates of behavior modification. They write about the use of all the various types and conditions under which behavior modification can be used. Where they depart from the behaviorists is in their stress on punishment as an equally vital and perhaps more effective tool than any others possessed by the teacher. We must caution the reader again to understand that to stress the use of punishment only as a conditioner, without equal stress on positive reinforcement, tokens, schedules, extinctions, and so on, would be doing the models formulated by Dobson and Engelmann a disservice. It would be wrong to think they are negativists rather than positivists in their approach to behavior. Yet, their uniqueness lies in their willingness and commitment to explain how a negative use of reinforcement might work. It is in this realm that we will focus our discussion.

In this model, punishment occurs, showing that the consequences of misbehavior are more costly than the consequences of behaving appropriately. Engelmann believes that punishment is very effective as a negative reinforcement and that a teacher should use it only to turn around a child's misbehavior; then the teacher can resort to positive reinforcement. He suggests that the teacher use negative reinforcement as a last resort, when all other means fail, and then quickly move away from it. Dobson, interestingly enough, disagrees with Engelmann. In our previously mentioned example of his rationale for using immediate physical punishment to save the child from later excessive harm, he urges the teacher to use such punishment of defiant behavior as an initial step.

As the reader may recall, all Relationship-Listeners and Confronting-Contractors disagree with the use of punishment. Rudolf Dreikurs and William Glasser in particular point out the difference between punishment and logical consequences. As for an adult using coercive force to inflict psychological or physical discomfort on a child, Dreikurs and Glasser believe it is not only wrong but totally ineffective. Dobson tries to link his interpretation of punishment with that of a logical consequence. He says that when an adult temporarily inflicts pain on a child who is defiant, then that action can be viewed as a logical consequence. He attempts to describe his argument as being compatible with Glasser's view, but we're afraid that one simply cannot link the two. Glasser and others make it clear that infliction of physical pain is not a logical consequence.[9]

What are examples of punishment? Punishment would include some of the following:

- Depriving a student of something of value (recess time, taking away pleasure books, or not allowing a child to see a movie or engage in a prized activity).
- Intimidating the child in a loud, clear, authoritarian voice.
- Isolating a child in a bare enclosure, where the student is forced to stay until the teacher decides when he or she may come out.
- Keeping a student after school.
- Giving the student repetitive and/or undesired work (write fifty times, "I will not do ———").
- Inflicting physical pain (paddling, spanking, shaking, or using pressure points).

Engelmann and Bereiter see such punishment as only the beginning of treatment. It is used only to stop the student's inappropriate behavior and should be followed by more positive methods of conditioning.

Physical Intervention and Isolation

Isolation: Engelmann, writing with Carl Bereiter, suggests that isolation should be another form of punishment. A child who is acting up should be told to cease. If it's necessary to speak to a child a second time, he or she should be warned that failure to comply will result in being put into the isolation room. The third time is "strike three," and out the child goes. They make it clear that isolation is not to be a pleasant or neutral experience:

> The "isolation room," if it is to be effective, should be an unpleasant place, providing an atmosphere that is far less enjoyable than that of the study room. A small, poorly lighted closet with a single chair will serve quite well.[10]

Dobson also sees the use of isolation from the teacher's point of view. A student who is constantly showing off and being a general nuisance should be put into an isolated area. This area should be away from all activity. However, the offending child should be able to see the activities that he or she is missing. Every time the child acts up, the teacher should increase the child's time in the area. When the teacher readmits the child, the teacher should attempt to use positive reinforcement (or what Dobson calls the "miracle tools of bribery") to give attention to correct behavior.

The teacher regulates the amount of time in isolation. Unlike models described by other writers, students in this model do not decide when they are ready to return. The child who fails to return to the classroom with acceptable behavior can expect to be kept in isolation for increasingly longer periods of time. Even though certain children might dislike school, most dislike being alone even more. Eventually, the disruptive child will decide to learn how to act in school in order not to be banished.

Physical Intervention: As previously explained, Dobson and Engelmann advocate the use of physical intervention, not only in the sense of isolating a child or preventing a child from hurting himself or herself and others, but also for the purpose of causing physical pain and thus "teaching the child a lesson." They agree that it is a particularly effective measure and that it works well with young children. Once a child has reached adolescence, physical punishment is no longer advocated. It causes older students who think of themselves as adults uncalled-for humiliation. A teacher who uses paddling or spanking with an adolescent is not only compounding the student's problem but is also setting up himself or herself for severe reprisals. We know of students who have lashed back physically, have slashed tires, and have used knives and firearms in retaliation. The teacher who uses physical punishment on a potentially violent adolescent is simply "asking for it."

Dealing with a younger child (up to fourth grade or about age ten) is a different matter. This child, according to Dobson and Engelmann, needs to be startled by pain as part and parcel of child rearing. Only when they are hurt as youngsters do they learn the boundaries of acceptable behavior to be remembered for adult life. This is why students who have had teachers who physically drew the line with them in the early and intermediate grades will theoretically not need to be physically "hurt" in adolescence. Reinforcement and reasoning at that age should do the job. Of course, as reasonable as this sounds, it does not help the middle-school teacher who is dealing with students who failed to learn the original lessons. For help, these teachers must return to the teacher behaviors and principles of behavior modification as described in direct commands, reinforcement, and isolation, in this and in the previous chapter.

How does the teacher of young children use corporal punishment? Let's begin with Dobson. He believes that the teacher must distinguish between intentional and unintentional behavior. The student who knowingly breaks a rule should not be "hit." It is only when the student is told *(direct statements)* to cease and the child openly defies the command that he or she deserves a little pain. Let us look at the example in the beginning of this chapter. If Mary Jane had stopped her finger waving and funny faces after the first (or even the second) time, then the matter would have been settled. Ms. Sieckle only spanked Mary Jane after the child was fully aware of what the teacher wanted her to stop doing and yet persisted in her behavior. Inflicting "pain" should only result when a child challenges the teacher's authority. It is the Rules/Rewards-Punishers' position that the teacher has to have power and control over the child's behavior. When the child challenges that power, the teacher needs to exert the necessary authority to show that he or she is indeed the boss. Following are examples of situations that *would* merit physical punishment:

- The child talks back to the teacher after being told not to.
- The child refuses to pick up or clean up after being told to.
- The child taunts the teacher by telling the class that the teacher is wrong and that the students should listen to him or her instead.
- The child knowingly lies to the teacher, and when confronted, refuses to confess.

Following are examples of situations that *would not* merit physical punishment:

- The child gets into an argument or fight with other students.
- The child does not finish his or her classwork (or homework) on time.
- The child breaks an object by mistake.
- The child spontaneously yells out of turn.

Once a teacher has clear evidence that the student is testing *(openly and defiantly)* his or her authority, the teacher should proceed in a three-step, restrained, calm manner. The first step is that the child should be taken away from the eyes of others. Second, the teacher should tell the child why the punishment is occurring and then spank or paddle the student once on the padded part of the buttocks. Dobson cites an alternative to spanking. It involves squeezing the shoulder muscle. He wrote that:

> The shoulder muscle is a surprisingly useful source of minor pain; actually it was created expressly for school teachers.[11] ... when firmly squeezed, it sends little messengers to the brain saying, "This hurts; avoid recurrence at all costs."[12]

The third step is that, after the punishment has been meted out, it is time to comfort, console, and give affection. The child will usually cry and feel badly; he or she is ready to be loved and told how to avoid such a recurrence in the future. *Dobson is adamant about giving love and warmth to the offending child.* The teacher should not remain angry, aloof, and unapproachable. The matter is over with and the teacher should welcome the child back.

Engelmann supports the use of physical intervention when a student is not attending to the lesson at hand. His concern is with children "catching up" academically. When a student is being disruptive, precious moments are being wasted. He also adds that one cannot begin to use behavior modification approaches with a student who displays no appropriate behavior to reinforce. Therefore, initially the child must be forced to behave properly. The student who is constantly out of his or her seat should be grabbed and forcefully put down.

Engelmann believes that the teacher should use physical punishment with a student who is engaging in habitual, unthinking behavior. This is a different criterion than Dobson's view of using such punishment for a student who is engaged in openly defiant behavior. Engelmann's opinion is that it is the unthinkingly loud, active, aggressive, or destructive student who needs immediate punishment. This child has no alternative behavior; he or she has always acted in this manner, and the teacher must forcefully stop it. Only then can new behaviors be learned. The use of verbal commands (directive statements) alone is not effective with this child. Bereiter and Engelmann say:

> In such a situation, the meaning of the teacher's words should be made clear by demonstrating the consequences that result when they are ignored. Sometimes the best definition comes in the form of anger—a slap or a good shaking.[13]

Comparing Engelmann and Dobson with Others

The one issue that clearly separates Engelmann and Dobson from the other authors of child management books is their belief in corporal punishment. The behaviorists cited in a preceding chapter urge the use of positive conditioning but resist the use of negative reinforcement or physical pain. The Relationship-Listeners and Confronting-Contractors are even more adamant in this view. They believe that the teacher does not have the ethical or moral right to use such force, and furthermore, its use merely adds to a student's problem. Glasser and Dreikurs take issue with Engelmann and Dobson over the effectiveness of punishment. They state that inflicting physical pain is totally *ineffectual* in changing a child's behavior. Engelmann and Dobson state that inflicting physical pain is the *most effective practice* a teacher has at his or her disposal.

Ct   cT

Silently Looking On	Nondirective Statements	Questions	Directive Statements	Modeling	Reinforcement	Physical Intervention and Isolation
(a) Observe, gather information on circumstances (What is the payoff?)			(1) Tell students the rules; repeat many times. —Tell student to stop misbehaving. —Tell student what to do.	(b) Teacher behaves in a businesslike manner.	(2) Reinforce appropriate behavior.	(3) Isolate for inappropriate behavior in uncomfortable place on teacher's terms.
					(5) Reinforce appropriate behavior.	or
						(4) If student is defiant (Dobson) or unthinking (Engelmann), inflict physical pain.

The Behaviorism/Punishment Model

Authors: James Dobson, Siegfried Engelmann

(numbers) overt behavior
(letters) covert behavior

FIGURE 10–1. Teacher Behavior Continuum (TBC)

Four "experts" have been presented with two diametrically opposed positions. Who is right? The reader will need to make his or her own determination.

SUMMARIZING ENGELMANN AND DOBSON

Although Engelmann and Dobson have some differences, we can extract some common procedures for dealing with disruptive children along the Teacher Behavior Continuum (see Figure 10–1). Covert teacher behaviors are as follows: (a) The teacher observes the circumstances surrounding a child's misbehavior. He or she judges what is reinforcing the behavior. (b) The teacher models behavior that is serious and businesslike, particularly during class work time.

The overt teacher behaviors are as follows: The teacher gives (1) *directive statements*. He or she tells the class repeatedly what the class rules are. The student who misbehaves is immediately told to stop and behave appropriately. If the child conforms, the teacher uses (2) *reinforcement*. If the child does not behave correctly, the teacher uses (3) *isolation* in an uncomfortable setting with the teacher deciding when the student can return. However, if the student's inappropriate behavior is an open challenge to the teacher's authority (Dobson), then the teacher needs to use (4) *physical intervention* by paddling, spanking, or squeezing. If the inappropriate behavior is habitual (Engelmann), the teacher needs to shake, slap, or spank. Once correct behavior is forthcoming, the teacher returns to (5) reinforcement.

NOTES

1. Carl Bereiter and Siegfried Engelmann, *Teaching Disadvantaged Children in the Preschool* (Englewood Cliffs, New Jersey: Prentice-Hall, 1966), pp. 90–91.

2. James Dobson, *Dare to Discipline* (Wheaton, Illinois: Tyndale House Publishers, 1970), p. 107.

3. Dobson, *Dare to Discipline*, Introduction.

4. James Dobson, *Hide or Seek* (Old Tappan, New Jersey: Fleming H. Revell Company, 1974), p. 158.

5. Dobson, *Dare to Discipline*, pp. 24–25.

6. Dobson, *Dare to Discipline*, pp. 98–99.

7. Siegfried Engelmann, *Preventing Failure in the Primary Grades* (New York: Simon and Schuster, 1969), p. 77.

8. Dobson, *Dare to Discipline*, p. 41.

9. William Glasser, "Disorders in Our Schools: Causes and Remedies," *Phi Delta Kappan*, January 1978, p. 331.

10. Bereiter and Engelmann, *Teaching Disadvantaged Children*, p. 83.

11. Dobson, *Dare to Discipline*, p. 26.

12. Dobson, *Dare to Discipline*, p. 24.

13. Bereiter and Engelmann, *Teaching Disadvantaged Children*, p. 87.

REFERENCES

Bereiter, Carl, and Engelmann, Siegfried. *Teaching Disadvantaged Children in the Preschool*. Englewood Cliffs, New Jersey: Prentice-Hall, 1966.

Dobson, James. *Dare to Discipline*. Wheaton, Illinois: Tyndale House Publishers, 1970.

Dobson, James. *Hide or Seek*. Old Tappan, New Jersey: Fleming H. Revell Company, 1974.

Engelmann, Siegfried. *Preventing Failure in the Primary Grades*. New York: Simon and Schuster, 1969.

INSTRUCTIONAL MEDIA

The following material is available from:

Media Five
3211 Cahuenga Boulevard, West
Los Angeles, California 90068

Films

New Approaches to Big Problems
29 minutes; color. Sale price $395; rental fee $45 per week.
Ideas on a variety of problem areas including discipline, human relations, author-ity, self-concept, truancy, and violence are presented in this film. Illustrated documentary segments.

Filmstrips

Dare to Discipline
James C. Dobson

Two filmstrips with two cassettes with Teacher's Guide; color. Purchase price $45.

Demonstrates the "take charge" approach to achieving discipline in the classroom. The approach enables teachers to set firm, consistent limits while recognizing students' needs for warmth and positive support.

11

Strengths and Limitations of Today's Teacher-Student Interaction Models

In the earlier descriptions of the teacher-student interaction models, the theoretical assumptions of student motivation and central overt and covert behaviors were described in the context of the Teacher Behavior Continuum. As yet, however, the individual strengths and limitations of these models have not been compared. In order to make these comparisons, it would be helpful to first review these models by scanning the outlines (see Figures 11–1 through 11–8), where one will find a more concise summary of the basic assumptions on motivation, overt teacher behaviors, key vocabulary, and educational insights that have been developed in Chapters 3 through 10. With this content in mind, we can now focus on the strengths and limitations of each model.

RELATIONSHIP-LISTENING

Thomas Gordon, Louis Raths, Merrill Harmin, Sidney Simon, Thomas Harris, Eric Berne, and other Relationship-Listeners share a belief in the inner rationality of the student. They believe student misbehavior is the result of obstacles that block the full expression of rational thought. The goal of each of these Relationship-Listeners is to use methods to remove those obstacles.

In discussions of the Relationship-Listening models, there are questions common to all. Three such questions are:

1. Do all students, regardless of age or intellectual capacity, have an inherent rationality?
2. Are all students, regardless of language ability, able to verbalize their thoughts and feelings?
3. Inasmuch as an approach predicated on language and reasoning is time consuming, does the teacher have such time to spend with one student?

THE SUPPORTIVE MODEL OF THOMAS GORDON

It is difficult to take issue with Teacher Effectiveness Training's emphasis on a warm, accepting relationship between teacher and students and the subsequent need to help students to acquire healthy, positive self-concepts. Gordon is concerned with the teacher being, foremost, a person who is sensitive, warm and noncritical. The strength of his model is that he goes beyond the vague descriptions of becoming a "good" person and instead prescribes specific teacher actions and methods to attain that end. He tells the teacher how to use critical listening, acknowledgment responses, door openers, active listening, and "I" messages as tools for helping a student to verbally reflect upon his or her emotions and behavior. He also provides the teacher with *Method III* ("no lose") problem-solving techniques and the six problem-solving steps to resolve conflict in a democratic equalitarian manner. These techniques free the teacher and student from the common outcome of disciplinary actions where one party loses and feels inferior while the other wins and feels superior. Other strengths of Teacher Effectiveness Training are embodied in the concepts of "areas of freedom" and the problems of

---

Basic Assumptions on Motivation

　　　Child is motivated by internal desire to be good. He or she is helped by a warm, accepting relationship with another that enhances his or her self-concept. The child is rational—capable of solving his or her own problems.

Overt Teacher Behaviors
—Critical Listening
—Acknowledgment responses
—Door openers ("Do you want to talk more?")

FIGURE 11–1.　Outline of Gordon's Teacher Effectiveness Training

—Active listening
—"I" messages
—Influencing ("Watch your step.")

Covert Teacher Behaviors
—Method III ("no lose")
—Daily actions
—Reorganizing space
—Reorganizing time: diffused, individual, and optimal
—Six steps to problem solving
—"Areas of freedom"

Key Vocabulary
—Ownership of problems
—Active listening
—"I"/"you" messages
—Door openers
—Method III ("no lose")
—Teaching-Learning area
—Six steps to problem solving
—Twelve roadblocks to communication
—Diffused time
—Individual time
—Optimal time
—"Areas of freedom"

Educational Insights
—"Areas of freedom"
—Organizing time as diffused, individual, and optimal
—Organizing space

Strengths
—Child solves his or her problem, thus developing responsibility
—Democratic rule-setting practice
—No bad feelings while solving problems (no winners or losers)
—Helps teacher to decide problem ownership

Limitations
—At what age is a child rational?
—Is the mentally retarded child rational?
—What about the child without language?
—The time required for the teacher to administer TET is prohibitive
—TET cannot be used in every conflict situation (i.e., violent child)

FIGURE 11–1. Outline of Gordon's Teacher Effectiveness Training (cont.)

Basic Assumptions on Motivation
—The brain functions as a high-fidelity recorder; it records feelings that become fixed—recording, recalling, reliving
—People will change if hurt, bored, or convinced that they can
—When people transact they send messages from one of the ego states (PAC)
—Because of a person's childish feelings of being "not OK," his or her actions with others are for the purpose of receiving strokes

Overt Teacher Behavior
—Confronting the student with the game he or she is playing and speaking to his or her *Adult*
—Asking "adult" questions
—Sending "adult" directive statements
—Responding at suitable times with parent to parent or child to child to give "strokes"
—Responding to potential crossed or ulterior transactions with his or her *Adult*

Covert Teacher Behaviors
—Silently looking on to determine the inner state of the student
—Determining game being played
—Recognizing his or her own state (PAC) being used

Key Vocabulary
Parent, Child, Adult	—Warm fuzzies
—Strokes	—Cold pricklies
—Tapes	—I'm OK, You're OK
—Hooking	Games
—Transaction	—Uproar
—Transactional Stimulus	—Chip on the shoulder
—Transactional Response	—Stupid
—Crossed-transaction	—Schlemiel
—Ulterior-transaction	—Make me
—Complementary-transaction	—Clown

Educational Insights
—Teacher use of language (PAC)
—Student use of language (PAC)
—Types of stroking

FIGURE 11–2. Outline of Berne and Harris's Transactional Analysis

---

Strengths
—By helping children through the stages you help develop your own maturity
—Provides a construct that enables teacher to critically evaluate his or her verbal-nonverbal interchange with students
—Helps student to learn to communicate with his or her *Adult*
—Separates feelings into states of PAC

Limitations
—May be hard to distinguish which of the three constructs is speaking
—The *Adult* as a rational state in the early years of life is weak and can be easily displaced by *Child's* or *Parent's* demands
—Ne3ds training or constant reflecting in order to begin implementation
—No clear plan for changing students' misbehaviors
—Works only with children with language

FIGURE 11–2. Outline of Berne and Harris's Transactional Analysis (cont.)

ownership. Thus the teacher need not feel responsible for every student problem that occurs. The teacher can determine those behavioral problems that belong to administrators or legal officials and thus be able to narrow the focus of his or her attention.

The stress on a warm and supportive environment has been mentioned as a strength; yet, as is often the case, a strength can have dimensions of weakness. Gordon gives teachers concrete actions for allowing a student to verbalize his or her actions and feelings, but solutions for dealing with students who are violent are not readily apparent. Gordon's "I" or influencing messages may not be strong enough when a student explodes in rage and strikes another student. Gordon's techniques can be helpful before or after the act, but what can be done during the student's actual act of violence? Doesn't the teacher have to win and the student lose if physical harm is to be avoided?

Another limitation of Teacher Effectiveness Training is that Gordon's underlying assumption of rationality can be questioned. Do students of all ages possess the cognitive structures to make rational and positive social decisions? Cognitive psychologists suggest a student is not truly rational (i.e., considerate of others) until around the age of adolescence. It may be unfair to expect a young pupil or an intellectually limited (i.e., mentally retarded) student to make wise choices. Such students may need the teacher to *tell* them what is best. Furthermore, Gordon's approach of having students verbalize their emotions reflects an obvious problem for the nonverbal student. Some students will refuse to talk, and some may have such a limited vocabulary that they cannot communicate what they are feeling. It would appear that the teacher can use entreaties such as door openers for verbal discourses with only those students who already have a degree of language proficiency.

Finally, perhaps the most frequent criticism of Teacher Effectiveness Training by teachers is that it takes a lot of time to listen and solve problems when working with a misbehaving student. When a teacher has thirty students in a class, is it feasible to use nondirective statements and personal conferences with a misbehaving student? Would it be simpler to deal with a student in a direct manner and return to the rest of the class?

THE COMMUNICATION MODEL OF ERIC BERNE AND THOMAS HARRIS'S *TRANSACTIONAL ANALYSIS*

Transactional Analysis has great value in helping teachers and students decode and analyze the messages they send to each other. Normally, people speak according to how they feel at the moment. Such talk is so much a part of one's everyday behavior that it is difficult to "stand back" and listen to oneself. It is Berne and Harris's contention that language emanates from various aspects of personality (*Parent*, *Adult*, and *Child*) and can facilitate or hinder reasonable decision making. In other words, the use of language between the teacher and the misbehaving student can facilitate or impede realistic solutions. Therefore, the strength of Transactional Analysis is providing the teacher with the means of 1) decoding his or her messages, 2) teaching the student the code, and 3) having a common framework for further student and teacher communications.

The limitation of Transactional Analysis for teachers is that it is basically descriptive. It helps in analyzing and using prescriptive language, but it does not provide any clear plan for changing student misbehavior. Furthermore, the *Adult* as a rational state in the childhood years is weak and can be easily displaced by the *Child* and *Parent* states. Therefore, it may not be of much value to a student to know what those states are if he or she can exert little control over the *Child* or the *Parent*. It may make a student feel more inadequate when he or she knows how he or she is acting (i.e., the *Child*) but does not have the inner control to do otherwise. This criticism of Transactional Analysis is similar to one of Teacher Effectiveness Training in that students, developmentally, may not have the language or cognitive skills to use the reasoning necessary to employ such abstract and categorical knowledge of personality states. Another problem is that it is sometimes difficult for a teacher to make the fine distinctions between the *Parent, Adult*, and *Child*. For example, when a student says, "No one is going to stop me from going outside," is that the impulsive *Child* meaning, "I feel like running away!" the *Parent* meaning, "Every student is supposed to go outside fifteen minutes every day," or the *Adult* meaning, "I feel lousy and need to clear my head"? A teacher cannot know unless the circumstances are readily apparent or there is time to discuss the message thoroughly. Teacher and student need train-

---

Basic Assumptions on Motivation
   —Values as well as emotions and I.Q. influence behavior problems
   —When values experiences are given to children with certain behavior problems, the problems often ease in intensity and/or frequency
   —Students can arrive at values through a rational process of choosing, prizing, and acting
   —The process will lessen apathetic, confused, and irrational behavior and increase more positive, purposeful, and enthusiastic behavior

Overt Teacher Behaviors
   —Modeling
   —Questions
   —Listening carefully and patiently
   —Clarifying responses
   —Formal exercises

Covert Teacher Behaviors
   —Establishing a mood of acceptance
   —Developing respect for student values
   —Focusing attention on an issue in life
   —Looking for value indicators
      1. attitude statements
      2. aspirations
      3. purposes
      4. interests
      5. activities

Key Vocabulary
   —Values-clarifying discussions
   —Role-playing, contrived incidents, zig-zag lessons, devil's advocate, values continuum, thought sheets, weekly reaction sheets, open-ended questions, overdissenters, role players, values confusion
   —Process of valuing, choosing freely, choosing from alternatives, choosing

FIGURE 11-3. Outline of Raths and Simon's Values Clarification

---

after considering consequences, prizing, affirming, acting, repeating
—Values indicators, clarifying responses, activities, worries, problems, apathetic, flighty, uncertain, inconsistent, drifters, overconformers, positive, purposeful, enthusiastic, proud, aspirations, attitudes, feelings

Educational Insights
—Values clarification should be infused in the curriculum
—Misbehavior should be viewed as a lack of values

Strengths
—Helps underachievers to improve:
   1. attitudes toward learning
   2. active participation
   3. raising of questions and alternatives
   4. perseverance
   5. self-direction
—Students become more purposeful
—Can be used anytime and anywhere
—Stimulates thinking

Limitations
—No ideas are given for what to do when faced with disruptive behavior
—May delve too much into students' personal lives
—Does not add to knowledge base about problems

FIGURE 11–3. Outline of Raths and Simon's Values Clarification (cont.)

ing and continued retraining with Transactional Analysis in order to use it. In a busy class, the time is not so readily available to stop and assess the deeper meaning of what the teacher or student has just said before taking action.

THE VALUING MODEL OF LOUIS E. RATHS, SIDNEY SIMON, AND OTHERS

These writers claim that some student misbehavior can be viewed as a lack of personal codes or values of conduct. Students who are given the opportunity to clarify their values will be more consistent and rational in correcting their behaviors. The use of valuing questions, values indicators, modeling, clarifying responses, and formal exercises enables the student to explore his or her reasons for actions. It is the position of values clarification that a student will not internalize and act upon values unless he or she has freely chosen them.

A supportive, nonjudgmental environment is needed for free choice. If a teacher imposes his or her thoughts and standards and thus coerces a student to act according to someone else's judgments, then the valuing process as a guide for consistent action is for naught.

The strengths of this model are based on the infusion of the valuing process into the everyday, ongoing curriculum. It provides every student, particularly the low achiever, the opportunity to participate actively, raise questions, explore alternatives, and make individual choices, without the usual fear of being corrected. The process stimulates thinking and can be used informally and formally anytime and anywhere during the school day.

The major limitation of the valuing model is its advocacy of nonjudgmental teacher support toward any student value. For example, in a discussion about physical violence, the teacher needs to be just as acceptive toward the student who says, "One should not use physical violence, as the ends never justify the means," as the student who says, "If someone's standing in the way of my getting a good job, I'm going to tear that person apart limb from limb." The teacher can explore the latter student's rationale and listen to other alternatives, but, according to the values-clarification process, he or she should not say or indicate in any way that "tearing a person apart limb from limb" is wrong. Even if a teacher were to agree completely with using such an approach, it still seems difficult to be acceptive of all values. For those teachers who have strong personal beliefs, it could be a terrible strain not to make one's beliefs known. Furthermore, some teachers may object philosophically to the position that all values are acceptable and instead point out that, in a classroom, the teacher has the responsibility for enforcing certain rules, standards, and values regardless of what a pupil thinks.

Another limitation of the valuing process is that it is basically an indirect method of dealing with misbehavior. It provides no immediate solutions for solving a disruptive student's problem; rather, its "payoff" is over a long period of time. Thus, it must be employed with other methods. The teacher has to use the valuing process on a continual basis for an extended amount of time before he or she can detect results. What happens if, after all this time, the student's behavior still does not change? Was such a time-consuming endeavor worthwhile, or, instead, could the teacher have used other models that would have been implemented and evaluated much sooner?

CONFRONTING-CONTRACTING

The Confronting-Contractors believe that appropriate behavior is learned as a result of a student coming into contact with the needs of others. The student learns the reciprocal relationship of individuals who accommodate each other in order to live in a social group. The appropriate medium for such learning is interaction with others. The student does not propose solutions that are wholly in his or her own self-interest, but rather finds answers that are acceptable to the teacher and the classmates. The teacher is not the nonjudgmental facilitator as espoused by the Relationship-Listeners, but instead delineates boundaries of behavior. Within those boundaries, choices can be made.

Basic Assumptions on Motivation
  —People are social beings and desire to belong
  —People are decision-making organisms
  —All behavior is purposeful and directed towards social goals
  —People do not see reality as it is, but only as they perceive it to be
  —A person is a whole being who cannot be understood by some particular characteristics
  —A person's misbehavior is the result of faulty reasoning on how to gain social recognition

Overt Teacher Behaviors
  —Confrontation
  —Engaging child in friendly conversation
  —Disclosing and confirming mistaken goals to the child
  —Asking the following questions:
    1. Could it be that you want special attention? (attention getting)
    2. Could it be that you want to be boss? (power)
    3. Could it be that you want to hurt others as they've hurt you? (revenge)
    4. Could it be that you want to be left alone? (inadequacy)
  —Class group discussion about all types of behavior (scheduled weekly)
  —Confrontation about goals and misbehavior
  —Continued encouragement to increase child's confidence (belief in self)
  —Avoiding criticism so true motives can be learned and behavior corrected
  —Use encouragement techniques such as:
    1. Work for improvement, not perfection
    2. Commend efforts
    3. Separate the *deed* from *doer*
    4. Build on strengths, not weaknesses
    5. Show your faith in the child
    6. Mistakes should not be viewed as failures
  —Developing logical and natural consequences, logically structured and arranged by the adult, that must be experienced by the student

FIGURE 11–4. Outline of Dreikurs's Social Discipline

Covert Teacher Behaviors
—Four goals of child's misbehavior:
  1. Attention getting
  2. Power seeking
  3. Revenge
  4. Display of inadequacy
—Preventing above behavior by following these steps:
  1. Observe child's behavior in detail
  2. Be psychologically sensitive to your own reaction
  3. Confront child with questions
  4. Apply appropriate corrective procedures

Key Vocabulary
  —Attention getting   —Recognition reflex
  —Power and control   —Role playing
  —Revenge   —Classroom discussion
  —Helplessness   —Sociometric test
  —Encouragement   —Reading stories
  —Hidden motivation   —Informal plays
  —Natural and logical conse-
    quences

Educational Insights
  —Classroom as collective group
  —Sociometric tests for analyzing individual's relationship to group
  —Classroom operated as a democracy

Strengths
  —Develops system of mutual respect (rewards and punishment *not* needed)
  —Allows children time to solve their own problems during class discussion
  —Involves whole class in decision making
  —Helps to aid in socialization of individual
  —Step-by-step procedure according to goals to follow
  —Self-worth developed by teacher and child
  —Has natural and logical consequences

Limitations
  —Teacher may not always be able to determine child's true goal
  —Some children refuse to talk about incident
  —Passive child is always very difficult to help using this method
  —At times, it can be hard to determine consequences

FIGURE 11—4. Outline of Dreikurs's Social Discipline (cont.)

Questions of application that critics might raise include the following:

1. If the student and teacher make mutual plans, do not these in reality become merely teacher plans to which students agree?
2. If interaction is based on communication, what happens to the nonverbal student?
3. Do all students want to belong to a group? After all, if it is true that some individuals enjoy being alone, then is social motivation going to work?
4. Isn't using the group to confront and solve a student's problems "heavy-handed," manipulative, and emotionally damaging to a student with an inferiority complex?

THE SOCIAL MODEL OF RUDOLF DREIKURS

Dreikurs's social model is based on the underlying assumption that every student (or human) wishes to belong. Misbehavior is a student's misdirected goal of belonging. Therefore, if a teacher can ascertain the student's misdirected goal (attention getting, power, revenge, or inadequacy) he or she can counter with a plan to enable the student to use appropriate behavior to belong successfully.

The strength of Dreikurs's model is in the concreteness of application. He tells the teacher how to uncover the student's goal and how to plan according to that goal. Among the techniques a teacher can employ are role playing, classroom discussions, sociometric testing, and story telling. He advocates a system of mutual respect where natural or logical consequences are used rather than arbitrary punishment or systematic reinforcements. The model is predicated on an optimistic outlook by the teacher who does not "give up" on a student. Rather, the teacher becomes sensitive and appreciative of a student's attempts to improve rather than the improvement itself.

The limitations of the social model are varied. Determining a student's social goal may not be as simple as it appears. What if a teacher has a mixture of feelings toward a student, which include feelings of hurt (revenge), being beaten (power) and helplessness (inadequacy)? What if the teacher asks the student the four verifying questions and receives no recognition reflex? Another problem with verifying the goal lies with a student who does not want to know why he or she behaves as he or she does.

The use of encouragement and personal attention also can be viewed as rewarding a student for misbehavior. There are those who believe, for example, that a passive student needs to be drawn out forcefully by physically showing him or her how to raise one's hand, by demanding that the student finish work in a certain length of time, and so forth. Dreikurs's techniques put little pressure on a student to achieve. Another concern is the question of dealing in a caring way with a student who is hurting others. Will not other students see the special attention such students receive for being "bad" and act accordingly?

A further limitation is that the choice of logical consequences is at times difficult to make. What should happen to a student who incessantly talks but still finishes all of the assigned work? What is a logical consequence for this student? Certainly it is *not* having his or her mouth taped shut, staying after school, or taking a note home. After all, the student is doing all that is expected except for talking too much. It is not readily apparent what the teacher should do.

THE REALITY MODEL OF WILLIAM GLASSER

Glasser believes that every student has the capacity to be rational and responsible. However, the student does not acquire this capacity by himself or herself. The teacher provides a classroom of relevant activities so that a student will want to succeed. The teacher then confronts the student by asking him or her to look at the behavior that is keeping him or her from succeeding. The student is asked to make a commitment to a future plan that will be enforced by the teacher.

Reality therapy provides the teacher with an understanding of human motivation based on the concepts of love and self-worth. Glasser provides the educator with covert behaviors for assessing the relevance of one's classrooms. The strength of the model is in the clear delineation of what a teacher needs to do for every misbehaving student. The student must be confronted with "what" questions and must be pressed for a plan. The success or failure of the plan becomes the responsibility of the student, not the teacher. Yet, if the initial effort results in failure, the teacher can keep the responsibility on the student by isolating him or her until another plan is developed and agreed upon. Again, if the plan is unsuccessful, the student and teacher can start again. Behavior that is having a detrimental effect on all class members can be handled in a classroom meeting where all classmates can develop a mutually agreeable plan with the misbehaving student.

The criticisms of Glasser's model first revolve around the educational

Basic Assumptions on Motivation

Relevance, responsibility, and reality are necessary for schools without failure. The child is rational. The child has the capability to be responsible, but needs to learn moral or acceptable boundaries of living successfully in society. Persons must live in a world of other human beings and must satisfy their own needs in a way that does not infringe upon others. Each person has two basic needs, the need for love and the need for self-worth, which must be fulfilled in order to have a successful identity. Behavior problems are a result of these needs not being met. A person must be helped to acknowledge his or her behavior and then take actions in making it more logical and productive. A person must make a commitment to responsible behavior.

Overt Teacher Behaviors
  —Confronting transgressions ("Stop that," "The rule is . . .")
  —Asking "what" questions ("What are you doing?" "What are the rules?" "In what way is your behavior helping you?")
  —Pressing for a plan ("I'll help, but you're responsible.")
  —Agreeing on natural consequence of plan
  —Failure of plan—isolating in class (repeat 1–4)
  —Failure of step 5—isolating in school (repeat 1–5)
  —Failure of step 6—isolating outside of school (repeat 1–6)
  —Referring to outside agency

Covert Teacher Behaviors
  —Observing the student and the situation
  —Assessing what the teacher is currently doing and what success the student is having
  —Starting fresh by reversing classroom organization and/or activities

Key Vocabulary
  —Heterogeneous   —Signed statement
  —Reality therapy   —Behavior
  —Identity   —Consequences
  —Nonjudgmental   —Value judgment
  —Class meetings   —Tight circles
  —Intense counseling   —Failure
  —Open-ended   —Thinking vs. memorization
  —Problem solving   —Commitment
  —Responsibility   —Relevance
  —Success   —Class meetings
  —Self-image   —Love
  —Involvement

FIGURE 11–5. Outline of Glasser's Reality Therapy

Educational Insights
—Class meetings for 1. Problem solving, 2. Open-ended, 3. Educational-
  diagnostic
—Superior system of grades; do away with standard A–F
—Upward Bound program
—Strength teaching
—Seminars for small groups
—Enrichment programs
—Tutors and counseling
—Community contact
—Make curriculum relevant
—No ability grouping

Strengths
—Behavior is student's responsibility
—It has no failures
—Has a step-by-step procedure for all students
—Child must take responsibility for own actions
—Involves all those responsible
—Is a specific use of isolation

Limitations
—Doesn't work well with child who doesn't care
—Class meetings are hard to fit into secondary school
—School changes may be hard to accomplish within school structure
—It is difficult to start fresh each day

FIGURE 11–5.   Outline of Glasser's Reality Therapy

problem of having to create a relevant classroom environment where a student has successful experiences. There are teachers who teach subjects that they know misbehaving students do not perceive as interesting or relevant. Yet due to external circumstances (i.e., in situations where the principal, superintendent, or school board dictate all policies affecting curriculum and environment), the teacher can do little either to change the subject matter or reorganize the classroom environment. Therefore, these educators have difficulty with the first step of Glasser's approach. They want the students to behave properly in their classroom regardless of whether or not they enjoy what is going on. A second limitation is the use of classroom meetings for a misbehaving student. Again there are classrooms and class schedules, particularly on the secondary level, that make such meetings improbable. When a teacher meets with a group of thirty students for one forty-five minute period a day and has specific learning outcomes for each class, he or she will be hard pressed to find the time to have ongoing meetings that take twenty to thirty minutes to conduct. Another criticism applies to the student who does not care about school: making a plan and using isolation with this student are not likely to be successful. A student who would rather not be in school might welcome the chance to be isolated in a comfortable area. Glasser suggests that a student will eventually choose to come out, and the teacher should not allow the student to reenter until a plan is made. If the student does not choose to return, how long is a teacher to wait? Additionally, there is the concern about "making a plan." The strategy is based on the student having a certain degree of organized thought and language proficiency; therefore, it does not address the student who may desire to be in class but does not know how to verbalize or systematize that desire. A final weakness may be the unrealistic hope that a teacher can begin each new plan with an optimistic outlook. It may well be unrealistic to expect a teacher to continue to be optimistic when a student repeatedly breaks contracts.

RULES/REWARDERS-PUNISHERS

The Rules/Rewards-Punishment writers believe that people are shaped by external stimuli. A teacher needs to be aware of the stimuli a misbehaving student is receiving and should then change the environmental conditions so that appropriate behavior will be more rewarding than inappropriate behavior. The teacher is therefore very much in control and should express explicit standards of conduct for the student.

The basic argument against Rules/Rewards-Punishment approaches is not whether they work but whether the ultimate consequences for the student are beneficial. For example, reinforcement programs implemented as part of a piloted national experiment in 1972[1] showed that some severely underachieving and delinquent junior high school students would make drastic changes in behavior if the rewards were great enough. Students who were constantly late and who whistled, moved around, and talked incessantly during class suddenly became the picture of punctuality and docility. They would arrive on time, sit down with folded hands, and be attentive to the teacher when they knew they could earn "tokens" redeemable for record players, transistor radios, bicycles, tickets to concerts, and the like. The questions debated are whether students should learn to behave for such materialistic reasons, and if so, what happens to a student when the obvious rewards for appropriate behavior end?

THE BEHAVIOR MODIFICATION MODEL

The behavior modification model is based on the use of positive reinforcement. General behavior is broken down into smaller parts so that students have insured success. A student can feel successful and competent as he or she learns appropriate behaviors and receives verbal, social, or material rewards. Standards of behavior are uniform, consistent, and clear to all students. The teacher does not need to spend any time in class discussions

---

Basic Assumptions on Motivation
—Children are not born with self-control—we must help them mold it
—Deal only with outward (external) behavior
—Use scientific techniques to demonstrate effectiveness
—Be concerned with unacceptable behavior the child exhibits and what interventions can be applied to change it
—The cause of the behavior exists outside the child, in the environment
—Motivation-reinforcers:
   Positive—something we like
   Negative—something we dislike
   Primary—relating to basic body needs
   Secondary—abstracts, symbols
—The consequences, more than any other factor, determine the behavior the individual exhibits

Overt Teacher Behaviors
—Teacher controlling the situation, imitation and shaping, fading, and directive statements for contingency contracting
—Explicit modeling for imitation, forward and backward chaining, saturation, time out, rewards for reinforcement of desired behaviors; commands as directive statements
—Using conditioners in form of material and verbal rewards; child definitely knows what he or she will receive as a result of his or her behavior
—Using variable intervals and variable ratios

Covert Teacher Behaviors
—Reinforcing only the behavior to be increased
—Before beginning behavior modification:
   1. Select the behavior to be changed
   2. Collect and record baseline data

FIGURE 11–6. Outline of Axelrod, Homme, and Others' Behavior Modification

3. Identify appropriate reinforcers
4. Collect intervention data
—Graphing baseline and intervention data to evaluate effectiveness
—Changing reinforcers periodically
—Reinforcing the behavior on a variable reinforcement schedule

Key Vocabulary
—Baseline data reversals
—Contingency contracting
—Positive and negative
   reinforcement
—Shaping
—Fading
—Operant conditioning
—Behavior
—Extinction

—Intermittent reinforcement
—Tokens
—Time out
—Differential reinforcement of other
   behaviors (DRO)
—Discrimination stimulus generalization
—Chaining

Educational Insights
—School subjects can be taught in a sequential reinforcing manner
—Stimulation of physical environment (positive and negative) should be
   considered
—Positive stimuli are most effective in all dimensions of schooling

Strengths
—It is positively oriented, and reinforces good feelings and self-concept
—Encourages success
—Gives a structured setting for learning
—Eliminates constant/continual contact with a child
—Capitalizes on nonverbal communication
—It works (scientifically tested)
—It can work with all children
—It is efficient.

Limitations
—Many people feel behavior modification practices are unacceptable and
   unethical
—It can have harmful effects if not used correctly; can be abused by insen-
   sitive and unethical practitioners
—Does not accept emotions as important
—Does not let the child use his or her own rational abilities
—Needs precise record keeping to determine its success

FIGURE 11–6. Outline of Axelrod, Homme, and Others' Behavior Modification (cont.)

about rules or to conduct individual conferences dealing with problem solving. He or she can spend more time on instructional matters. Behavior modification can be used with all students, regardless of their age or cognitive and language abilities. A reinforcement schedule can be implemented with a nonverbal, passive student as well as with a highly articulate, aggressive student. Although, at first, reinforcements need to be used frequently, the teacher can eventually use a random interval schedule. Positive use of behavior modification can be scientifically tested by the classroom teacher. This technique usually will work, and it is an efficient way of reversing a student's disruptive actions.

The limitations of the model are both philosophical and practical. Behavior modification is an approach that attempts to change a student's observable behavior. However, some misbehavior may be the result of "inner" problems. A student who is being physically abused at home may be taking his or her hostility out on classmates. A reinforcement program that conditions cooperative class behavior and extinguishes physical aggression may be beneficial to the teacher, but it does not help the student (or parents) resolve the underlying home problem. Therefore, in many cases, behavior modification approaches may change the symptoms but do little to alleviate the actual problem. There is also the argument that, in a democratic society, it is unethical and unacceptable for schools to control an individual's behavior. Limiting behavior so that destruction or harm can be avoided is necessary in any society, but the notion of conditioning specific behavior would be more applicable to a totalitarian society. Educational concerns with behavior modification are that learning "to behave" is an important cognitive task, just as important as learning such school subjects as reading and mathematics. Therefore, if a student is not allowed to bring his or her mental operations into use by learning to clarify emotions, to weigh alternatives, and to decide upon solutions, then a major area of intellectual or rational development would be neglected. Another concern is more immediate to teachers in that such a scientific approach is predicated on precise delineation and measurement of a student's pretreatment behavior. To do this, a teacher needs to write down misbehavior in clear terms and to keep an accurate tabulation of frequency. Some teachers would resist spending the time and effort that this ongoing record keeping involves.

THE ASSERTIVENESS MODEL

Some of the same strengths and limitations of the behavior modification model apply to the assertiveness model (see Figure 11−7). Canter and Canter

Basic Assumptions on Motivation
   —All students can behave regardless of their family histories, socio-economic background, or physical/mental exceptionalities
   —Student misbehavior continues when teachers do not enforce the same standards for all students
   —Teachers have the right to request behavior from students which meets the needs of the teacher and ensures an optimal learning environment
   —Teachers have the right to ask assistance from parents, principals, and other school personnel

Overt Teacher Behaviors
   —Determine differences among assertive, nonassertive, and hostile behaviors
   —Establish a uniform classroom discipline plan of relatively few but specific rules and consistent actions for enforcing them
   —Write the plan down and share it with principal
   —Use mental rehearsal to explain the classroom plan and enforcement procedures and to prepare for handling student violations

Covert Teacher Behaviors
   —Use hints to alert students that there is a problem with their behavior "Class, we should be doing..."
   —Disguise directive statements as a question: "Would you stop...?"
   —Give "I" messages (If you don't stop, then you have chosen...") and "broken record" demands to avoid being side-tracked
   —Use a steady gaze and low voice when talking to students
   —Give rewards for appropriate behavior (positive notes, calling on a student, token coupons, marble system to reward whole class) and punishments for inappropriate behavior (loss of privilege, detention, note home)
   —Use systematic exclusion (to another classroom, principal's office, home)

Key Vocabulary
   —Assertiveness
   —Teacher rights
   —Uniform standards
   —Classroom plan
   —Hints
   —Demands

   —Rewards
   —Punishments
   —Broken record
   —Systematic exclusion
   —Roadblocks
   —Mental rehearsal

FIGURE 11−7. The Assertiveness Model of Canter and Canter

Educational Insights
—A teacher's job is to teach and therefore he or she has the responsibility and right to have his or her own needs met in order to do the job
—The purpose of school is for students to learn; misbehavior keeps students from learning
—Expecting less appropriate behavior from some students because "they simply can't behave" is a self-defeating prophecy
—It is best for students to know that the teacher is in charge

Strengths
—Use of class time is more efficient. Problems are handled quickly and consistently; the teacher can spend more time teaching academic subjects
—A single system of rules, rewards, and punishment can be used for all age levels and kinds of students; there is no need to vary one's approach
—The teacher can be confident and efficient with discipline because he or she has a set program to follow

Limitations
—It may fail to recognize "circumstantial" evidence for misbehavior and the need to give special attention to or plan for an individual student
—It releases the student from personal responsibility and rational decision making
—Punishments may not work
—It is undemocratic and authoritarian. Students have little say in rules and procedures

---

FIGURE 11–7. The Assertiveness Model of Canter and Canter (cont.)

believe in the use of positive behavior modification, but they also emphasize punishment (loss of privileges, detention, notes home). The Canters' discipline model is concerned with a teacher asserting his or her rights and putting together a plan of rewards and punishments that will enforce the teacher's authority. Again, many of the behavior-modification advocates take issue with the use of punishment on the basis of research showing that positive and negative reinforcement (systematic avoidance of an undesirable event) works but that punishment does not work.[2] Since punishment is commonly used in schools, most teachers would probably side with the Canters' position that even though punishment may not have long-term benefits, it does at least give temporary comfort to a teacher to be able to use the threat of punishment with a student.

The Canters' emphasis on a teacher's being assertive and clear in directions and expectations appears to be a major strength of the model. The use of a uniform plan for all students appears to be the model's greatest liability. Those who believe that a classroom should be a model of democracy, that students should take responsibility for their own behavior, and that misbehavior is often symptomatic of underlying problems will find little comfort with the assertiveness model. Total teacher control, uniform disciplinary actions without regard to individual differences, and a low priority for communicating and understanding a student's behavior are all limitations to those who believe that discipline should include learning about oneself, one's relationship with others, and the attempt to behave according to one's own standards.

THE BEHAVIORISM/CORPORAL PUNISHMENT MODEL

Some of the same strengths and limitations of the behavior modification model exist with the Behaviorism/Corporal Punishment model. These writers propose all the positive behavior modification approaches, but they also include the use of negative measures such as stern commands, physical intervention, and, at times, physical punishment. They advocate concern and patience with students, but establish as a firm base that the student must accept a teacher's authority. Their premise is that students go to school to learn academics, and therefore a teacher needs to deal with disruption quickly and efficiently. Although positive reinforcement is encouraged, it must be immediately effective or the teacher should directly take steps to make the consequences of a student's misbehavior unpleasant and not worth doing again. In other words, misbehavior should be less positively rewarding than more appropriate behavior. A major strength of the model is in its point of view that discipline is not in opposition to love and respect for students. To provide specific rules and to enforce those rules is to provide a structured environment where love and security can flourish. When teachers take the opposite view that care and sensitivity are shown by allowing students to do and say whatever they wish, the results can often be erratic and even volatile behavior on the part of student and teacher.

The most prevalent concern with this model is whether punishment really works. Scolding or paddling would indicate to a student what he or she should not be doing, but it does not tell him or her what should be done instead. Punishment therefore would need to be administered in conjunction with positive reinforcement. If this is so, then why not simply ignore the misbehavior rather than punish it? Also, punishment can have the effect opposite of its intent. To have a student stay after school for refusing to obey the teacher can make the student more resentful and more disobedient. Another concern is that the teacher would be providing a model of behavior to the student that he or she may not wish the student to emulate. For example, if a teacher believes it is inappropriate for students to use physical means to resolve a conflict, but that students should use calm language to

---

Basic Assumptions on Motivation
  —Respectful, responsible children result from families where the proper combination of love and discipline is present
  —Developing respect for the adult is critical in student management
  —The best time to communicate often occurs after punishment
  —Control without nagging
  —Don't saturate with excessive materialism
  —Avoid extremes in control and love
  —The adult is in charge—he or she must win

Overt Teacher Behaviors
  —Identifying the rules well in advance; letting there be no doubt about what is and what is *not* acceptable; when the child cold-bloodedly chooses to challenge those known boundaries, giving him reason to regret it; at all times demonstrating kindness, love, and understanding (discipline is not an antonym of love and discipline is not a synonym of punishment)
  —Controlling child behavior by reinforcement (reinforcement *must* be immediate)
  —Using directive statements (contingency contracting): if you do X, then you do or get Y; even though one gains points for following the contract, he or she is also penalized if he or she does not follow it

Covert Teacher Behaviors
  —Seeing behavior modification (positivist)
  —Reminding yourself to maintain your "power," to use discipline, and to use kindness and love
  —Reminding yourself to be immediate and consistent with reinforcers
  —Reminding yourself to never let the child have the "upper hand"
  —Reminding yourself to be patient!!!

FIGURE 11–8. The Behaviorism/Punishment Model

Key Vocabulary
—Discipline
—Control
—Reinforcement
—Consistency
—Responsibility
—Self-discipline
—Self-control
—Kindness
—Love
—Understanding
—Respect for authority
—Miracle tools
—Family and God
—Defiance

Educational Insights
—Discipline needs to be quick with the late bloomer, slow learner, and underachiever
—Grades need to be viewed as reinforcers
—The purpose of schools is for students to learn; misbehavior keeps students from learning
—It is better to be strict at the beginning; "don't smile till December "

Strengths
—Use of class time is more efficient; Problems are handled quickly; the teacher spends a lot of time teaching academic skills
—Behavior Modification is a scientific method; results can be proven
—It is effective for all age levels and kinds of students

Limitations
—Such techniques need to start very early when the child is young
—It is undemocratic and authoritarian
—It may fail to recognize "circumstantial" evidence for misbehavior
—Releases child from personal responsibility and rational decision
—Limits on physical punishment are established by the school board
—Punishment may not work
—It models teacher behavior that is inappropriate for students to engage in

FIGURE 11−8. The Behaviorism/Punishment Model (cont.)

make their needs known, then the use of "punishment" by the teacher would be incorrect. If a teacher grabs or paddles a student for fighting, then he or she would be clearly showing the student that "might does make right." The student would feel justified in continuing to fight, because he or she has seen that the teacher has resolved his or her frustrations in the same manner. Aside from the issues of whether punishment works or whether punishment is a poor model, there is also the reality that the matter of punishment is often strictly regulated by school board policy. Many school systems do not allow, or severely restrict, various forms of punishment (such as paddling or detention after school).

SUMMARY

There are no teacher-student interaction models today that, to our knowledge, do not have their critics. There is not now, and there possibly never will be, research that provides indisputable documentation that one model is superior to others. It has instead been the purpose here to refresh the reader's memory of the significant features of each model through the presentation of skeleton outlines (Figures 11—1 through 11—8) and then to present some of the debated issues concerning each model.

NOTES

1. "Performance Contracting Experiment in Remedial Education," Conducted by the Office of Economic Opportunity, Carl D. Glickman, Education Analyst for the Portland, Maine Project.
2. Axelrod, S. and Apsche, J. *The Effects of Punishment on Human Behavior.* (New York: Academic Press, 1983.)

Introduction: Beyond Models to Professional Decisions

To read about models, techniques, theories, and strengths and limitations can be, for the teacher that needs help in discipline immediately, somewhat overwhelming. As a result, you may be asking yourself a host of questions,

"Which one of these models is correct"
"Which one should I use?"
"Will my principal 'tell me' which one to use?"
"Can I use one model when the teacher next door is using another?"

The answer to these questions will vary depending on what you believe, where you are in your professional development as a teacher, and what kind of situation you teach in. The idea of stages of professional development may be a new idea for many, but as a student teacher or intern, a first-year teacher, a five-year teacher, or a thirty-year teacher approaching retirement, you will have changed in how you think, teach, and act towards students. With increased experience and maturity, you begin to rethink past practices and may decide other ways to approach your teaching.

The answers to the above questions will vary from teacher to teacher, depending on their particular stage or time period of professional development; there is no one correct way to decide discipline approaches, techniques, or skills. Following are five possible ways to determine answers to the above questions.

Decision Making Based on a Single Approach

Selecting one model as your model of discipline infers that no outside authority—principal, expert, colleague, school official—can truly tell you what is the best single discipline approach. A person from outside your classroom simply does not know the day-to-day realities that you face. To impose a model or techniques on a teacher without giving that teacher the opportunity to adapt it to his or her own situation belittles teachers as professionals. This is not to say that others cannot help, but when you as a teacher are in a conflict with a student, you can not be someone else and practice techniques that are uncomfortable and different from your own values. This would be doomed to failure. But your own beliefs can provide you with a screen for considering the widest possible choices about discipline systems, models, and techniques to obtain an effective working atmosphere for you and your students. The simplest way to begin is by making a determination of the model(s) closest to your own beliefs. This can be done by looking at your score in the Beliefs on Discipline Inventory (see the Introduction to Section One) and by recalling what you thought while reading each of the models. You may have felt that a certain model "fit well." Identifying and using one particular model is a common choice for an undergraduate who is just learning to be a teacher or a teacher in a new classroom situation (such as the first-year teacher, or even experienced teachers who find themselves in a new grade, a new subject area, or a different group of students). If this is you, then, you may decide to stop right here. You could simply go back and reread the model of your choice and then read the original books and resources listed at the end the chapter. You might even form a cooperative study group with fellow teachers who have a similar attachment to that model. The films, filmstrips, and other media listed at the end of chapters will help you gain deeper understanding of how to use the techniques found in the model.

Decision Making Based on an Eclectic Approach

An eclectic approach is a second way to proceed. Your response to the choice of a single model may be, "There is no one model that I like totally; however, I see a few techniques from some of the models that I already use and I would like to acquire some other techniques to add to my skills." If this is how you are thinking, then you may wish to piece together an eclectic approach, taking from various models to create your own unique model. The negative side of the sword of eclecticism is that an unthinking "shotgun" or "smorgasbord" application of techniques could produce an erratic, disorderly series of teacher behaviors that lead to inconsistency with students and increase, rather than decrease, student misbehavior. The problem becomes one of finding orderliness within the process of creating an eclectic selection of teacher behaviors. Eclecticism can be most positive if the teacher thinks of how to use desired techniques along the Teacher Behavior Continuum (TBC) and to plan strategies based on a long-range goal of escalation or deescalation of power. By this, it is meant that a teacher's behavior with a misbehaving student should be rational. With success with a student, the teacher should determine if a decrease in teacher power is appropriate and with failure, whether an increase in teacher power is in order. The gradual progression up and down a continuum of power techniques gives consistency and orderliness to teacher actions. Chapter Twelve provides a process for creating one's own eclectic discipline model.

Decision Making Based on the Degree of Seriousness of Student Misbehavior

It seems obvious to state that all discipline incidents are not at the same level of severity. To cite an extreme, the misbehavior of dropping pencils repeatedly to annoy the teacher cannot be compared to the misbehavior of a student selling heroin or carrying a dangerous weapon in school. None of the models fully account for the severity factor that is a practical consideration in the day-to-day running of a classroom. Thus teachers may be responding to questions about discipline with the statement, "I do not choose an action towards a student until I look at the seriousness of the misbehavior and then I make my own judgment as to what would be an appropriate action." Taking appropriate action is a difficult process for teachers to decide "on the spot." For example, a teacher may have begun to get the "sinking" feeling that control is being lost in their classroom, and a small incident such as a student dropping a pencil might ignite actions of a "drowning" teacher that would be much too extreme for the crime. Such action is seen by students, parents, fellow teachers, and the principal as unreasonable and over-reacting. On the other hand, an unthinking teacher could fail to take a firm or strong enough measure to respond to a serious misbehavior such as a fight, drug selling, or the display of a weapon. If the teacher ignores the act or does not act decisively the students will see the teacher as someone who can be easily pushed around. More serious misbehavior will probably result. Chapter Twelve provides a system to help the teacher plan and choose disciplinary actions appropriate to the misbehavior.

Decision Making Based on Student Social Development

Still another answer to discipline might be helpful to teachers who think to themselves, "Although I have strong beliefs about overt behaviors of discipline, I do not choose techniques based on my values alone but instead consider the student and his or her development." These teachers feel that misbehavior by a student must be placed within the context of all the student's behavior. They believe that misbehaving students have not yet developed mature social skills. With understanding of developmental changes in students, a teacher can choose techniques that are appropriate to a student's current social stage and move the student to more mature social behavior. Chapter Thirteen provides a construct for looking at students and a guide for matching techniques from the models to the individual student.

Decision Making Based on a Professional Team Approach

Finally, teachers may reason, "I at times need others such as the principal, school psychologist, and fellow teachers to help me with certain students. In the past, getting such help has been time consuming and simply inadequate." When a student's misbehavior flows outside of an individual teacher's classroom and affects others, a team approach towards that student would be most beneficial. Chapter Fourteen gives the teacher a system and set of procedures for using the resources of others to benefit the misbehaving students.

What follows then in Section II goes beyond a single answer to discipline. The reader is given four ways to make professional decisions about dealing with student behavior. It is for the teacher to make his or her own choices.

12

Decision Making Based on an Eclectic Approach

Having gained an understanding of the various teacher-student interaction models and how they are positioned on a "power" continuum, we may look at ways that a teacher might use these methods in a unique, creative manner. The discipline methods a teacher uses will be based initially on his or her beliefs about his or her role as a teacher. A statement such as "I simply do not like the controlling and mechanistic techniques used by the Rules/Rewards-Punishment models," indicates a clear value position. The teacher making this kind of statement may feel that Rules/Rewards-Punishment models dehumanize students, treating them as if they were simply stimulus-response animals lacking in rational thought. Such a teacher who feels strongly against such an approach, might be more comfortable and effective using the techniques of Relationship-Listening or Confronting-Contracting. A teacher with the opposite belief will feel equally strong. He or she might think "Students must show me first that they can be trusted! Until that occurs I will decide on appropriate rules and then I will make sure that students learn to follow those rules." This teacher who believes that his or her role is to be in charge might be humorously called the "don't smile until Christmas" teacher. He or she would naturally gravitate to the Rules/Rewards-Punishment models and would have difficulty in using Relationship-Listening or Confronting-Contracting techniques.

It is important that a teacher clarify his or her own beliefs and use those beliefs as a starting point in developing an action theory. What each discipline model is first, is a theoretical view of what motivates a student to behave and then a series of techniques and teacher behaviors to put the theory into

213

"The magic has gone out of my discipline model!"
Cartoon by Ford Button

action. Each theorist—Gordon, Harris, Raths, Glasser, Dreikurs, Axelrod, Canter, and Dobson—advocates "the way." But it is "the way" according to each writer's own beliefs about students. The common-sense question for a teacher would be: Will one model of techniques be sufficient for me with all my students?

Another way of looking at espoused discipline models contrasted with the real classroom is to ask when is the last time that you have seen a teacher in the classroom who was a 'purist,' or uses only one pedagogical model? The answer is probably rarely, if ever! One principal stated, "Our district began using the Glasser model five years ago and we have been working on it ever since and only 40 percent of our teachers are using it today." One possible reason for this was that the other 60 percent of the teachers valued Relationship-Listening or Rules/Rewards-Punishment models and could not carry out a model dictated by administrators. What we more likely will find, in practice, is that teachers with effective discipline have "pieced" together an orderly discipline plan with techniques that cut across several models.

Many school districts have attempted to impose a particular model of discipline on all teachers in their district and, then, three to five years later impose another. This happens because administrators sometimes look for a "quick fix" to discipline problems in their district. Often in response to a nasty discipline incident which has made the news, the district wants to assure the concerned public that discipline is improving. Thus we see the local school principal on the 5:00 o'clock TV news shaking hands with the "expert from afar" as he or she announces that the school district has brought in, from a thousand miles away, a nationally known expert on discipline, who will provide one day of in-service training to help improve discipline throughout the district. What such a "quick fix" does, even when well intentioned, is to disregard the beliefs, concerns, and struggles of the individual teacher.

The resolution of conflict between teacher and student in a discipline situation involves the deepest structures of a teacher's personality. It is related to one's own values about how we, ourselves, were raised and disciplined as children and students and how we personally deal with others. When administrators force discipline models on practicing teachers, these teachers in good faith attempt to put them into practice but because these techniques do not relate to their own value system, they are carried out as a recipe. The techniques "do not work" for the teacher and the teacher often declares the model totally useless.

One answer, then, is not to accept or reject a discipline model in total, but find a process whereby the teacher can design his or her own plan that fits their own values. To coin even more educational-babble, we may suggest that a teacher could create his or her own individualized discipline plan (IDP) by accepting the theoretical idea of escalation-deescalation of teacher power according to one's own values. But why more theory?

Let's use a homey example. Tuesday morning, your alarm failed to go off, and you yourself are late for school. If you can believe it, you are giving midterm exams this morning! You turn the key in your Mercedes XKL and nothing happens. You make the brilliant move of getting out of the car, opening the hood and peering down into the engine—without knowing what in the world you are looking at! Carburetor, farburetor, it's all the same to you—because you don't have theory or a plan based on that theory! No theory to tell you how the fuel system works, no theory to explain the electrical system, and most importantly, no theory on how all the systems work. Without a theory, you can not create a plan and action to start the car. You're now beginning to have doubts on whether buying the Mercedes was wise; maybe you should have taken the Ford Escort instead. So you slam the hood shut, kick the tires, call an automotive expert, and prepare to sell your firstborn to pay the bill that you are about to receive.

The same inability to make a rational decision when teaching students results from a lack of theory. Pretend that you are a teacher of primary children. Carol knocks over Jim's block tower, Jim kicks Billy, Billy grabs the paint brush from Sally, and Sally throws up. The classroom situation is becoming a game of "discipline dominoes"! You sagely conclude that things are not going well in your classroom, but what are you going to do about it? Without a theory, then there is no plan of action.

In the Mercedes example, the driver gives up by becoming depressed or aggressively slamming, kicking, and swearing. As Dobson reminds us, there are many teachers today who passively give up or slam, kick, and swear when they are faced with a student or group of students that misbehave. The Canters label such teacher behavior as nonassertive or hostile (in "slam-kick-swear"). Such teacher behavior develops heightened anxiety in students because they see the teacher as unpredictable and erratic. An individualized discipline plan based on one's own theory gives order to teacher behavior and allows the teacher to know how to act before misbehavior occurs. In this way the teacher can "open the hood," look in, take out a wrench, and get things running again.

Your own theory of discipline begins by understanding that when you as a teacher act toward a student, that action projects a certain degree of power that you wish to use towards the misbehaving student. This behavior can be placed along the previously introduced Teacher Behavior Continuum and can be classified as emanating from Relationship-Listening, Confronting-Contracting, or Rules/Rewards-Punishment points of view. Observed over a period of time, a teacher generally conveys one of these three orientations with its accompanying degree of power. Relationship-Listening behaviors give students maximum power and teacher minimal power; Confronting-Contracting behaviors share equal student and teacher power; and Rules/Rewards-Punishment behaviors give maximum teacher and minimal student power. Thus, every teacher has a starting point related to his or her own degree of power that they wish to use with students. The difficulties that point to the need for a theory come when behaviors that a teacher has been using habitually with success don't work with a particular student or group of students. When these comfortable techniques don't work, the teacher is on the spot. We as teachers must do some "gear shifting" to try new behaviors towards, with, or at the misbehaving student. If we habitually turned the key with the Mercedes and it failed to respond, we would need to think of what to do next—a second response to get the car started. Without trying a second response, we are left using behaviors that do not work. Unless we move on to some new behaviors, we can become emotionally flooded and, at worst, are left with a "yell, slam, kick, swear" approach; unfortunately the problem is not our Mercedes this time. The "yell, slam, kick, swear" approach to discipline will leave us with students who tend to "yell, kick, swear" back, a principal giving us a poor evaluation, and, in the extreme case, a potential law suit.

To avoid this, we can make our theory for new behaviors into an individualized discipline plan. At the practical level we can envision three starting points that focus on teacher power and "gear shifting." (By gear shifting, we mean using more or less powerful behaviors.)

Plan 1—From Relationship-Listening to Increased Teacher Power

The teacher when first responding to a misbehaving student can use Relationship-Listening techniques; then, after a period of time if the techniques do not seem to be working, the teacher can "gear shift" to Confronting-Contracting techniques. Again, if the teacher is unsuccessful, he or she might escalate the degree of power to Rules/Rewards-Punishment techniques. This progression of "gear shifting" upward can be viewed as follows:

> Starting
> Relationship-Listening———→(unsuccessful)———→Confronting-
> Contracting———→(unsuccessful)———→Rules/Rewards-Punishment

Student: "Mr.(s.) Anderson, my father is angry at you. He wants to know why I am failing this course!"

Teacher: "You're having difficulty explaining your lack of success in my class?" (behavior: active listening)

The teacher has taken a Relationship-Listening stance as a starting point in working with this student. From a transactional-analysis perspective (see Chapter 4), the student's remarks may be viewed as communication from student's *Parent* to the teacher's *Child*, thus trying to intimidate the teacher or make the teacher feel guilty. The natural tendency would be for the teacher to respond with a *Parent* statement to the student's *Child*, thus causing a cross transition with the teacher falling into the student's game. If the teacher had fallen for the game, he or she would have said "Listen, wise guy, you haven't done one 'stick' of homework in the last two months and you have failed the last three exams completely. You know very well why you're failing this course. Don't give me any threats about your father." Teacher Effectiveness Training theory (see Chapter 2) views the student as attempting to shift the problem of win-lose problem ownership to the teacher or attempting *Method II* problem-solving (when the student attempts to beat the teacher). The teacher refuses to fall into the student's game or accept ownership for the student's problem. He or she has countered instead with "active listening" and merely reflects an understanding of the student's problem.

Student: "Yeah, I am getting B's and C's in all my other classes, except this one. My old man says that he doesn't want a 'turkey' like you stopping me from graduating."

Teacher: "Failing my class would stop you from graduating." (behavior: active listening) "Well, we still have half a semester to go, I want you to master the content in this course and you want to graduate, let's see if we can find some way of using the remainder of the school year so that you will be able to pass the course." (behavior: *Method III*, "no lose" problem solving)

We see the teacher consciously avoiding the student's game playing which is trying to provoke the teacher with verbally aggressive names. The teacher has continued with active listening and then attempts win-win problem solving. At this point, the student might start to behave more constructively by participating in the negotiation of a new plan of study and committing to it. On the other hand the student might continue to be belligerent.

Student: Listen, man, I don't want to talk———— with you. My old man plays golf with two members of the school board; either you change my grade or you'll be finished when he is done with you."

For the purist Relationship-Listening teacher, abusive language from a student would not cause him or her to break the minimal teacher power stance; the teacher would continue with an "I" message.

Teacher: "When you swear at me, I become angry. Such language blocks my ability to problem solve with you." (behavior: "I" message—behavior, effect, feeling)

The purist teacher would continue with Relationship-Listening behaviors such as active listening, "I" messages, value questions, and transactional analysis of language for as long as it takes. Many practicing teachers would find it difficult to maintain such a purist stance, possibly because they feel that such continued student misbehavior is simply inappropriate and requires more direct teacher action, or, although they may still value the Relationship-Listening techniques, with thirty to one hundred other students, they simply do not have the time to patiently counsel one student.

The nonpurist teacher has many more tools and techniques available in dealing with such students. The next step of the individualized discipline plan would be to do some "gear shifting" by moving to Confronting-Contracting (Glasser's and Dreikurs's techniques). Both of these theorists view the misbehaving student within a social context. The verbally abusive student is showing hostility not just at you as a teacher but instead towards you as an authority. Perhaps from earlier childhood experiences, the student has been unsuccessful in finding acceptance from others and therefore has learned to use the misdirected goals of attention, power, revenge, or, helplessness. The Confronting-Contracting stance is to let the student know the limits of behavior in a social setting, to have the student re-evaluate what he or she has been doing as destructive, and confront the student to come up with a plan to change. At the same time, the teacher can help the student find ways of improving interaction with others and find the acceptance that he or she seeks.

Teacher: "Stop this! This behavior is unacceptable! What are you doing?" (behavior: directive statement, "What" question)

Student: "What? I'm not doing anything."

Teacher: "What are you doing?" (behavior: "What" question)

Student: "I am telling you what my old man said."

Teacher: "No, what you are doing is using unacceptable language and your father to make me change your grade. It won't work; I will not be intimidated. Maybe you have learned to get your way with such behavior, but it will not work with me. I am willing to work with you to find ways for you to complete my course successfully. I cannot talk any longer; I need to get to my next class, but I will meet with you today at noon in my room—bring your lunch and you can eat it there. In the meantime, you will need to think about how your current behavior is helping you and what you are going to do in the future." (behavior: directive statement; "What" question).

(In such situations with very powerful students, we, as teachers, can become fearful and afraid, and the tendency is to respond aggressively (give strong punishment), or passively (helplessness). Dreikurs as a Confronting-Contracting theorist has suggested that we disengage and not view the student's hostility and manipulation as personal, but instead as simply a student's erroneous attempts to gain acceptance. If we as a teacher do not disengage our feelings toward that student, we may become so angry that we become incapable of dealing with the student in a constructive manner. At times, the best immediate solution is to correct the student, ask him or her to think about the misbehavior, and make a contract later.

Teacher: (During lunch period with student) "Now, we must find a way to work this out. What is your plan?" (behavior: press for plan)

Student: "I don't know. Hey, what you want from me?"

Teacher: "Your actions by swearing and threatening are unacceptable to me and if we are going to be together for the rest of the semester, I want to know what will your plan be?" (behavior: directive statement; press for plan).

The teacher confronts the student and pushes the student to come up with a contract. Notice that the teacher does not accept ownership of the student's difficulties by suppressing the tendency to tell the student how to behave and change; instead, the teacher keeps the "ball in the student's court" by saying in so many words that I'm here to help but you need to tell me what you are going to do.)

Student: "Man—get off my case!"

Teacher: "Yes, I can get off of your case, but not until I know what you are going to do about your behavior. You should be aware of the logical consequences of your action. One, if you continue to fail to do your work then you will fail my class and you will not graduate—this is, of course, one of your choices. Second, if your name calling and swearing disrupts my teaching then you are showing me by your actions that you do not know how to be a member of a classroom, and the consequences will be removal from the classroom—but that is your choice. What is your plan?" (behavior: directive statement; press for plan; logical consequences)

Here we see the confronting process and the discussion of logical consequences. The situation can be resolved by the student responding to the teacher's Confronting-Contracting technique, or the situation can worsen. Following are two possible scenarios:

Successful Scenario

Student: "Man, I want to graduate, my old man will kill me if I don't."

Teacher: "And your actions now are not helping you reach that goal. What is your plan to change?"

Student: "Could you help me catch up?"

Teacher: "You're in my fifth-period study hall; I could give you a few minutes of tutoring during that time. But what about homework?"

Student: "I could stop going to town right after school and get it done. I think my friend Pat is good at this stuff—maybe Pat could help me."

Teacher: "What about this swearing, intimidation, and name calling?"

Student: "Ah, man, I just want to pass this class, man, and graduate."

Teacher: "OK, I have been taking some notes here, and I would like to go over our contract:
1. I will not go to town until my home work is finished.
2. Mr.(s.) Clark will help with some tutoring in study hall.
3. I will get Pat to tutor me.
4. I will not swear or "smart off."
Now let's decide on the consequences for the contract. What will happen if you do what we agree to and what will happen if you don't? After we decide that, I will need your signature to complete our agreement and I will sign it. I also will be glad to have a meeting with your father and go over this contract and possibly get his signature, if you think that will be helpful for you."

Student: "No, let's work it out ourselves. I can explain things to him."

Unsuccessful Scenario

Teacher: (During lunch period with student.) "Now, we must find a way to work this out. What is your plan?"

Student: "Listen, ———, get off my case—who do you think you are dealing with here? I don't want any of your ———.

Teacher: "Yes, I can get off your case, but not until I know what you are going to do about your behavior. You should be aware of the logical consequences of your action. One, if you continue to fail to do your work then you will fail my class and you will not graduate—this, of course, is one of your choices. Second, if your name calling and swearing disrupts my teaching then you are showing me by your actions that you do not know how to be a member of a classroom, and the consequences will be removal from the classroom—but this is your choice. What is your plan?

Student: "Hey, listen, man, you know where you can put your plan!"

The teacher continues to press for a plan but without success. If the teacher wishes to maintain the Confronting-Contracting position, he or she may ask for a conference to include the student, school principal, and parents; and repeat the call for an acceptable contract. If this step is unsuccessful and the student's behavior is not improving, the teacher again can "gear shift" to a Rules/Rewards-Punishment stance and use behavior modification, assertiveness, and punishment techniques.

Teacher: "Ok. I now need to make it clear regarding the rules in my class. I will not let you disrupt my class or stop me from my teaching. I want you to:
1. Stay in your seat and raise your hand if you wish to talk.
2. Stop using profanity or being discourteous.

3. Have all your materials and supplies ready when class begins, with no class disruptions on your part.

If you break one of these three rules, I will put your name on the board as a warning. If you break the rules a second time, I will put a check by your name as another warning. If this occurs a third time I will send you to the office and call your parents for a conference. I am also notifying the principal of this discipline plan and sending a copy to your father. If assignments are completed and I do not have to speak to you about obeying the rules, then I will tutor you during fifth-period study hall, if you wish. You choose! Now, in regards to your homework: we will have fourteen more assignments over the next seven weeks. Each assignment will be worth 10 points, making a total of 140. There will be two more tests amounting to 100 points, each making a total with the fourteen assignments of 340 possible points for the remainder of the course. If you miss more than 30 percent of these points (that is, 238 points), you will get an F as a grade; 239 to 264, a D; 265 to 289, a C; 290 to 314, a B; and 315 to 340, an A."

Once the teacher has "gear shifted" to Rules/Rewards-Punishment, the teacher has concluded that the student is incapable of rational reasoning for solving and being responsible for improving his or her own behavior, as is required for Relationship-Listening and Confronting-Contracting methods. Negotiation is no longer appropriate. The behavior desired is made clear and positive reinforcement and punishments are established. In the example above, the teacher could also have set daily small behavioral goals and shaped behavior with positive reinforcement (praise and special responsibilities as tokens) for appropriate behavior. If the student continues to misbehave, it will be necessary for the teacher not to back down and follow through on the negative reinforcements and punishments in the plan.

To summarize, Plan 1, action theory, begins with Relationship-Listening; when this is unsuccessful over a period of time, the teacher escalates to the techniques of Confronting-Contracting; and with continued lack of success, finally escalates to Rules/Rewards-Punishment. This is an individualized discipline plan that began from minimal teacher-power techniques and escalated to maximum teacher power-techniques.

Plan 2—From Rules/Rewards-Punishment to Lessening Teacher Power

A teacher could start an individualized discipline plan with Rules/Rewards-Punishment, and with success move down to using less teacher power

(Confronting-Contracting techniques) and then again move to less power (Relationship-Listening techniques). This can be diagrammed as:

> Starting
> Rules/Rewards-Punishment⟶(with success)⟶Confronting-
> Contracting (with success)⟶Relationship-Listening.

Many teachers use Rules/Rewards-Punishment methods as a way of beginning their school year. Once the students understand and obey what the teacher expects, the teacher begins to give them some freedom to make decisions by moving to Confronting-Contracting techniques, and finally, with continued success, to give a greater amount of freedom by using Relationship-Listening techniques. The idea is to maintain a well-disciplined classroom throughout the year but have students take on greater responsibilities for their own behavior. It is important to realize that if a teacher starts with the most powerful techniques and is unsuccessful, then he or she cannot escalate any further and is left without any recourse but punishment and possibly removing disruptive students from the classroom and/or school. (Of course, a wise teacher may think that if the beginning powerful techniques are not working, why not try less powerful ones. What's to lose!) The objective of this book is to provide teachers with a smorgasbord of techniques from minimum to maximum teacher power, increasing the repertoire of the teacher as a discipline problem solver. Shouting "Sit down, shut up, or get out of my class!" is evidence of a teacher with limited willingness and understanding of the available techniques for creating a well-disciplined classroom.

Plan 3—From Confronting-Contracting to Less or More Teacher Power

Finally, there are teachers who wish to select, for their starting point in dealing with misbehavior, a midpoint in the power continuum of Confronting-Contracting methods. With success, the teacher begins "gear shifting," de-escalating to the less powerful techniques of Relationship-Listening or, if unsuccessful, "gear shifting" by escalating to Rules/Rewards-Punishment techniques. We may diagram this plan as:

> Starting
> Relationship-Listening⟵(with success)⟵Confronting-
> Contracting⟶(unsuccessful)⟶Rules/Rewards-Punishment

AN ORDERLY PLAN

What is important in designing an individualized discipline plan is that teacher behavior will not be random if the teacher thinks through the current practices to use with a student and then plans what to do next in the event of success or failure. Although the teacher appears eclectic in the discipline techniques used, students begin to understand that the teacher has a purpose and thus become secure in knowing that they will be treated fairly. Like the person whose Mercedes will not start, the teacher will not need to regress in his or her own behavior to "yell, slam, kick, swear," but can go about conducting the class in an orderly manner.

To create an orderly plan we start with Chart 12−1, which is a matrix crossing the teacher behavior continuum in the right-hand column with all the models going across the rows.

For example, looking from left to right, across from Directive Statements in the TBC column, we find influencing (Gordon); adult responses (TA); tell logical consequences and confronting (Dreikurs); make a mutual plan (Glasser); contingency contracting (behavior modification); "I" message, demands, and broken record (assertiveness), and tell rules-stop-what to do (behavior modification with punishment).

A teacher can read the overt behaviors within each box and place a check in the box containing the behaviors that he or she finds acceptable and would like to put into practice. Think about one of the more common but annoying discipline incidents that occurs in your classroom or with a particular student. The question to ask is: "Would I start with Relationship-Listening, Confronting-Contracting, or Rules/Rewards-Punishment techniques?" Refer to the worksheet for developing an individualized discipline plan.

Now write in outline form the more powerful techniques that you would use if you need to "gear shift" to increase power. You can also write out the techniques to use if you need to "gear shift" to reduce the display of power. You are thus building an individualized discipline plan. Such a plan should produce actions clearly related to your own values with the greatest probability of working for you. The following are case studies of individualized discipline plans that three teachers have used with particularly troublesome students.

CASE STUDIES

The following are three actual cases of how teachers with different beliefs made beginning choices and developed their own plans for dealing with a

CHART 12–1.

	Relationship-Listening			Confronting-Contracting			Rules/Rewards-Punishment		
Models	Gordon's Supportive	Communication (TA)	Valuing	Dreikurs's Social	Glasser's Reality	Behavior Modification	Canters assertiveness model	Behavior Modification with Corporal Punishment	TBC
Overt Behaviors				as a part of logical consequences	(4)institution (3) out of school (2) school off to (1) class	time out nonreinforcing area	systematic exclusion	isolation in uncomfortable area	Isolation
							rewards: marble system. token coupons. positive notes & calls punishment: choice—"either behave or... deprive of activities. stay after school. note home	punishment (physical)	Physical Intervention
				as a part of logical consequences		saturation			
	affirm student OK feelings			reap natural or logical consequences encouragement	reap consequences of plan	positive shaping		negative / positive	Reinforcement
	6 steps to problem solving Method III	class discussion and exercises with PAC	group exercises	class discussion	classroom meetings	positive model with (+) reinforcement	steady gaze voice low and composed light touch	businesslike attitude by teacher	Modeling
	influencing	adult responses		make a plan corresponding to goal / tell logical consequences confronting	make a mutual plan	contingency contracting	"I" message ("I want you to....") demands: promise. not threat broken record	tell rules / tell to stop / tell what to do	Directive Statements
	door openers	adult responses	confronting, probe for value	verify questions 1, 2, 3, 4	confronting "stop" confronting "what?"		disguised directive statement: "would you...?"		Questions
	"I" messages active listening		active listening				hint: "We should be doing..."		Nondirective Statements
	acknowledgments critical listening	adult responses				extinction reinforcing (−)(+)			Silently looking on
Covert Behaviors	determine problem of ownership	diagnosis teacher and student PAC	look for value indicators	observe the student ask oneself questions 1, 2, 3, 4	observe the student		establish classroom discipline plan avoid roadblocks mental rehearsal	observe (what is the payoff)	

225

WORKSHEET
Individualized Discipline Plan

Give one example of misbehavior that is causing you the most trouble in your classroom.

_____

_____

_____

Give the starting point(s) techniques that you currently use.

_____

_____

_____

_____

Would you classify these above techniques as (circle) 1. Relationship-Listening; 2. Confronting-Contracting; 3. Rules/Rewards-Punishment?

Unsuccessful Resolution
If student behavior does not change, will you escalate or "gear shift" to (circle) 1. Relationship-Listening; 2. Confronting-Contracting; 3. Rules/Rewards-Punishment.

List those techniques that you would use:

_____

_____

_____

_____

If you need to escalate or "gear shift" again, list your techniques.

_____

_____

_____

_____

Successful Resolution
If the student changes behavior in a positive way, will you continue with the same techniques, or de-escalate ("gear shift") to: (circle) 1. Relationship-Listening; 2. Confronting-Contracting; 3. Rules/Rewards-Punishment?

List the new techniques that you would use.

_____

_____

_____

_____

Now, based on the above, circle one of these individualized discipline plans as your general plan of operation.
• Plan 1: RL, to increase power
Starting
   RL——▶ (unsuccessful) ——▶ CC——▶ (unsuccessful) ——▶RRP
• Plan 2: RRP, to less power
Starting
   RRP ——▶ (with success) ——▶ CC ——▶ (with success) ——▶ RL
• Plan 3: CC, to less or more power
Starting
   RL ◀—— (with success) ◀—— CC——▶ (unsuccessful) ——▶ RRP

"misbehaving student"* We asked the teachers to develop and report their cases using a standard format of gathering information about the student, interpreting the student's behavior according to their beliefs, fixing a plan,

*We would like to thank public school teachers Susan Dice, Donna Lawrence, and Tommy Jo Galbreath, along with thirty other teachers for field-testing the ideas of this book and allowing us to use their reports.

selecting beginning overt behaviors for two weeks, assessing the two-week progress, and considering future overt behaviors for the next two weeks. (The teachers' original words have in some cases been edited to read consistently with the writing style of this book.) Following each study are some of the authors' notes.

A Relationship-Listening Teacher—Plan I: Description of Student Behavior:

Georgette's misbehavior occurs most frequently during silent work periods in the classroom. She talks to her neighbors during such work times, her work is incomplete at the time the class period is finished, and she plays with items brought from home during this time.

This behavior occurs daily, most often in the morning reading periods. Georgette also gets out of her seat, walks to different people, and talks to them during the work period. This occurs two or three times in the hour-and-a-half work period.

In interpreting Georgette's behavior, I feel I must first describe the work periods in which Georgette's problem is centered. The students are given their assignments to complete at their desk. After their work is finished, there are various learning centers located around the room where the children can go. There has never been any strict rule about staying in their seats. However, Georgette is up talking to people five minutes after work period has begun. She is not asking directions for the work; I have asked her if she needs help and she has said no.

She is an above-average student in all her work, and when she completes her seatwork, it is usually done correctly. She often does not complete it until she hears me call for the paper; then it's done hurriedly and turned in.

I realize that some of the problem is mine (Gordon's problem of ownership), as she is a good student. Yet she is also bothering other students and keeping them from their work. I interpret her behavior as the Relationship-Listeners would. Georgette has simply not been aware of or thought about her behavior. If she could verbalize her actions, and if I could verbalize my problem with her actions, then she would change her behavior.

Fixing the Pathway

I will use Plan I, "From Relationship-Listening to Increased Teacher Power."

Overt Behaviors

- Use Adult (TA) Language when talking to Georgette; don't be the *Parent*.
- Engage Georgette in discussions by using critical listening, acknowledgments, and door openers.
- Give "I" messages.

Assessment of Two-Week Implementation

The first step I took in trying to correct the behavior was to use "I" messages when Georgette walked over and distracted students and myself during work time. I would say, "Georgette, I have to stop listening to students in this reading group when you get up and talk to others. I can't hear what is being read to me." After such "I" messages, at a recess time I would have private talks with Georgette, asking her if she wanted to talk about her work being late or me getting annoyed. I remembered not to scold or lecture her, and if she didn't want to talk, not to pursue it. Well, after two weeks Georgette's behavior is the same: she has never responded to any of my door openers; she simply clams up and shrugs.

Future Overt Behaviors

I am going to continue private discussions with active listening, but I'm also going to ask the four questions of Dreikurs to see if she gives a recognition reflex. I suspect her goal might be attention, and if it is, I am going to make up a plan where she will have daily opportunities to receive special attention when her work is done.

Authors' Comments: We see that this teacher tried to use a combination of Relationship-Listening techniques to help the child to clarify her own behavior and to propose her own solution. Since the student did not respond, the teacher continues Plan I, by now also employing some of the Confronting-Contracting techniques of verifying the social goal and making a plan to help the student acceptably to achieve the goal. The strategy has obviously worked, for after two more weeks the teacher reports,

After evaluating the progress shown by Georgette during the previous two weeks, I felt that Georgette was ready to re-evaluate and talk about her own progress. After talking to Georgette, we both felt the special attention wasn't needed any more. Georgette was very pleased with the good remarks she had been getting on her papers and thoroughly enjoyed my stopping at her desk once or twice a morning to encourage her. She felt she could now do her work without any trouble, but I could tell she really enjoyed the extra attention given during my stops. I then suggested that perhaps she might want to help around the classroom. She decided she would like to keep the arithmetic center straightened up and would like that to be her daily job. I agreed and told her we would talk again in a couple of weeks to see if she could handle getting her work finished and being in charge of the learning center.

I feel Georgette has come a long way in dealing with her own problems and in understanding that we all must work together. I feel, in working with Georgette, she and I have turned a somewhat shaky relationship that could have made us both unhappy, into a positive, working relationship that is not only productive but satisfying to us both.

A Rules/Rewards-Punishment Teacher—Plan II: Description of Student Behavior:

René reluctantly came to school in September. She was withdrawn, did not smile, and would not interact with other students. Her attendance was poor. The only time she talked to me was to ask when the school day would be over.

During the next few months of school, René's behavior did not change. She would not communicate with me or other classmates. She would sit alone in the same location at each recess. If someone spoke to her, she would lower her head and not respond. She is not regarded as attractive and her clothes are old and shabby. Her schoolwork is poor; however, she will attempt any work that is given her. The school psychologist has tested René and reports that she is within the average IQ range. She has had medical checkups, and records indicate she is physically normal.

Interpretation of Behavior

We must look to her environment for the cause of misbehavior. All behavior can be explained as responses to environmental stimuli. I believe René acts the way she does because she's never been positively rewarded in the past when she has attempted to engage others. In fact, she probably has been shunned, teased, and scorned when she has tried to make friends with her new classmates.

Fixing the Pathway

I am a Rules/Rewards-Punishment advocate and believe in using Plan II. I want to follow a pathway to put the teacher in control until the desired behavior is accomplished. I realize improvement will be slow, but I am confident some improvement will be seen by the end of this year.

The steps along the pathway are to observe, collect baseline data, classroom rearrangement, positive reinforcement, modeling and shaping.

Overt Behaviors

There was one girl in our class who was attractive, outgoing and considerate. I suspected she might be able to get through to René. I decided to begin by rearranging the classroom and moving René beside Sue. I talked to Sue about befriending René, and she agreed. I arranged their seats so I could easily observe them.

My baseline experiment was very easy to do since René rarely ever talked.

For reinforcement, I smiled at her whenever I caught her quick glance. I touched her more often and talked to her just as I would the other students. However, I never put her on the spot for a reply that would take more than a nod of the head.

My long-range goal for René was for her to communicate and interact socially. To do this, she needed self-confidence. Every day for the first two weeks we had a class discussion about a story I read to the class for modeling. René has a weight problem that may make her feel different from the rest. The purpose of these stories was to show that everyone has a place and will be accepted as they are.

Assessment of Two-Week Implementation

Moving René beside Sue showed fast results. René would whisper occasionally but then look around to see if anyone was watching. When I caught René's eye, I would smile to show my approval.

Improvement was slight but successful, since she did say a few words occasionally. At the end of the two weeks I did a baseline experiment again. During the day she was speaking to me a minimum of four times and telling me about her former school.

Future Overt Behaviors

Now that René is beginning to interact with others, I plan to move towards greater student control. I plan to set up group projects so I can conduct classroom meetings (as Glasser suggests) with René and a small number of students. This way she may, after some time, feel free to talk in such a non-threatening situation and eventually even propose ideas for the group.

Author's Comments: Here we have a case of a Rules/Rewards-Punishment beginning with positive reinforcement both in verbal and social form. This teacher has obviously eliminated the idea of using the more powerful techniques of punishment, or isolation because of sensitivity to this particular student. Since the reinforcement is successful, the teacher continues along Pathway II by next employing Glasser's classroom meetings.

A Confronting-Contracting Teacher—Plan III: Description of Student Behavior

The student is neat in appearance, well dressed, robust, and healthy looking. I have no reason to suspect that there is a health problem or other physical disability. However, the student does seem very tense, loud, and he handles materials, equipment, and games roughly.

He sometimes stays outside from five to ten minutes after lunch is over or remains in the restroom after the class has gone upstairs after the break. He then enters the room after the other students are quiet and settled into whatever activity they are doing. He always has a companion, though not always the same student. They come into the room making a lot of noise and disrupting whatever activity is taking place.

The student likes to take his time getting into lines in the room whenever the class is moving to another room. He usually then ends up, by his own design, at or near the end of the line. As soon as the teacher (who is at the front of the line) turns the other way to lead the class to its destination, the student in question knocks over displays in the room, takes things off the bulletin board by the door and drops them into the wastebasket, drops books from the box of books to be returned to the library into the wastebasket, kicks, pushes, fights, or otherwise causes a commotion at the end of the line, or leaves the line and takes another route to the place the class is going.

During class time, he talks without raising his hand and talks back to the teacher.

During class discussion periods or when the teacher is reading to the class or explaining something, he rocks back and forth in his seat.

Although the tardiness takes place mostly in the morning, the other misbehaviors take place about every fifteen to twenty minutes throughout the day.

This student always involves at least one other student when he comes in tardy or when he misbehaves outside the classroom. It isn't always the same student, but it is always one or several of the same five or six boys. Many of the students who frequently misbehave admire the student with whom I am working and will do just about anything he suggests, even though he always is the boss and frequently ends up screaming or physically fighting with them. He is both physically and verbally very aggressive.

Academically, the student has few problems. He seems to like most of the subject matter and his work is above average. He does, however, hurry through projects and assignments and, as a result, much of his work is below his best efforts. He does get right to work after assignments are made, works best under very structured circumstances, and loves to help with classroom housekeeping duties. He does, however, frequently undo some of the cleaning and straightening he has done so well in an effort to make these jobs last longer.

He responds well to positive reinforcement and encouragement.

My efforts to change his misbehavior up to the time this case study formally began included ignoring first offenses, conferences, directive statements, lost recesses, and isolation. None of these was effective for more than two days.

The student loves to draw, is interested in cars, trucks, motorcycles, science-fiction characters, and looks forward to his visits with his father, who lives in another state and takes him home with him every other Saturday.

Interpretation of Behavior

In attempting to interpret my student's goals in his behavior, I asked myself the four questions Dreikurs suggests that teachers covertly ask themselves concerning their own emotions when this child misbehaves. I do feel annoyed and I sometimes feel beaten and intimidated. I think most of Mark's misbehavior is directed toward the goal of attention getting from his peers and from me, but I feel sometimes his goal is power.

In conference later, I asked my student the four sequential questions Dreikurs suggests:

Could it be that you want special attention?
Could it be that you want your own way and hope to be boss?
Could it be that you want to hurt others as you feel hurt by them?
Could it be that you want to be left alone?

From his reactions, I concluded that my first interpretations seemed correct, and I must try to find ways to give this student attention when he is not behaving appropriately and ways that he can have power that are useful to the class and rewarding to him, without engaging in a power struggle with the teacher.

Fixing the Pathway

I am a teacher who believes as the other Confronters-Contractors do that boundaries must be established and that students must be made aware of what those boundaries are. I like to share responsibilities, decision making, and power with my students, but I also reserve the right to clarify the rules and, once they are agreed upon, to enforce them.

I try to be actively involved with my students in warm, caring relationships, and I strive always to give them as much freedom as they can handle without hurting others or hampering the atmosphere for learning for others.

The plan I chose to use after I used Dreikurs's model for interpreting the student's behavior was Plan III, beginning with the techniques of the reality therapy model by William Glasser. Having earlier in the year tried methods using less teacher control and finding them not successful with this student, I liked the idea of helping the student to acknowledge the reality of his own inappropriate behavior and of giving that student the responsibility for making an acceptable plan for his own future behavior that will not infringe on the rights of others.

Overt Behaviors

After interpreting Mark's behavior and evaluating my past behavior with him and the approaches that did not work, I listed the changes I thought we could start with.

The changes desired first were:

Line up without fighting, kicking, or pushing.
Raise his hand when he wants to talk.
Come to class when the bell rings.
Take time to work carefully and to do a good job.

Overtly, I will:

- Ask him the "what" questions; press for a plan; have him sign the agreement.
- Tell him that I will give him the attention he wants when he is not talking out of order. Then I will make it a point to talk to him before school starts and again when he returns to my class from English at 11:30. I will call on him at least once every half-hour during the afternoon for at least two weeks. I will also give him time to share his drawings once each day for one month.
- Talk to him eight times each day when he is not talking out of order. Give him attention when he is behaving.
- Praise him for promptness when he comes to class on time and when he doesn't linger in the restroom after the rest of the class has returned to the room.
- Make sure this student lines up near the front of the lines when going to the restroom, to lunch, or to the library, since most of the misbehavior in lines occurs when this student is at the back of the line and I am at the front.
- When papers are very carelessly done, hand them back to be redone.
- When the student takes his time, works carefully, and turns in papers that are 90 percent accurate, post the papers on the bulletin board.

- Have class meetings the last fifteen to twenty minutes each day so that all the students can discuss anything that is bothering them at school or anything that pertains to them that they'd like to talk about.

Assessment of Two-week Implementation:

I think giving Mark attention before he misbehaves has helped him to fulfill his need for recognition and attention. He has worked hard to keep his commitment to raise his hand when he wants to speak. My goal those first two weeks was for him to raise his hand at least half of the time when he wanted to talk. He has reached this goal.

He has not, during these two weeks, been late to class. I have made sure this student was at or near the front of the line whenever he must line up. So far, this has decreased the number of problems in lines by about half. However, he still gets involved in fights once he enters the restroom.

His papers have been done more carefully, and all except two math papers have been at least ninety percent accurate. I have returned only one writing paper to be redone.

This student chose to have fifteen minutes free art time every Thursday afternoon if he has kept his agreement all week. He also gets to help me do bulletin boards when they need to be changed.

The student has agreed to stay after school for fifteen minutes to re-evaluate his behavior when he doesn't keep his plan. So far, we haven't had to do this.

The class meetings held the last fifteen to twenty minutes each day have improved the whole class's overall behavior and concern for one another. During this time, students have been very frank about how this student's misbehavior has hurt them. This, as much as any single thing, I think, has helped the disruptive student to see that students he felt he was impressing did not like having their thinking interrupted and did not like to be pushed and bullied in line and on the playground.

While classroom behavior has improved, behavior on the playground is still quite aggressive from this student, both physically and verbally.

Future Overt Behaviors

I will continue to re-examine my classroom behavior and my use of classroom time, and I will continue to strive for activities that motivate the students, capitalize on students' interests, and that help each child to fulfill his or her needs to feel worthwhile and to be involved with a teacher who cares about him or her. Specfically, with Mark I will continue to help him to achieve his goals for attention and power in ways that are acceptable and not disruptive to the class. Our conversations before class will continue, with the emphasis being Mark telling me what he wishes to talk about and what he values.

For the next two weeks, I will press for Mark to raise his hand seventy percent of the time for when he wants to talk, while giving him attention when he is behaving without talking out and giving him time to share his interests and his art with the class, through demonstrations and displays. I'll continue to let him know I appreciate his coming to class on time so that we can all begin our work without the interruptions caused by late-arriving students.

I think it is now time for us to sit down together to work out a new plan to improve aggressive behavior that is still taking place in the restroom, in the art room, at the library, and on the playground. If need be, I will make a contingency contract for him. Since Mark is seldom alone in the aggressive activities, I feel the conference now should involve him and the other five boys who are from time to time involved with him in the negative acts or who follow his misbehavior and disruptions by disruptive attention-getting behaviors of their own. They are all strongly influenced by his leadership.

The class meetings will continue, but from now on we will meet just on Mondays and Thursdays from 2:40–3:00, except when there is a special need to meet more often.

I will continue to believe that these students can and will improve their behavior when our relationships to each other are warm and trusting and when they are meeting their needs to feel worthwhile and successful.

Author's Comments: This Confronting-Contracting teacher pursuing Plan III has given us a good example of the "fork in the road." She chose to begin with overt behaviors, Dreikurs's questions, Glasser's "what" questions, making a plan, and classroom meetings, as well as a liberal dose of behavior-modification praise. After two weeks of having some techniques be successful, she proposed to have more individual conferences with Mark now that he felt free to vent his feelings and attitudes. Now she used active listening and value questions to let Mark explore his inner feelings. Yet, in areas where Mark has not made satisfactory progress, the teacher increased her power by making his group come up with a plan or abide by her contingency contract.

SUMMARY

In summary, all the plans described suggest that the teacher advance and retreat across the power continuum using techniques based on whether they succeed or fail to change student behavior. We have used the three individualized discipline plans as constructs to demonstrate how we can carry out such a progression and regression of teacher power. The teacher should not employ these constructs as rigid recipes and should not move mechanically through the techniques without real thought or sensitivity. It becomes both the teacher's responsibility and challenge to use the constructs and techniques in a sensitive manner. The creative teacher will, at times, devise his or her unique plans based on personal values, professional skill, the realities of the situation, and uniqueness of the student.

13

Decision Making Based on the Degree of Seriousness of Student Behavior

In the day-to-day school life of a teacher, he or she is repeatedly approached, even inundated, by students. Questions, remarks, behaviors, and misbehaviors as students knock on the door or pull at the teacher's shirtsleeve are signals that alert the teacher to student needs. What is a way of making sense of this barrage of demands, prioritizing severity of needs, and making reasonable responses? Each discipline model described in earlier chapters provides a limited range of responses to student behavior. Teachers who say that their starting point in reacting to student behavior is not their own needs and beliefs but instead the needs of the student, must first determine the seriousness or severity of student misbehavior. Only then can these teachers determine the degree of power and overt behaviors that should be used. For these teachers the criteria for decision making focus on the student and the situation. In the following four situations, would your behavior to the students be the same or different? What is the information that you would use in deciding to act?

Situation 1: Carol has recently come to school unclean, improperly dressed, and today you discover that serious burn marks are on her body running from the neck down to her back. The burns are discolored and in need of immediate medical treatment.

Situation 2: Tom, who has never been a problem student, starts a fight in the cafeteria. You discover that last night his alcoholic father kicked him out of the house and he spent the night sleeping on the floor in his sister's home.

236

Situation 3:   Anita, who has been identified as a gifted child, has recently because of a busing mandate been transferred to your school where she is now a minority student. She has complained of nausea, fails to complete her work, and has repeatedly fallen asleep in class. Her behavior is in complete contrast to reports from her previous school where she was a straight-A student and involved in many school leadership activities.

Situation 4:   Beth today is belligerent to you. She cursed you when you made a normal demand on her. You know her to be a most competent and popular student. In the fall semester, she was elected Queen of the Christmas Ball. However, you now know that two weeks before the ball, she and her boyfriend broke up and no other boy has asked her to the dance.

Most teachers will realize that some of these situations are clearly discipline problems, while others may call for counseling and legal action and others may be seen as no real business of the teacher. However, each situation, although varying in the degree of severity, demands teacher help and intervention. Each situation requires the teacher to make a reasoned and orderly decision. The way of responding to these situations is to determine the degree of power conveyed by the techniques in the Teacher Behavior Continuum that is appropriate to the situation. Various incidents may call for a Relationship-Listening response, others a Confronting-Contracting response, others a Rules/Rewards-Punishment response, or even a legalistic-coercive approach that goes beyond the teacher and the school's authority. The following construct may give some clarity to the problem of determining appropriate teacher responses to particular situations.

Needs of the Students

Let's review the four examples previously mentioned: Carol's bodily injury; Tom's fighting and being kicked out of his home; Anita's passive, emotional response to adjusting to a new school; and Beth's irritability and outburst due to her inability to secure a date to attend the dance in which she will be honored. Obviously each of the situations is related to a need of the student. An analysis of this need by a construct such as Maslow's (1970) hierarchy can give order to what appears to be unrelated behaviors of students.

From a Maslovian position, in order for students to gain self-fulfillment or become self-actualized (Level IV), the person's lower needs must be met before higher needs can become a focus of interest. In other words, one must first meet the physiological needs of food, water, and basic physical health

TABLE 13–1. Maslow Needs

Levels	
IV	Self-Actualized
III	Belonging
II	Security
I	Physiological

care as seen in Situation 1—physical injury (Carol). Once these physiological needs are attained, security can become the focus for a student's energies and the teacher can attempt to establish a safe, dependable future such as seen in Situation 2—loss of home and fighting (Tom). Having obtained some sense of security, the student next needs belonging: to become a member of a group, a place—or school. We can see the need for belonging in Situation 3—a gifted child without friends. Anita is having difficulty adjusting to a new group. Moving still higher along the Maslow hierarchy to the level of self-esteem needs, the attainment of respect by one's peers, we see Situation 4 can be related to the self-esteem of Beth—how will she appear to her peers with no date for the ball to honor her as Queen? A teacher can analyze the behavior of the student and identify what particular need is being blocked and where this need falls in the Maslovian hierarchical arrangement. The teacher is then ready to evaluate the degree of crisis of these problems.

DEGREES OF CRISES

When looking at needs based on Maslovian hierarchical levels, the teacher will see that the degree of seriousness of the situation will vary from life-threatening (injured child) to limited seriousness (Beth and the lack of a date for the ball). We may classify degrees of crisis, moving from most to least serious, as a) imminent crisis; b) developing crisis; and c) potential crisis (McMurrain, 1975).

a. Imminent Crisis

Imminent crises would be those situations where *physiological* needs are involved. At the extreme level, this means a life-threatening or bodily-harm situation. If Carol's burns are not immediately treated with medical care, irreversible damage will occur. Time is of the utmost importance with this incident. Witout immediate and forceful teacher action, the most serious consequences could occur to the student; the situation is life threatening.

b. Developing Crisis

The developing crisis is generally related to the blocked needs of Level II: *security*. The consequences are serious, but there appears to be more time to stop the event from moving to an imminent crisis. Tom's fighting and the loss of his home is a developing crisis. If changes do not occur to enable him to reestablish a secure home, we can speculate that his behavior will continue to regress into more destructive behavior with the real likelihood that Tom (or a target of Tom's) could become physically harmed. The case of Anita, the gifted child in a new school, also can be seen as the blocked need of belonging and be labelled as a developing crisis. She appears to be in turmoil but, according to evidence from her former school, the condition is not typical of Anita.

c. Potential Crisis

In the case of Beth, the queen of the ball and without a date, the need level is *self-esteem*; this is only a potential level of crisis. The situation is causing seriousness and anguish to a student such as Beth, but the seriousness is related to a blow to her self-esteem. With empathetic support from an adult, Beth can probably find an answer to her dilemma, and in time the crisis will pass.

THE TEACHER'S HELPING BEHAVIOR

With the understanding of the two related constructs, Maslow's hierarchy of needs and the levels of crisis, we come to the question of what actions or "help" the teacher should take in response to such student behaviors. The answer is found in the construct of the continuum of discipline approaches previously described. Chart 13−2 displays the relationship among needs, crises, and discipline approaches.

TABLE 13–2. Needs, Crises, and Discipline Approaches

Needs	Crises	Model

Level IV
Self-esteem
	P
	  O
	    T
	      E
	        N
		Relationship-Listening

Level III
Belonging
	T
	   D I
	    E A
	      V L
	        E
	          L
		Confronting-Contracting

Level II
Security
	O
	         P
	        I
	         N
	          G
		Rules/Rewards-Punishment

Level I
Physiological
	I
	   M
	    M
	      I
	        N
	         E
	          N
	            T
		Coercive/Legalistic

The degree of power of the teacher's intervention would escalate or deescalate according to the level of need and the severity of the crisis. In other words, rather than being model-oriented (always using TET, reality therapy, etc.), the teacher's approach becomes eclectic, based on a needs-crisis-seriousness construct.

In the case of Beth, the queen of the ball, the need level is self-esteem, and we have a potential level of crisis. The helping techniques for the teacher are found in the Relationship-Listening models. Gordon's TET talks about problem ownership and the need to establish an accepting relationship to help the student come to some emotional control over a problem and use "no lose" problem solving. The teacher could also give TA strokes and help Beth to think about *Adult* responses to finding a date for the dance; value-clarification techniques might also help her rethink her problem in terms of long-range goals.

TET
Critical listening
Acknowledgment responses
Door opener
Active listening
Method III ("no lose"):
  six steps to problem solving
"I" message

TA
Respond with the *Adult*
Give strokes

```
********************
*                  *
*      BETH        *
*  Queen of the Ball *
*                  *
********************
```

Value Clarification
Value-clarifying discussion
Question based on valuing
  choosing freely
  choosing from alternatives
  choosing after considering consequences

  prizing
  affirming
  acting
  repeating

FIGURE 13–1. Needs: Level IV—Self-esteem Crisis: Potential Models: Relationship-Listening

In the case of Anita, the gifted new student, the blocked need is belonging and suggests a developing crisis. The techniques of confronting and contracting seen in Glasser or Dreikurs's models would be most useful and appropriate for the teacher in dealing with such situations. Both models place a high value on getting needs met in a social context and give clear suggestions on how to accomplish a positive sense of belonging. The teacher could determine by the use of Dreikurs's questions that Anita needs attention and assign her to a "buddy"—seat her with a gregarious student or engineer special classroom group activities where Beth would have positive interaction with classmates. Another possibility would be using Glasser's steps of

Dreikurs
Confronting
Question motivation
    attention-getting
    power
    revenge
    helplessness
Make a plan based on motivation
Use encouragement
Design class activities or class meetings
Do sociogram

```
************************
*                      *
*      Anita           *
*  Gifted new student  *
*                      *
************************
```

Glasser
Ask "what" questions
Help child develop a plan
Sign agreement
Intense counseling
Class meetings
With a lack of success,
    bring in principal, parent,
    outside agency

FIGURE 13–2. Needs: Level III—Belonging Crisis: Developing Models: Confronting-Contracting

establishing a mutual contract after finding out what Anita enjoys doing or conducting small classroom meetings to acquaint Anita with other class members.

In the case of Tom, whose problem was loss of home and fighting, the need level is security and the level of crisis can be considered a developing crisis. The teacher in this instance may choose techniques from the Rules/Rewards-Punishment model. This means that with Tom *and his parents*, the teacher (probably also with the help of the school administration) would specify actions to be followed by Tom and the parents. To stop Tom's fighting, the teacher could set up a contingency contract based on earning points for good behavior or a punitive plan for known defiance involving levels of isolation, detention, etc. At the same time the teacher would need to

Behavior Modification
Set up contingency with Tom
Establish positive and negative
  reinforcers
Set up contingency with Tom's father
Establish positive and negative reinforcers

```
***********************
*                     *
*       Tom           *
* Loss of home/fighting *
*                     *
***********************
```

Assertiveness
Establish rules for Tom's behavior
Establish rules for Tom's father
Tell both Tom and Father the discipline
  action you will follow
Use broken record if necessary
If necessary, Tom may be removed from
  school

Behaviorism with Corporal Punishment
Identify rules
If student knowingly breaks rule, give
  him reason to regret
Immediate reinforcement

FIGURE 13–3. Needs: Level II—Security Crisis: Development Models: Rules/Rewards-Punishment

be assertive and follow up with Tom's parents, the principal, or a social worker to see that Tom's needs for security are being met.

If Tom and his parents are fulfilling expectations, every effort should be made to be positively reinforcing. If these techniques do not work, the developing crisis will become an imminent one, and physical harm is a real possibility to Tom and others. The teacher would move to the coercive/legalistic approach mentioned in the next case. The coercive/legalistic approach acknowledges that help must be sought beyond the teacher and the school and may include using a social service agency or mental health facility to get family counseling, or even involve legal authorities.

In the case of Carol, the injured student, the need level is physiological and the crisis is imminent. This life-threatening situation calls for very powerful intervention that is really beyond any particular discipline model. We call such emergency actions coercive/legalistic behavior. When time is of utmost importance and the danger is so great, the teacher can use assertive-

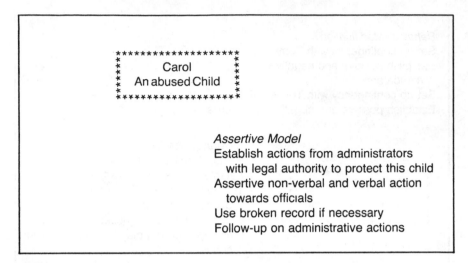

FIGURE 13–4. Needs: Level I—Physiological Crisis: Imminent Models: (Coercive/Legalistic)

ness techniques to get immediate help and legal protection for the child. Usually in such a serious case, the steps required by the teacher are set down by law and the teacher is bound to take assertive legalistic/coercive actions for the student's welfare. To clarify, coercive/legalistic is not a model but a process whereby the teacher's actions are clearly defined by law. To carry out this responsibility, assertive techniques can be a reassuring way for the teacher to confront authority.

The teacher assertively demands of the administration that legal actions be taken. If necessary, broken-record statements can be used to keep from being sidetracked. The teacher should check to see that the agreed-upon action, whether by the social welfare agency, the school board, or the police, has been taken.

SUMMARY

Teachers may find that assessing the degree of seriousness of student behavior is a helpful way to identify the type of crisis intervention needed. With a less serious situation (*possible* crisis), the teacher can behave in a less powerful way than in a dangerous situation (*imminent* crisis). It is not always easy to make a clear discrimination among crisis situations, but a teacher should still try to prioritize student behavior and act accordingly.

REFERENCES

Maslow, A. *Motivation and Personality*. New York: Harper & Row, Publishers, 1970.

McMurrain, Thomas. *Intervention in Human Crisis*. Atlanta: Humanics Press, 1975.

14

Decision Making
Based on Student
Social Development

After looking at the choices available from the three individual discipline plans and the degrees of seriousness of student behavior described in the previous chapters, there may be some teachers who reject those decision-making processes based on these described teacher values. Such teachers resist aligning themselves with Relationship-Listening, Confronting-Contracting, or Rules/Rewards-Punishment models. Instead, they say, "I do not accept any single model or school of thought. I see value in all models and would like to choose techniques based upon what I know about the individual student." Through their years of experience and professional training, such teachers believe that students (even those of the same age) grow, behave, and respond differently according to varying stages of growth and maturity. As suggested by Dreikurs, development of all behavior is an orderly process. This process is somewhat akin to the acquisition of motor skills: children learn to wiggle before they crawl, to walk before they run. If human behavior is orderly in its development, then generalizations can be made about what can be expected from a student at a certain time in his or her development. With knowledge of this developmental order, specific teacher interventions, based on models or pieces of models, can be judged to be the most compatible with certain times, conditions, and developmental stages of student behavior. With an understanding of these developmental patterns of socialized growth in their students, teachers can work in tune with these growth patterns. Conversely, there exists the possibility that, unknowingly, teachers may be using methods that are beyond a student's ability to comprehend, and thus the techniques being

246

employed will fail or, worse, their use will retard the student's growth toward maturity.

The material that follows on moral and social development may not seem, at first, meaningful to the upper elementary and secondary teachers who may question the relevance of focusing on the early development of their older students. Such questions are understandable because the study of social development stresses the early years of a youngster's life; however, it is only with an understanding of this period in a child's life and the *sequence* of the child's social and moral development (the sense of right and wrong), that the teacher can assess what stages a student has undergone and what stages are to follow.

Only then can the teacher be on target with disciplinary or intervention techniques *appropriate to the development stage and not the chronological age*. A quick example should suffice. It will soon be explained that, at the beginning stage of moral reasoning, a child (usually four to seven years old) will behave according to his or her egocentric view of the consequences of his or her behavior. Behavior is judged to be right or wrong by the child only in terms of whether he or she will be rewarded or punished. If the behavior is not punished, then it is all right to continue. The effects of such reasoning can also be seen among teenagers and adults. During the New York City blackout, when many adults went on a rampage of looting, the nation was provided with ample evidence of such first-stage moral reasoning. A television interviewer asked a looter carrying off a stereo set, "Why are you doing this?" The answer was, "Because it's dark, and I won't get caught." To try to reason with a person not using adult ethical principles would be for naught. Teachers who deal with students *of any age* can make a diagnosis and determine appropriate teacher action based on knowledge of the student's moral stage acquisition. The description that follows of social and moral stage acquisition will set a foundation for the making of decisions on appropriate teacher intervention.

SOCIALIZED BEHAVIOR: A DEVELOPMENTAL PROCESS

The acquisition of socialized behaviors by students, like all other forms of development, goes through stages. This development begins in early childhood (infancy through preschool), when the child is considered to be *prerational* and *egocentric* (self-centered). The child is highly demanding, shows little restraint in his or her interaction with others, and displays an attitude of, "I want it when I want it." This self-centeredness dissipates dramatically during the early elementary grades, when the school-age child generally becomes a cooperative, well-socialized worker. This school-age student learns to control his or her body impulses and refrains from using materials destructively, and he or she can carry out agreed-upon tasks with others to achieve a common goal (i.e., team games or group projects).[1] Although the elementary student has become a stable, cooperative rule-player and worker, it will not be until he or she has reached middle school, junior high school, or adolescence that the student will acquire sufficient intellectual abilities to be able to discuss and analyze *fully* his or her values and moral behaviors as they might relate to such issues as stealing, violence, drugs, sex, and prejudice.

What, then, is misbehavior from a developmental perspective? At the beginning, there is an infant living between two large islands of pleasure and discomfort. When the infant needs to be cared for (fed, diapered, or held), he or she expresses the need by crying and screaming. Obviously, for an infant, these forceful bodily demands cannot be labeled as "misbehavior," but as appropriate behavior for that stage. It would be unrealistic to expect an infant not to cry. The term "misbehavior" can only be applied when the behavior related to a stage is used at an age beyond the appropriate time. For example, parents would not become concerned about a baby who cries frequently at the age of two, but they would become increasingly concerned with episodes of frequent crying when the child is eight years of age. Parents and teachers usually can expect a student to be a socialized worker by the age of seven. This age serves as a general reference point for judging good behavior and misbehavior. We then ask, "How does this development proceed through the first seven years?"

THE FIRST SEVEN YEARS OF SOCIAL DEVELOPMENT

Passive Body-Centered Behavior

We have already mentioned the first year of life, when the child can be viewed as a relatively passive organism who reacts through bodily impulses. The infant's energy is directed to having bodily needs met. The infant, without mobility or coordination, is almost totally dependent on his or her caretakers.

Physically Aggressive Behavior

In the second year of life, the child learns to walk, and, as a result of his or her new-found mobility, can put distance between self and parents. As a result, the child often has to be supervised when he or she walks beyond the adult's immediate grasp. Parents, attempting to protect the innocent child from potential danger, inundate the two- or three-year-old with prohibitions in the form of such "no's" as, "*No*, you cannot play with mother's sewing kit," "*No*, give me the dangerous scissors," "*No*, don't ever run near the street," "*No*, stay away from the electric outlet!"[2]

These "no" commands continually interrupt the child's natural curiosity to see, touch, taste, and feel everything in sight. Remember, during the first year of life, the infant needed only to whimper or cry before the adult world would run to provide care. Suddenly, the tables are turned. Instead of parents accommodating the child, the child is being asked to accommodate the wider world. This is not an easy change to make. Imagine what it must be like for a child to be told, "Wait until after supper before you eat that piece of candy," or, "Use your spoon instead of your hands to eat your mashed potatoes." These commands, which delay immediate gratification and help in the socialization process, are necessary, but so are the child's early predictable responses to prohibitions.

Initially, the child reacts to those repeated "no's" and demands for delayed gratification with the first stage, *passivity*.[3] A child who is caught pulling the leaves off a house plant and is told "no" will often become immobile, possibly with thumb sucking, and will look at the adult with a glassy-eyed stare. However, this passive retreat does not last for long. With repeated prohibitions or "no's," the child lashes back with physical aggression.

In another example, when a child's father stops the toddler from exploring his shaving cream can, the child screams, cries, and strikes at the father by kicking, biting, or hitting. When the child previously responded with passivity, his or her energy was directed inward. With continued adult interference and socializing "no's," that energy is now directed outward in the form of physical aggression. For the immature toddler, as with the infant, it is accepted that such *aggressive behavior cannot be labeled as "misbehavior," but simply as a reflection of the toddler's immature abilities to understand and perform "correct" behavior*. This aggression is seen simply as energy turned outward, however misdirected it may be.

Verbally Aggressive Behavior

In late toddlerhood, this development of impulse control and physical aggression reaches a third phase called "verbal aggression." As an example, three-year-old Tommy discovers a five-pound box of Christmas chocolates. He rummages through the box, pushing large handfuls of candy into his mouth while scattering the excess across the living room rug. His mother suddenly appears from the kitchen and finds him in his full, chocolate-spattered glory. Upon seeing his mother, her expression, and the sudden movement towards him, Tommy begins to shout, "No, no, no!" at her.

How does one interpret his words? Children are not born with an understanding of how they are to behave and what they may and may not do. They must learn these prohibitions primarily from adults, either directly or by example, and the process is one of *setting limits*.[4] When we see Tommy saying "no" to his mother in this incident, we see that he is beginning to internalize or learn the prohibitions. Although, at this immature stage, they are easily forgotten, Tommy *at least* remembered the prohibition when his mother appeared. This is only one step away from remembering "no, no" beforehand, or for Tommy to intellectually say "no" to himself and thus inhibit his own behavior. The child verbalized what the adult would say. This internalization of "no's" or prohibitions is not fully complete until about the age of seven, when a rigid conscience is acquired (a reflection of early moral reasoning to be described later).

Children have a need to use language in an aggressive way to attempt to learn how language can be used to control their world, have their needs met, and to precipitate action. Children's use of verbal aggression such as "no" or the use of profanities toward adults may not be pleasurable by the adult's standards, but the child is learning an important lesson.[5] He or she is learning that language can be the vehicle for expressing actions, and that in turn it will inhibit the need for physical aggression. This use of language as verbal aggression is in direct contrast to the previous phases of physical aggression, when children attempted to "be the cause" through direct physical aggression toward others or when they experienced the initial phase of retreating into helpless passivity (i.e., immobility, staring blankly). Now that a child can use language outwardly to attack, it will not be long before he or she can use it inwardly to think about his or her behavior before taking action and in turn to censor his or her own behavior.

From a developmental perspective, one would prefer to have the pre-schooler or kindergarten child who has lost his toy to a classmate show such verbal aggression as, "No! No, you poopie-pants boy" rather than to show physical aggression by striking the classmate with a large building block. This can also hold true for the much older student who, when experiencing frustration, shows greater socialized stage of development by swearing rather than physically striking out. Although it may be difficult to accept that verbal aggression is more mature than physical aggression and that physical aggression is more mature than passivity, this structure provides the teacher with the "building blocks" for matching intervention techniques with the socialization scale and its accompanying behavior. In other words, a teacher needs to facilitate verbal aggression when a student continually displays physical aggression, and, to facilitate controlled forms of physical aggression when a student displays passivity, even though the actions being facilitated are not viewed as "correct" adult behaviors.

Effecting Social Interaction Through Language—
The Socialized Cooperative Worker

With the internalization of limits in the form of "no's" and the development of socialized language, the child can use this language to encode his or her strong feelings and to satisfy his or her needs.[6]

Internal language, as thought, is used to prohibit or censor certain actions before their enactment, and external language is used to ask for or to discuss with others ways of achieving desired ends. At the beginning of the elementary grades, the student has acquired these skills and has generally matured to the cooperative worker stage.

Reaching the acquired worker stage does not mean, however, that the socialization process is at an end. The student can work with others, but only within a framework of rigid adult rules that have been imposed and internalized. First-grade teachers can attest to this fact with their steady stream of students earnestly tattling on others who "broke the rules." It is not until much later that students become social persons or "adults" in the sense of having true consideration for others as well as a sense of moral principles.

Conceptualization Through Language—
The Attainment of Adult Maturity

At the approximate age of adolescence, most students acquire well-developed language and cognitive skills that enable them to think in terms of abstract concepts.[7] With this increased conceptual ability they can reflect on their behavior in relation to others and establish some guiding and individual principles. When they can understand why and how others act as they do and when they can clarify their own behavior in the context of long-range goals, they will emerge as truly "social persons" in their adult forms.

The Developmental Socialization Continuum (DSC) shown in Figure 14–1 illustrates the developmental progression from the stage of passivity to that of physical aggression, to the stage of verbal aggression, to the facilitation of social interaction through language. The span of time from passivity to

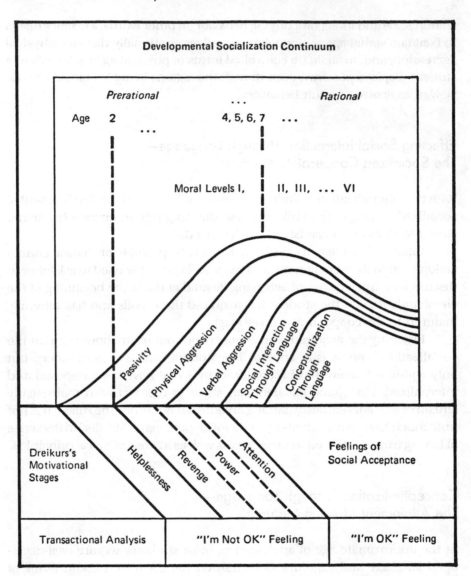

FIGURE 14-1. Developmental Socialization Continuum (DSC)

social interaction through language generally covers the first seven years of
life and is described as the prerational period. It is the period comparable to
that of Dreikurs's "misdirected goals"[8] or one's immature attempts to have
one's needs met. The stages evolve as the passive child withdraws from
prohibition, growing into a physically aggressive child who attacks the prohibitions through vengeful action. The child then becomes verbally aggressive,
using language as a powerful tool to overwhelm the prohibition, and finally

develops into the beginning social child who uses language as a means of expressing to others his or her needs. Through these prerational stages, the child behaves in descending degrees of conflict with others, as indicated by Harris's[9] "I'm Not OK" feeling of the *Child*.

The period from social interaction to conceptualization through language, from age seven to and through adulthood, can be called the rational period. It is the period of expanding moral reasoning and when such reasoning is no longer based on conflict but on mutual understanding. The student now acquires an "I'm OK" feeling of the *Adult* and the sense of Dreikurs's *Belongingness* or *Social Acceptance*. The key to this rational evolution is higher cognition, language abilities, and emotional security. For a more detailed explanation of the substages of moral reasoning, the reader may wish to refer to the Appendix.

SUMMARIZING DEVELOPMENTAL THEORY

For the first seven years of life, the child behaves without the use of rational language. All developing children go through the phases of *prerational* behavior (passive, physically aggressive, and verbally aggressive) that eventually fade away and are replaced by the *rational* levels. (See Figure 14–1).

From approximately the age of seven onward, the normal child will begin to use language and thought to understand his or her current behavior and to direct future behavior. As he or she moves from concrete to abstract thinking, reasoning as to the correctness of one's behavior similarly moves from self-centered standards ("What is going to happen to me?") to other-centered standards ("What would my teacher or friend say?") to societal standards ("What is the law?") and finally to individual standards based on self, others, and society ("What is morally right?").

Although these stages are described as distinct, it would be incorrect to view them as totally separate. In each case, the maturing child will show "carryover" examples of behaviors from previous stages. With the attainment of new stages, behaviors of previous stages will become less frequent; yet, such behaviors will still appear. These appearances may at times be appropriate. For example, when we are under great danger, such as being held at gunpoint, it might be prudent to be passive. We may even need to be physically aggressive to remove the traveling salesman from our door. Verbal aggression may also be needed before this salesman will finally leave. Fortunately, though, most mature adults can hold their impulses and strong feelings in check and deal with each other in a conflict by using socialized language. In our churches, courts of law, gatherings of friends, and in class-rooms, adults can exchange opinions with each other in order to conceptual-ize ideas about today's social or moral problems and thus manifest a higher level of moral behavior towards others.

In many cases, the dilemma of working with misbehaving students is that they are behaving at a level of development that is inappropriate. For example, a physically aggressive fifteen-year-old is of much greater concern than a physically aggressive five-year-old. The teacher who has a knowledge of development could more readily tolerate the five-year-old, but must act quickly to move the fifteen-year-old to the next, less harmful stage of verbal aggression.

Teacher-Student Interaction Models and Developmental Theory

With the Developmental Socialization Continuum (Figure 14—1) as a con-struct for viewing how children grow socially, two questions need to be asked.

1. What models will be the most effective at what ages of a child's development?
2. What models will permit the child to move to higher levels of moral understanding?

With some general brush strokes (Figure 14—2, Moral Centeredness and Intervention Models), the following suggestions can be made:

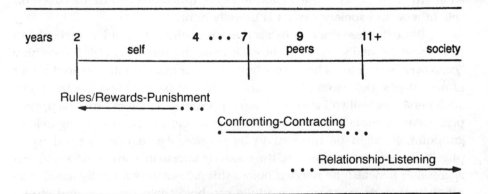

FIGURE 14—2. Moral Centeredness and Intervention Models

1. Rules/Rewards-Punishment models that are not based on the rational capacities of students might be highly effective with young children (prerational period) who have limited cognitive and language abilities.
2. The Confronting-Contracting models that are predicated on negotiation and peer collaboration might be ideally suitable for students in middle childhood (approximately ages seven to eleven). At this age, the student's reasoning is moving from Levels I and II or "What's in it for me?" to that of Level IV, "What are the rules of our society?" The student is becoming increasingly concerned with others and the larger social order.
3. The Relationship-Listening models, which assume rational and independent thought on the part of the student, might be most suitable for those in the age group of adolescence to adulthood. During this period, the student can think abstractly about his or her behavior and its present and future consequences.

Placing the schools of thought (Relationship-Listening, Confronting-Contracting, and Rules/Rewards Punishment) on this age continuum related to rational and prerational thought would create an overlap onto various stages of moral centeredness. With these developmental concepts and constructs in mind, we may now turn to specific techniques and various models to apply with stages of social development.

RATIONAL AND MORAL PROGRESSION AND REGRESSION

The developmental socialization processes and continuum (DSC) described earlier chart the ideal development path and are based on the normative or "average" behavior of children as they progress and mature through age levels and stages of development. But it is not the "average," well-socialized student who gives the classroom teacher behavioral problems. It is the one or two nonsocialized children in every classroom who "keep the teacher awake at night."

We hypothesize that these children have had their socialization retarded and have not progressed from passive or aggressive defensive behavior to that of employing rational abilities with their accompanying socialized behavior. This implies that elementary and secondary students, or even adults, demonstrate acting-out, destructive behavior that is prerational, much like the young toddler or preschool child.

We also suggest that these children or students have progressed or developed to the more rational forms of social behavior, but, because of some immediate emotional frustration or pressure, they have temporarily been emotionally "flooded" by their inner feelings. Thus, they have regressed to a more immature prerational behavior that erupts in the form of passive resistance, physical aggression, or verbal hostility to those whom they must deal with in a classroom environment.

We accept the position of the Rules/Rewards-Punishment school: that simply labeling a student (poor academic background, deprived home, low socioeconomic status, or even mentally retarded) does not change the situation; the teacher still needs to deal with the student's acting-out behaviors in the classroom. It is therefore our intention to select those overt and covert behaviors suggested by the many models presented to intervene with our "misbehaving" student whose actions place him or her somewhere from prerational behavior (passive, physically aggressive, and verbally aggressive) to rational behavior on the developmental continuum. This intervention, it is hoped, will help the child to attain the growth necessary to achieve a conceptual understanding of his or her own values and moral behaviors.

THE PASSIVE STUDENT (HELPLESSNESS)

The passive student, if viewed on our Developmental Socialization Continuum (DSC), has either not been able to find social acceptance or has retreated from the social world of peers, family, or school and appears to maintain himself or herself as if "hidden inside a shell." Dreikurs, we will remember in Chapter 6, suggested that such students could have retreated into a state of helplessness, where they want to be "left alone" and wish for the world to make no demands on them. We further suggest that Berne and Harris, in the Transactional Analysis model, characterize such passive students as having an "I'm Not OK" view of themselves (see Figure 14–3).

Characteristics: Generally such passive students or children are described as:

- Being in a dream world and appearing flat and expressionless in faciaɪ expressions and body behavior.
- Rejecting comfort, both in physical and verbal forms, from teachers and peers.

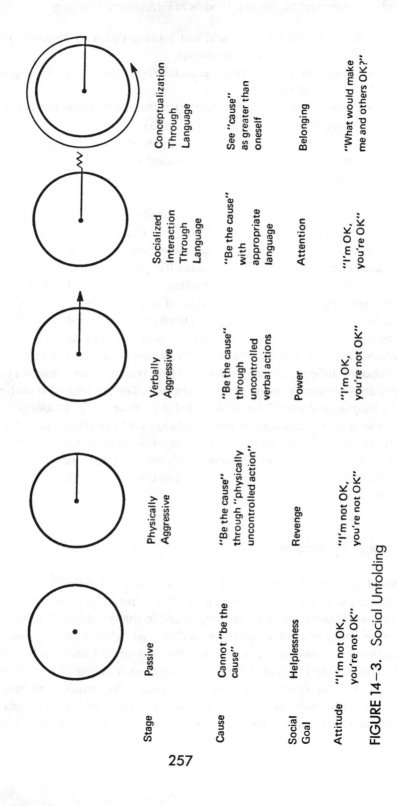

Stage	Passive	Physically Aggressive	Verbally Aggressive	Socialized Interaction Through Language	Conceptualization Through Language
Cause	Cannot "be the cause"	"Be the cause" through "physically uncontrolled action"	"Be the cause" through uncontrolled verbal actions	"Be the cause" with appropriate language	See "cause" as greater than oneself
Social Goal	Helplessness	Revenge	Power	Attention	Belonging
Attitude	"I'm not OK, you're not OK"	"I'm not OK, you're not OK"	"I'm OK, you're not OK"	"I'm OK, you're OK"	"What would make me and others OK?"

FIGURE 14—3. Social Unfolding

- Being social recluses and not joining peers in activities or games appropriate to their age group.
- Being difficult to arouse, stimulate, or motivate and being afraid to tackle new tasks.
- Usually drifting from activity to activity, never completing anything.
- Doing the opposite of what is asked.
- Saying, "I can't," rather than trying to do what is requested, with the request often having to be repeated.
- Being "lazy" and listless in class.

Often these passive children are described by parents and by some busy teachers as "well behaved," which suggests that they are not generally causing disruptions or engaging in aggressive conflict, and, therefore, they seem to "fade into the woodwork." Because the passive, nonaggressive behaviors exhibited by these students during a busy school day generally go unnoticed, the more aggressive acting-out student is in the "limelight" and gets the teacher's attention. If we accept our Developmental Socialization Continuum (DSC), we might suggest, along with the support of Dreikurs and the Transactional Analysis theory, that it is the passive student who has the greater emotional difficulty. It can be inferred that such passive students are in the grey area between normality and pathology. The teacher who wishes to use the techniques would be wise initially to have such students evaluated by a school psychologist or neighborhood child development clinic to see whether the child needs more skilled psychiatric intervention or therapy. We suggest that there may be some students who are outside the teacher's "sphere of competency," a subject we will discuss in greater detail at the end of this chapter.

Teacher Techniques

Based again on the Developmental Socialization Continuum, we hypothesize that the passive student of any age seems either to be locked into immature prerational behavior or to have regressed to that position. The teacher techniques or models that would provide the most help for this student are those that we have labeled Rules/Rewards-Punishment, as these are *not* based on the cooperative rational abilities of the student. If the passive student will not speak, we would have little success with such nonintrusive (minimal teacher power) techniques as found in the Relationship-Listening models such as Thomas Gordon's Teacher Effectiveness Training and its approach of "active listening." Our central goal in intervening with passive students is to have them turn their energies from the *inward* destructive behavior of excessive daydreaming and self-absorption to the *outward* energies directed toward an active social involvement. We suggest the covert and overt teacher techniques recommended in the behavioral model of the Rules/Rewards-Punishment school, with gradual movement to those of the Confronting-Contracting school, such as Glasser and Dreikurs. Chart 14–1 provides a list of teacher behaviors that would be appropriate for working with the passive student.

Keeping in mind the goal of having passive children turn their energies outward, we can experiment or more systematically use these teacher behaviors in our own creative way and approach.

The Rules/Rewards-Punishment people employ the powerful use of reinforcement to help passive students to engage with the outside world. Covertly, the teacher collects baseline data, establishes terminal behaviors, breaks down the terminal behavior into sequential steps, and mentally rehearses. For example, Caroline's passive behavior is reflected by her resting her head on the desk and by her failure to respond, either verbally or nonverbally, when addressed. The teacher sets the terminal behavior of Caroline responding (verbally and nonverbally) to others. This behavior is broken down into sequential steps, as follows.

1. Caroline will hold her head up and keep it off her desk for periods of five minutes.
2. She will look at the teacher when she is asked a question.
3. She will verbally respond when her name is called.
4. She will answer the teacher's questions with more than one-word responses.
5. She will initiate conversation by raising her hand and asking questions.

After identifying the sequence for shaping, the teacher will now use overt behaviors. Beginning with Caroline's first behavior (holding her head up for five minutes), the teacher will reinforce the desired behavior with a *continuously fixed schedule*. Once that behavior is conditioned, a random schedule can be used and the next behavior can be reinforced. The teacher can also use forms of modeling, through adult and peer examples, those behaviors that should be imitated. The most intrusive form of teacher behavior would be commands. "Caroline, get your head off the desk and hold it up" could be combined with physical modeling, such as, "Hold it up like this." The teacher physically holds Caroline's head up along with his or her own.

COVERT BEHAVIORS	OVERT BEHAVIORS

Rules/Rewards-Punishment

Assertiveness

COVERT BEHAVIORS	OVERT BEHAVIORS
a. Mental rehearsal	1. Give systematic rewards
b. Make a plan	2. Assertive nonverbal and verbal praise

Behavior Modification

a. Count student behavior (baseline experiment)	1. Shaping—Reinforcement
	2. Modeling
b. Establish terminal behavior desired	—peer
	—adult
c. Break down terminal behavior into sequential steps for shaping	3. Commands
	4. Avoid negative reinforcement or physical punishment

Confronting-Contracting

Glasser

a. Observe	1. Make classroom reorganization
—the student	
—the situation	
b. Assess	
—what the teacher is currently doing	

Dreikurs

a. Observe and collect information about the student	1. Questions of social goals: "Do you want to know why you are behaving like this?"
—with peers	
—with family	"Could it be that you want to be
—with other teachers	left alone?"
b. Ask oneself	2. Encouragement
"Do I feel . . .	—recognize student's attempt to
1) annoyed—attention getting	improve
2) beaten—power	
3) hurt—revenge	
4) incapable—helplessness	
c. Watch for recognition reflex	
d. Plan to incorporate student with others	

CHART 14–1. Passive Student and Teacher Techniques

Once Caroline imitates correctly, the teacher returns to reinforcement. Negative reinforcement or physical punishment should be avoided, as the passive child already feels worthless, and punishment may drive such a student into further despair.

The Confronting-Contracting techniques applicable to the passive stage can be found in both Glasser's and Dreikurs's work. Glasser's contributions are largely covert teacher behaviors, as his overt use of confronting questions and classroom meetings is predicated on a student actively responding. However, having the teacher observe the passive student and the situations where passivity is most or least evident can be very helpful. The teacher can assess what he or she is currently doing with the student in terms of instructional activities, materials, grouping, and physical placement. A determination can then be made as to whether certain materials, groupings, and so on, might be changed. Overtly, changes in the classroom can be then made that would be of greater interest and comfort for the student.

The Dreikurs model appears to provide some further understanding of the motivation behind passivity and how a teacher can help to redirect that motivation. Dreikurs's point of view is that the passive child has the mistaken goal of "helplessness," reflected in a desire to belong, but has given up. The teacher can help that student to learn to belong. The behaviors used would be directed toward affirming the student's goal of helplessness before determining a plan. The teacher would collect information about the student's interaction with peers, family, and other teachers. The teacher would ask, "How do *I* feel toward the student?" If the answer is "incapable," then helplessness can be suspected as the student's goal. The student would then be asked the verifying questions, and the teacher would look for the *recognition reflex* rather than for a verbal response. With the goal established, the teacher would then develop a plan for the passive student that would include a lot of encouragement from the teacher for the slightest attempt by the student to improve. The plan would also provide the student with tasks that he or she could handle successfully and that would help the class, and it would show other students that the student can be a contributing member.

Transition from Passivity to Physical Aggression

Fortunately or unfortunately, when the teacher is successful in turning the inner energies of the passive student outward, the student's behavior becomes physically aggressive. The student has a new awareness that he or she can have an impact on those outside persons from whom he or she previously had withdrawn. This new-found euphoria of control manifests itself in a testing of the limits and of finding out how much of a controller one can be. When the previously passive student comes out into the world and is then frustrated or denied by an object or person, it would be common for the student to lash out by kicking, spitting, or hitting. The student would try "to ram his or her will" against others.

THE PHYSICALLY AGGRESSIVE STUDENT

Description: It may be a difficult premise for some teachers to accept, but the expression of physical aggression by a previously passive student is a desired collection of behaviors that indicate the student is moving up the stages of socialization. The goal for a physically aggressive student is to help the student channel those physical acts into expressions of language. In the process of channeling those acts, the teacher must carefully guard against driving the student back into passivity.

The physically aggressive student finds the world a prohibitive place. Persons are always trying to stop the student from gratifying his or her desires, and the student feels that the way to get something is to attack. According to Transactional Analysis, the student has an "I'm OK; You're Not OK" attitude, and, according to Dreikurs, the student is operating with the misguided goal of *revenge*, to get back at those who prohibit.

This student needs little introduction to the experienced classroom teacher. He or she stands out and causes the teacher to always be wary. The teacher likens the student's presence to sitting near a keg of dynamite. Unlike dynamite, the student does not explode once and disintegrate; instead, he or she continually explodes with irrational, physical outbursts of behavior. As a result, this student often endangers others, personal and school property, and, at times, himself or herself.

Characteristics: Physically aggressive students usually display the following behaviors:

- When asked to move, look at their work, or any other similar request, they will physically refuse to do so.
- When frustrated because they do not get their way, they will throw a temper tantrum.
- If physically restrained by the teacher, they will fight back.
- They will constantly punch, kick, or trip other students.

- They will hurt themselves by taking unreasonable risks; e.g., jumping across a large hole, running into a wall, scaling and balancing from dangerous heights, or driving a vehicle to the edge of disaster.
- They will misbehave during classwork sessions, throwing spitballs and airplanes, grabbing books and papers, and throwing chairs to get the teacher's constant physical attention.

Teacher Techniques

Keep in mind that the teacher's task is twofold: first, to restrain the student's actions from hurting others or destroying property; second, to transfer physical action to verbal action. This brings back memories of a primary school teacher who had the following two classroom rules:

1. No hitting or swearing.
2. If you are going to hit, then swear instead.

Intuitively, this teacher knew that verbal aggression was to be valued over acts of violence.

As shown in Chart 14–2, the assertive approach would be to give the rules, let the student know that they will be enforced, not allowing the student to side track by use of broken record, and, if necessary, firmly asking the principal and parents to help. The *behaviorists'* approach of covertly collecting baseline data and deciding on a reinforcement plan would use the specific teacher behaviors of shaping, modeling with language, "time out," saturation, and extinction. *Shaping* would be targeting one desirable behavior at a time and reinforcing it. *Modeling with language* is a technique where the teacher stops a student from attacking and shows the student how to verbalize his or her feelings. For example, a student who begins to fight after being shoved by another student is stopped by the teacher and told (to state with Gordon's "I" message), "When I am shoved, I'm afraid I will fall and injure myself; that makes me frightened and then angry" (behavior effect-feeling). *"Time out"* is a technique that can often be used by removing the student from classroom activities to an area void of any stimulation. A time period should be established. If the student returns to the class and behaves in the same manner, the student should be removed again and the time period increased. The teacher can also use the process of *saturation*, where the student is made to repeat his or her aggressive act until it becomes tiring and negatively reinforcing. Such a case is the student who destroys the papers and work of others. This student could be required to take a large stack of old newspapers and tear page after page into little pieces. Obviously such techniques involve a great deal of teacher power, and they may come close to becoming negative reinforcement. On the other hand, if a student's aggressive behavior is not causing human or property damage, a less intrusive approach such as *extinction* can be used. The teacher simply withdraws any attention from the misbehavior. Such withdrawal usually causes an initial increase in the misbehavior before it begins to decline.

COVERT BEHAVIORS	OVERT BEHAVIORS

Rules/Rewards-Punishment

Assertiveness

a. Mental rehearsal	1. Give rules
b. Make a plan	2. Use broken record
	3. Carry through on plan
	4. Involve principal and, if need be, the parent
	5. Give systematic rewards

Behaviorists

a. Collect baseline data	1. Shaping
b. Decide on reinforcement program	2. Modeling with language
	3. "Time out"
	4. Saturation
	5. Extinction

Confronting-Contracting

Glasser

a. Observe	1. Make classroom reorganization
—the student	2. Confront the student with
—the situation	commands. "Stop that." "The
b. Assess	rule is . . ."
—what the teacher is doing	3. Confront the student with "what"
—what success the student is having	questions in private or *classroom meeting:*
	"What are you doing?"
	"What are the rules?"
	"In what ways is your behavior helping you?"
	4. Press for a plan
	5. Reap the consequences
	6. Levels of isolation
	—repeat steps 2, 3, 4, and 5

Dreikurs

a. Observe and collect information about student
—with peers
—with family
—with other teachers
b. Ask oneself "Do I feel . . . hurt? revenge?"
c. Recognition reflex after verifying question

1. Questions of social goals:
"Do you want to know . . . ?"
"Could it be that you want to hurt others?"
2. Make a plan; protect the student from being hurt.
3. Use the whole class for support
4. Natural/logical consequences
5. Encouragement

Relationship-Listening
Gordon
1. Verbalizing student actions
Harris
1. Teach TA, emphasizing the *Child* construct

CHART 14–2. Physically Aggressive Student and Teacher Behaviors

Confronting-Contracting approaches attempt to help the student to verbalize concerning his or her actions. Glasser tells the teacher to observe the classroom situation covertly to decide first whether any reorganization of the student's environment should be attempted. The teacher then proceeds to force the issue. This is done by confronting the student with commands and repeating the rules. The student is asked to describe his or her behavior, explain the rules, determine the effectiveness of aggression, and detail a collaborative plan. This is followed by being held accountable for the agreed-upon consequences of the plan. Failure to comply results in being placed in a level of isolation (in class, in school, at home, or in an institution), with the student having the opportunity to remake a plan at every level. It is important to note Glasser's advocacy of *classroom meetings* and how they apply to the physically aggressive pupil. The student who is ruled by his or her bodily impulses thinks of no one else but self (egocentric, prerational thought). The classroom meeting, as a forum for an all-class plan, may facilitate a student's thinking about others. All students have the opportunity to tell the physically aggressive student point-blank the effect that his or her behavior is having on them. Such a group encounter, wherein the offending student is put on the spot, might seem overly harsh, but it could be just what the student needs to hear.

Dreikurs's use of collecting information and then using social-goal questions is another way of introducing language as a substitute for physical aggression. Once the teacher has verified revenge as the misdirected student goal, he or she can develop a plan that will incorporate a lot of care, attention, and protection for the student. The teacher will not play into the student's game by showing hurt, but instead will try to remain calm and friendly. The teacher could privately ask the class for help by having them be responsive to the student, by including the student in their activities, and by walking away from any conflict with the offending student. Any aggressive behavior by the student should be met with natural or logical consequences rather than with punishment, such as having the student repair the broken chair (and standing at his or her desk until the glue sets) instead of being required to stay after school or being scolded. The process of encouragement, including recognition of the student's attempts to improve and having faith in that improvement, should be an ongoing one.

A few of the Relationship-Listening writers' techniques are also suitable to this stage of development. Gordon's use of nondirective statements, wherein the teacher gives verbal meaning to a student's action, facilitates social growth. For example, the teacher who says, "Tina, you must be mad at Charles to tear his sweater," enables the student to see the relationship between thought and action. Likewise, Harris's *Child* construct is similar to the actions of the physically aggressive student, and the terms *Parent, Adult,* and *Child* can be taught to the student to permit the child to reflect on his or her actions.

Transition from Physical Aggression to Verbal Aggression

One form of "adult misbehavior" replaces another as a student moves up the ladder of social development. The physically aggressive student who learns to use verbal aggression is making progress. The teacher should support (within realistic limits) students who fight with their mouths instead of their hands.

THE VERBALLY AGGRESSIVE STUDENT

Description: The consolidation of this stage is evident by the student who "leads" with his or her mouth. He or she is the boss, commanding, scolding, yelling, and demanding. The student is using words to get his or her way. The louder and more violent the language, the student reasons, the greater will be his or her success. This posture, according to Transactional

Analysis, is still an "I'm OK; you're not OK" view. According to Dreikurs, the misguided social goal is now control, to manipulate others through language. The student is still prerational and egocentric, thinking only of his or her needs rather than the needs of others. Students of this stage are perhaps seen as the most common "problems" in elementary and secondary schools. Be of good cheer, as this is only one stage from rational, socialized thought.

Characteristics: The verbally aggressive student displays some of the following behaviors:

- Makes fun, teases, and ridicules other students.
- Swears at other students.
- Jokes and laughs when asked to be serious.
- "Sasses" or is sarcastic toward the teacher.
- Yells out with inappropriate comments during class instruction.
- Gets into frequent shouting matches.
- Laughs and is openly amused when other students are being reprimanded.

Applying Techniques

Unlike the physically aggressive student, these pupils generally do not cause physical harm or destruction. Instead, they are a constant nuisance and annoyance to the teacher and class. As a result, the teacher no longer needs the powerful controlling techniques of the Rules/Rewards-Punishment writers; instead, he or she may now want to employ techniques of the Relationship-Listening writers, who support the use of language, and then move to the Confronting-Contracting writers, who put language to use in a purposeful and constrained manner. Please refer to Chart 14−3.

Verbal aggression is the student's attempt to verbally *encode* his or her feelings and ideas. Statements like "I hate you" or "You're a turkey" are beginning efforts (however poor) by a student to tell someone what he or she really means and feels. In detailing techniques, teachers should believe that verbal aggression is a stage that must be temporarily accepted so he or she will respond (as Dreikurs suggests) in a way that is disengaged from the emotion, without feeling beaten and without verbally lashing back. If the teacher responds harshly, then the student's poor attempt to communicate is cut off and the child may be driven back to committing physical aggression as the only way to communicate his or her feelings and desires.

COVERT BEHAVIORS	OVERT BEHAVIORS
	Relationship-Listening
	Gordon
a. Reorganizing the space	1. Critical listening
b. Reorganizing the time	2. Acknowledgment responses
	3. Door reopeners
	4. Active listening
	5. "I" messages
	6. Method III ("no lose") problem solving

Harris

a. Diagnose interaction state—verbal aggression as a "child/or parent" state	1a. Ask the student questions, adult to adult
	b. Reply to student's verbal aggression with adult statements
	c. Use adult responses to clarify student's verbal aggression
	2. Affirm the student as "OK" with complementary transactions

Confronting-Contracting

Dreikurs

a. Observe and collect information about the student —with peers —with family —with other teachers	1. Confronting: "Do you want to know why you are behaving like this?"
b. Ask oneself, "Do I feel . . . beaten"—control	2. Verifying: "Could it be that you want . . . to be boss"—power
c. Recognition reflex after verifying question	3. Make a plan according to verified goal—let the student have power
	4. Use the class group
	5. Natural/logical consequences
	6. Encouragement

Glasser

a. Observe —the student —the situation	1. Confront the transgression: "Stop that, the rule is . . ."
b. Assess —what the teacher is currently doing —what success the student is having	2. Ask "what" questions: "What are you doing?" "What are the rules?" "In what ways is your behavior helping you?" "What is your plan?"

CHART 14–3. Verbally Aggressive Student and Teacher Behaviors

3. Press for plan
4. Have student reap the consequences of plan
   Use levels of isolation—repeat steps 2, 3, 4, 5
5. Classroom meetings

Rules/Rewards-Punishment
Behaviorists

a. Collect baseline data
b. Decide on reinforcement

1. Nonverbal extinction
2. Contingency contracting

CHART 14–3. Verbally Aggressive Student and Teacher Behaviors (cont'd)

The techniques of Teacher Effectiveness Training are a good starting point. Covertly, the possibility of classroom reorganization needs to be considered if circumstances exist that would trigger the child's verbal barrage. The overt techniques would be to listen to the student's emotional responses, remain detached, and wait for the student to calm down and think about what is being said. This can be accomplished through critical listening, acknowledgment responses, door openers and reopeners, active listening, and, if the behavior has a concrete effect on the teacher, the use of "I" messages. After the student has been supported in expressing his or her true feelings, socialized language can then be attempted by using *Method III* ("no-lose") problem-solving techniques.

The other Relationship-Listening model that speaks to verbal aggression is Transactional Analysis. Such language is conveyed through either the impulse-ridden *Child* or the overbearing *Parent*. The teacher should ask questions from the *Adult* state directed to the student's *Adult*. Affirming the student as "OK" with a complementary transaction is important, for if there is cross-communication (i.e., *Parent* to *Child*), then the student would retreat into an "I'm Not OK" view, give up using language, and resort to violence.

Once a student has become calm, then almost all the overt and covert behaviors of the Confronting-Contracting models could be used. Dreikurs's concept of the "power"-hungry child intertwines with the verbally aggressive stage. After verifying the goal, the teacher could then establish a plan that would give the student power in a socially acceptable manner. The teacher needs to avoid becoming involved in an escalating power struggle with the student, where one of them will win big and the other will be humiliated.

Only sections of Glasser's model would apply to this stage. His covert observations and assessments and overt classroom changes used as preventive measures are valuable; yet, the reader will notice how the uses of confrontation and isolation have been omitted in Chart 14—3. The student needs the opportunity to defuse his or her emotions through verbal communication; confrontation and isolation stop the student from doing so. On the other hand, after the student has gained some control over his or her strong feelings, then "What" questions, pressing for a plan, reaping the consequences, classroom meetings, and possibly isolation would be in order. In the same manner, the behaviorists' use of nonverbal extinction, wherein they ignore the child's behavior but still allow the student to express himself or herself and then reward social or appropriate language through a contingency contract, could also be justified.

Transition from Verbal Aggression to Social Interaction Through Language

The student begins to think not only of his or her wants but also of the consequences of his or her actions. The student's verbal aggressions become less frequent, and he or she settles down and is able to talk about why they occurred. The student's moral reasoning begins to emerge in its most elementary form at Level I—the punishment and obedience orientation—and Level II—instrumental-relativist orientation. Previous prerational explanations for verbal aggression such as, "He's a jerk! I hate him!" change to concrete statements such as, "Because I wanted that pen, I thought it was mine!" or "I don't like to be pushed around," or "It's not *fair* for them to do it when I can't!"

THE SOCIAL-INTERACTION-THROUGH-LANGUAGE STUDENT

Description: At this stage of development, it is difficult to classify behaviors as disruptive. Students will fight, they will verbally attack, and they will not always respond to the teacher's commands; yet, these students are seen as "normal" because the teacher can reason on a basic level with them. Dreikurs would classify their goal as attention, and to achieve it they will annoy the teacher from time to time; yet, they have enough language ability, self-control, and reasoning to know how far they can go before the teacher will become excessively angry. In other words, they think through their actions. Harris would say that they have an "I'm OK; You're OK" attitude. The only missing aspect of true social behavior is logical adult reasoning that takes the standards and concerns of others into consideration.

Characteristics: Students possess some of these divergent characteristics:

- Being teacher's pet: they are over eager to please, and will volunteer for anything.
- Being the class humorist: they interject laughter or jokes that break up the class and amuse the teacher.
- Being the cause of occasional "accidents": someone gets tripped, or a chair falls backwards and disrupts the classroom decorum.
- Pretending to need help with their classwork, from the teacher or from other students, when none is really needed.
- Being quick to point out others who are breaking the rules.
- Conforming to peer standards of dress and manners.

Application of Techniques

The central goal of working with a student at this stage is to consolidate the student's awareness of his or her behavior and then expand the student's awareness of consequences to include a concern for others. The models that most closely represent this stage are the Confronting-Contracting writers and the comprehensive treatment of the Relationship-Listening writers. (See Chart 14–4.)

Glasser's step of asking the student "what" questions enables the student to focus on the outcome of his or her behavior (Level I—Moral Reasoning: the punishment and obedience orientation). "What" questions, followed by *Dreikurs's* verified goal of attention, help to formulate a plan that gives the student the attention he or she craves. A plan that incorporates logical consequences provides the student with further consideration of what he or she gains by acceptable behavior (Level II—Moral Reasoning: the instrumental-relativist orientation).

Aside from a disruptive incident, *Gordon's* use of active listening combined with certain *values-clarification* exercises enlarges the student's awareness of other criteria for behavior (Level III—Moral Reasoning: the interpersonal concordance, and Level IV—Law and Order Orientation). To help the student to further organize his or her thinking about present and fu-

COVERT BEHAVIORS   OVERT BEHAVIORS
                    Confronting-Contracting
                         Glasser
                              1. Confront the student with "what"
                                 questions:
                                 "What are you doing?"
                                 "What are the rules?"
                                 "In what ways is your behavior
                                 helping you?"

                          Dreikurs
a. Verify the goal—attention   1. Make a plan—give attention
                                    2. Logical consequences

                    Relationship-Listening
                  Raths, Harmin, and Simon
a. Avoid judging, influencing, or   1. Look for values indicators
   imposing teacher values   2. Informal values questions: seven
b. Look for values indicators   criteria
   —clues with teacher   3. Formal exercises:
   —clues with others   —ranking
                                       —sorting
                                       —role playing
                                       —literature
                                       —composition

                          Gordon
                              1. Active listening

CHART 14–4. The Social Interaction Through Language and Teacher
Behaviors

ture behaviors, the teacher can use values-clarification questions and formal exercises such as ranking, sorting, role playing, assigned reading, and
composition.

Transition from Social Interaction Through Language to Conceptualization Through Language

A student who is moving across stages will no longer be disruptive. He or she
may break a class rule, but it will be because of a rational decision to do so.
One of the signs that the student's use of language is becoming more abstract

and indicative of higher levels of moral reasoning (Levels III and IV) is when he or she shows obvious interest in listening to another student's ideas of how to resolve real-life dilemmas. Although the student's reasoning is still based on a "What's in it for me?" outlook, eventually the student will begin to reason according to considerations of others (i.e., "What would others think?" and "What are the laws of society?").

THE CONCEPTUALIZATION-THROUGH-LANGUAGE STUDENT

Description: This is the stage where most of us would like to see all our students. The student reasons as a mature adult and wishes to grapple with such value issues as war, sex, drugs, and crime. He or she is interested in knowing how these issues relate to society at large. The student may challenge the teacher's authority or label the rules of a particular class or society as being "unjust," but the student will be open to debating the issue. The teacher may need to be sufficiently flexible to change a classroom rule if the student has a valid point. A teacher who fails to use higher moral reasoning at this juncture and stands behind the "cloak of authority" could make a student retreat to previous stages.

Characteristics: Following are some behaviors of conceptualization-through-language students.

- They question the teacher and students about their own beliefs and behaviors.
- They actively listen and respond to group discussions about classroom and societal issues.
- They bring such considerations as "the good of all of us" into discussions.
- They attempt to reason with others who are practicing behaviors (stealing or drugs, for example) that they feel are detrimental.

Application of Techniques

The goal of the techniques involved is to facilitate a student's moral development from Level III (Interpersonal Concordance) and Level IV (Law and Order Orientation) to Level V (Social-Contract) and Level VI (Universal-Ethical). It would be unrealistic for us to attempt to describe or even profess the ability to know how to do this in a systematic way. These students are not disruptive and are therefore largely beyond the scope of this book; however, we would suggest the use of the Confronters-Contractors' classroom meetings, educational change for a democratic classroom, and the Relationship-Listening writers' group discussions of values, moral dilemmas, and "no lose" problem solving as particularly applicable. (Refer to Chart 14–5.)

Dreikurs's notion of reassessing for educational change is applicable when the teacher allows the individual student to choose many of his or her own activities and schedules, thus facilitating individual responsibility independent of imposed rules and regulations (Level V—Moral Reasoning-Social Contract). The same independence can be promoted by allowing students to engage in Glasser's classroom meeting, where real classroom problems are discussed and group rules are made. Group exercises of Raths, Harmin, and Simon that stimulate alternative actions through role playing or discussion of moral dilemmas can facilitate all levels of moral reasoning. *Gordon's* use of individual problem solving through *Method III* is an excellent means for a student to plan behavior according to personal codes of right and wrong.

COVERT BEHAVIORS	OVERT BEHAVIORS
Confronting-Contracting	
Dreikurs	
a. Reassessing for educational change for democratic living	1. Individual student choice of activities and schedules
	Glasser
	1. Classroom meetings
	2. Group rules
	Relationship-Listening
	Raths, Harmin, and Simon
	1. Group exercises —role playing —moral dilemma discussion
	Gordon
	1. Method III ("no lose") problem solving

CHART 14–5. The Conceptualization Through Language and Teacher Behaviors

THE CLASS AS A SOCIAL UNIT

After outlining stages of progression of individual social development, matched with applicable techniques, it can be hypothesized that groups show the same development.

We have previously described the assistance teachers can provide to individual students along the Developmental Socialization Continuum to help the students achieve more mature social behavior. Many readers probably have memories of certain classes in which the students created a collective personality. Often these classes would match their collective will against the teacher. This can be a natural tendency when a group of students who know each other first meets a new teacher and little trust exists. The teacher may see the same behavioral progression or regression in the class as a whole, as is seen through the stages of socialization. If trust is not quickly established, verbal aggression could be directed at the teacher in comments that might begin in a relatively mild way, such as, "Why do we always have these lousy assignments?" These aggressions could continue with harsher outbursts, such as, "Teacher, you're crazy!" or "We all hate this class!" If the teacher does not meet these verbal aggressions by "listening" to what the students are really trying to say, and instead uses either inappropriately harsh or permissive techniques, the class might regress into physical aggression by throwing objects at the teacher or each other, destroying property, or even making direct assaults on the teacher. If the teacher were to react with severe punishment that evokes fear, the class might further retreat into passivity, where little work is done, students do not talk, and the class becomes bored and expressionless. The teacher may have won the battle, but he or she has lost the war.

If a teacher finds this regression occurring, he or she can respond to the entire class as though he or she were dealing with one student. The goals would be to encourage activity at the passive stage, verbal aggression at the physically aggressive stage, and rational dialogue at the verbally aggressive stage.

SPHERES OF COMPETENCY

Previously it was mentioned that there might be pupils who are outside the teacher's *sphere of competency*. As Gordon, in *T.E.T. Teacher Effectiveness Training*, delineated "spheres of freedom" with concentric circles, so may "spheres of competency" be drawn. (See Figure 14—4).

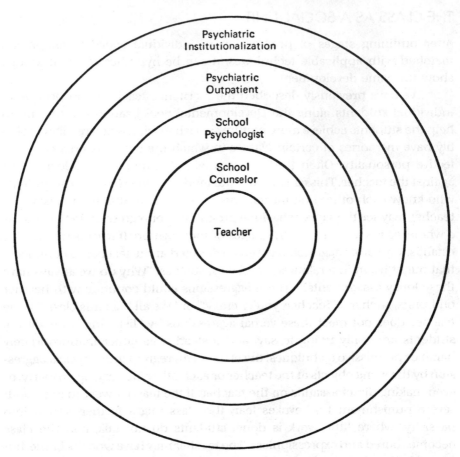

FIGURE 14–4. Spheres of Teacher Competency

Teachers have many skills for organizing educational experiences for students. With a further knowledge of management models, pathways of teacher choice, and the application of techniques to social development, the reader will have gained insights in how to help students acquire higher levels of socialized behavior. We hope this book will widen one's sphere of competency; yet, there may be a student who is outside a teacher's capability to help. In the course of one's teaching career, it is rare not to have a few such experiences. After having attempted many eclectic approaches, a teacher should not feel inadequate by seeking outside help. Chapter 15 offers a staff approach for gathering outside assistance for a student whose misbehavior is creating difficulties beyond the classroom. If such a team approach is not available, or if the student needs more specialized help, then referrals should be made to those with more specialized experience. Referrals would proceed to school counselors and, if necessary, would continue to further levels of competency, such as a psychologist, psychiatric outpatient clinics, and, ultimately, psychiatric institutionalization.

It would be self-deceiving for a teacher to think he or she can help every student. A teacher may have twenty-five to thirty students a day in an elementary school class or more than one hundred students a day in secondary school classes. The models and approaches of this book are based on what a teacher can do with an individual student within the constraints of regular teaching time. A teacher who has an eclectic knowledge of various models can find ways to help most students; he or she can help students who show an *orderly* unfolding of human behavior. Students who need psychiatric help are those whose behavior is *not orderly* and *not predictable*. Whether such a student is deeply passive or violently aggressive, the teacher would be doing the student and himself or herself a disservice by not asking for the needed help. A classroom teacher who must attend to many students and a multitude of tasks can become terribly frustrated from trying to deal with an emotionally deviant child. A student's failure to respond could even trigger a teacher's regression into irrational stages of action, such as a retreat to verbal and physical aggressions that are directed at the deviant student as well as the entire class.

SUMMARY

In review, it has been suggested that a teacher can decide upon using particular techniques from the various models that are applicable to the stage theory of social development. The teacher's goal is to facilitate the student's behavior from one stage to the next, although it will not be until the final stages are reached that "adult" social behavior will be seen. A mismatch of teacher techniques to stages could contribute to a student's regressing to more immature behavior. It was theorized that group behavior in an entire class could also move forward or backward along the same continuum. Lastly, "spheres of teacher competency" were described to allow for the assessment of those students who can be helped by a classroom teacher and those who need to be referred to more specialized help for their problems.

NOTES

1. Anna Freud, *Normality and Pathology in Childhood: Assessments of Development* (New York: International University Press, 1968).

2. Rene Spitz, *No and Yes* (New York: International University Press, 1957).

3. Anna Freud, *The Ego and the Mechanisms of Defense* (New York: International University Press, 1971).

4. Selma Fraiberg, *Magic Years* (New York: International University Press, 1959).

5. Susan Isaacs, *Social Development of Young Children* (New York: Schocken Books, 1972).

6. Charles H. Wolfgang, *Helping Aggressive and Passive Preschoolers Through Play* (Columbus: Charles E. Merrill Publishing, 1977), p. 6.

7. Jean Piaget, *The Construction of Reality in the Child* (New York: Ballantine Books, 1971).

8. Rudolf Dreikurs and Pearl Cassel, *Discipline Without Tears*, rev. ed. (New York: Hawthorn Books, 1972), p. 32.

9. Thomas A. Harris, *I'm OK—You're OK: A Practical Guide to Transactional Analysis* (New York: Harper & Row Publishers, 1969), pp. 37–53.

15

Decision Making Based on a Professional Team Approach

Once the classroom door is closed, the teacher enters a private world of intimate interaction with students that can be rewarding, dynamic, and exciting. This is teaching at its best. However, this relationship and interaction can also produce a hostile, frightening environment for the teacher and students, where little learning takes place. Teachers generally have been given the charge by parents, school administrators, and fellow teachers to be the "lion tamer" or to be an exponent of the "don't smile until Christmas" syndrome. The message is that you are given *this* number of students for *this* period of time, and—for "heaven's sake"—it is your responsibility to keep them under control. Your "long arm of control" should somehow even extend to those times when you are not supervising your students, such as on the school playground, in the school cafeteria, on the school bus, and during school assemblies and sporting events. "It was *your* Robert, Mrs. (or Mr.) Jones, who was causing a problem in the (whatever). *You* need to do something about him!" Such a demand on teachers suggests that they have omnipotent powers and are able to wave "the magical wand of fear" to get students to behave. (Often, this same demand is also unfairly asked of school principals, counselors, or school psychologists *by* teachers.) If you cannot appease your school administrator, fellow teachers, or parents, you will eventually find your teacher performance evaluation carrying such criticisms as "has difficulty with disciplining," a phrase that seems to reflect the ultimate sin of being a teacher. This causes teachers to feel they have been branded with the scarlet letter *D* for *discipline* and that they have been shunned by their colleagues who, in subtle ways, suggest to them that they are ineffectual and unworthy to be part of their profession.

279

"Mr. Walters sometimes has a little difficulty handling parent conferences."
Cartoon by Ford Button

We suggest that the larger a school becomes, the more rules and structure that seem to be needed, and, in turn, the teacher's "area of freedom" becomes more limited. Once these limitations and structures are established, they seem to become "sacred cows" and are rarely re-evaluated to see whether they are truly needed or are serving the purpose for which they were originally intended. This erosion of "freedom of the teacher" continues until one feels dehumanized or one has become a jailer rather than a creative teacher.

Let us therefore suggest that teachers turn from the view of the teacher as a "classroom island" to that of becoming part of a cooperative team effort involving some or all of the school staff. This support group would have a number of advantages:

1. The group could be supportive of the teacher who is, for the first time, attempting the various techniques suggested in the models previously presented.

2. They could recognize and work on the problem of the "difficult" student who rarely is a problem *only* in the classroom, but who also disrupts the school activities that generally affect the entire school staff.

3. The group could engage in a team effort that includes school administrators and permits a forum for re-evaluating the institutional rules that limit the teacher's "area of freedom," and they could arrive at rules that are based on what is best for the *individual* student rather than on what is administratively expedient.

4. The school staff, working as a team, could concentrate on the "difficult" student and, using the overt and covert techniques in the various models, the teacher behavioral pathways, and a developmental understanding and perspective, could gradually blend all these methods to create a common schoolwide mode of operation that would improve the atmosphere for all students.

5. They could engage in a team effort, based on the techniques previously presented, that will meet the new legal demand for "mainstreaming" the special or exceptional child into the social activities of the school, with the "least restrictive environment" for such children.

Although it is generally true that teachers who are mainstreaming exceptional children will have ranges of students with whom they might not have worked before, we are not assuming, and we do not wish the teacher to assume, that a mainstreamed student automatically will be a discipline problem. As with all students, most mainstreamed youngsters will exhibit a great degree of self-control, but a few will not. We do not view mainstreaming in the narrow sense of having "special" students from "educationally mentally retarded," "learning and behaviorally disabled," "perceptually impaired," "brain damaged," and "emotionally disturbed" classes entering the regular classroom. This is one aspect of mainstreaming, but its wider concept is more identical to the notion of a fully integrated democratic school. This is a school where all children, regardless of race, religion, sex, economics, ethnic background, and social, mental, or physical capabilities, have the constitutional right to be part of both the classroom and the school community. Therefore, in this discussion of mainstreaming, we are really talking about problems resulting from having a full, dynamic, heterogeneous classroom of students.

In having a variety of students in the classroom, there is a greater probability that a teacher will encounter a student whose behavior disrupts the class or the school as a whole. It might be a student who has an extraordinary intellect, a student from a culture that is foreign to the teacher, a student with a physical handicap, or possibly a retarded child. Hopefully, based on the content of this book, the teacher will have a range of strategies and models of student management to use with such students, to be both applied individually or by a team effort called "staffing."

STAFFING: A TEAM PROCESS

For the well-seasoned classroom teacher, the mere mention of being part of a team process brings forth shouts of, "Oh, no, not another meeting!" Such a verbal aggression from teachers seems to be justified, as every teacher can remember meeting after meeting that has dragged on with little or no results. The frustration produced from these futile attempts to work with others seems to drive teachers back into their classroom "islands" to "do their own thing." It can be hypothesized that the reasons for nonproductive meetings are the lack of a clear orderly process for solving problems, and the group members' lack of understanding regarding the possible solutions available to them. Teachers have sat in meetings for hours feeling unclear as to what the problem being discussed was, and finally they would become frustrated into a state of "helpless passivity" by their colleagues whose "personal wisdom" seems to be repeated at every faculty meeting. In order to overcome these "roadblocks" to good collective problem solving, a clear orderly process will be proposed based on the six steps for problem solving described in the Thomas Gordon model of *Teacher Effectiveness Training* (TET). This material is based on John Dewey's scientific problem-solving steps of (1) defining the problem, (2) generating a possible solution, (3) evaluating, (4) deciding on a solution, (5) implementing, and (6) evaluating the solutions. In order to minimize the personal wisdom or biased form of solution, we propose that the team use the overt and covert teacher techniques, pathways, and developmental constructs as a data base for reasoned solutions. The function of the team then becomes one of creative integration or application of these techniques and methods to fit the needs of their particular school or a particular student who is "difficult."

Individualized Socialization Plan (ISP)

As a result of federal legislation and some state laws, there are now demands for school personnel to create a specific plan, called the Individualized Educational Plan (IEP), to insure that the "exceptional" pupil who is now in school or is returning to the regular classroom from a special class will continue to have an individualized and focused program. In order to meet legal requirements, the IEP needs to include:

1. A statement of the student's present performance
2. Yearly goals
3. Immediate objectives
4. Services to be used (or who will work with the child)
5. A time line for such services
6. The amount of time to be spent outside the regular classroom
7. Objective criteria for evaluating achievement of objectives and goals.

Such a plan ordinarily needs to be developed by a team that includes, at the minimum, the classroom teacher, a second teacher (possibly the teacher of exceptional children), and the parents or guardian. (The student can also be a part of such a meeting and procedures.) The agreed-upon plan must be written and signed by those involved.

The process of staffing can be an ideal aid to be used by the team to develop a plan for the "exceptional" child as well as for the "difficult" student. Although the central goal of IEP is to establish an educational plan, in many cases the child's social behavior is such that his or her cooperative behavior needs to be established so that the teacher will be able to carry out the plan. The tools presented previously are applicable to all children and can be valuable for the teacher working with the exceptional student.

"Staffing" is a structured process whereby school personnel meet and formulate an individualized plan for responding to and assisting a "misbehaving" or "difficult" child to become a socialized part of the school and classroom. An agreed-upon plan for improving a student's social behavior can be recorded on an Individualized Socialization Plan, ISP (see Form 15–1). The staff meeting can include any of the school personnel who have contact with this child, including such people as the school bus driver, cafeteria workers, playground supervisors, guidance counselors, the principal, as well as the child's parents and even the child as participants. Such participants may wish to meet on a formal or informal basis every two weeks at a regular school meeting or during preparation periods. The number of participants

---

Student's Name: _____
School: _____
Date of Staffing: _____

I. *Student's Behavior*
   A. General concern:
   B. Specific improvements desired:

II. *Actions to be Taken*   By Whom   When
   1.
   2.
   3.
   4.
   5.

III. *Evaluation of Improvement*
   Information to be collected:
   Date of followup

Staffing Members

FORM 15–1. The Staffing Plan

can vary, but the ideal size of the group would be four to nine people. Hopefully, most of the staffing participants would already have an understanding of the ideas previously provided in the summarized models as well as the directional pathways and the developmental socialization continuum that is to be used as a content foundation or knowledge base. One might find that, in his or her group, members who represent all three theoretical positions (Relationship-Listening, Confronting-Contracting, Rules/Rewards-Punishment) would be involved. It is within a group where these differences among teachers of varying beliefs and classroom practices exist that the greatest range of options will be explored to determine how to intervene with the "misbehaving" or problem student. The value-clarification model suggests that choosing from alternatives provides the best forum for decision making.

In order to facilitate group problem solving, the staffing process or meeting is governed by specific rules that might initially appear to be rigid and arbitrary. However, these strict procedures as to who may speak and for how long are needed when a team attempts to work together, and the rules restrict the "personal wisdom chatter" that lacks direction and focus. Such rules also decrease the possibility of the process deteriorating into aimless meetings where nothing is resolved and no actions are taken, as such meetings quickly deflate the teacher's enthusiasm.

It has been described previously that when individuals begin to feel frustrated and unsuccessful, they also begin to retreat along the developmental socialization continuum from rational problem solving to a prerational behavior of verbal aggression, physical aggression, or helpless passivity. The structure of the staff meeting will hold to a minimum the "verbal aggression" and "not OK" view of students or parents, while at the same time it will maintain the support needed by staff members to generate rational solutions.

STAFFING AGENDA: STEPS AND PROCEDURES

It is helpful at the beginning of a staff meeting to appoint a "timekeeper" who will announce each step and goal and will identify those who contribute. The timekeeper serves as a monitor to channel the discussion to conform to the stated goals (see Form 15–3).

> *Step 1:* Definition of the problem: Overview of the student's be-
> havior
> Time: 15 minutes
> Purpose: Step 1 is to gather all necessary information about the
> student *before* moving to solutions
> Procedures:

A. The teacher who spends the most time with the student should begin with a general overview of the student, his or her behavior, and the changes desired. The teacher (or other staff member) will discuss any typical behaviors or incidents that have occurred and will describe the teacher's actions or approaches that have been attempted. This teacher will end the report with a list of behavioral changes that he or she would like to see in the student. For example, "I would like to see Carol (1) attend school on a regular basis, (2) work with peers without fighting or destroying their products, and (3) complete her homework."

B. The classroom teacher or any other member who has collected systematic data with the use of baseline methods suggested by the behaviorists or the observations of the student in relationship with

Student _____

Date _____

Name of Staff Member _____

Part I   Student's Misbehavior(s)
1.   Describe misbehavior(s)
    a.
    b.
    c.
2.   How frequent is each type of misbehavior?
    a.
    b.
    c.
3.   What time of day does it occur?
    a.
    b.
    c.
4.   In what physical surroundings?
    a.
    b.
    c.
5.   With which peers or adults?
    a.
    b.
    c.
6.   In what kinds of activities is student engaged before misbehavior occurs?
    a.
    b.
    c.

Part II   Teacher (or other) Actions
1.   What do you do when student misbehaves?
    a.
    b.
    c.
2.   How does student respond?
    a.
    b.
    c.
3.   When are your actions most successful?
4.   When are these actions least successful?

FORM 15–2.   Student Background Information

Part III Student Motivation
   1.   What responsibilities (assignments, tasks, or orders) does student fulfill?
   2.   What types of reinforcement (positive and negative) does student receive?
        a. positive (and/or encouragement)
        b. negative (and/or logical consequences)
   3.   How does student respond to reinforcement?
        a. positive (and/or encouragement)
        b. negative (and/or logical consequences)
   4.   How does student relate to the group (physical aggression, verbal aggression, passivity, or other behaviors)?

Part IV When Student *Is Not* Misbehaving
   1.   Describe positive behaviors.
        a.
        b.
        c.
   2.   How frequent is each type of positive behavior?
        a.
        b.
        c.
   3.   What time of day does each behavior occur?
        a.
        b.
        c.
   4.   In what physical surroundings?
        a.
        b.
        c.
   5.   With which peers or adults?
        a.
        b.
        c.
   6.   In what kinds of activities is student engaged before positive behavior occurs?
        a.
        b.
        c.

Part V Additional Questions
   1.   What does student enjoy doing (hobbies or subjects)?
   2.   What does student do well (hobbies or subjects)?
   3.   Are there any reasons to suspect health or physical disabilities?

FIGURE 15–2. (*cont.*)

peers, family, or school staff as suggested by Glasser and Dreikurs is given the opportunity to report. A student background information form (see Form 15–2) can be developed by the school staff to organize information gathering. It is advisable that only the member with the organized data be permitted to report and that questions and discussion be held for later. This procedure will provide an avenue to get the information on the table, not to clarify it.

C. Any members of the group who have contact with the student present their background information. It is urged that they try to use the same reporting criteria as those found on the school's student background information form to determine whether the student's behavior is consistent from situation to situation or with staff member to staff member. Again, the staff members simply report their information and withhold discussion of the information until later.

D. All members of the staff now have the right to question the teacher or each other to discuss the student and his or her problems in greater detail. This is also the time to identify and explore what overt techniques have previously been tried with this student by the teacher or others. *These questions should be concerned with asking and not presenting solutions in disguise.* Such questions as, "Have you tried 'active listening'? It might work." or, "Last year, I had the same type of problem and I found that the classroom meetings worked. Do you think you could do that?" are really disguised

---

STEP 1.   Definition of the problem   (15 minutes)
           A. Teacher statement
           B. Teacher background information
           C. All members contribute to background information

STEP 2.   Generating and evaluating possible solutions   (20 minutes)
           A. Writing solutions by all members
           B. Reading solutions by all members
           C. Discussing advantages and disadvantages of various solutions

STEP 3.   Deciding on a plan of discipline   (20 minutes)
           A. Agreeing on action
           B. Write plan—who will do what, when

STEP 4.   Set evaluation meeting   (5 minutes)

FORM 15–3. Staffing Agenda

solutions and will find their place in Step 2. The group can add to, modify, or alter the behavioral changes first proposed by the teacher. Step 1 is complete when all members agree upon the desired changes for the student being discussed.

Hints to Timekeeper: Let the group know when ten minutes are up. If they are not already at the point where members are presenting their own background information, urge them to move on. At the fifteen-minute point, ask the group to begin questions of each other to clarify information.

> *Step 2:* Generating and evaluating possible solutions: Coming up with alternative actions
>
> Time: 20 minutes
>
> Purpose: Step 2 is to provide an open forum for each member to propose his or her own ideas about actions that might be taken to improve a student's behavior and finally concludes with group "brainstorming" on how the ideas can be brought together into a comprehensive, collectively agreed-upon plan of action.

Procedures:

A. All staff members will write down, without talking to each other, their solutions in terms of what actions they or anyone else could take to help the student. It is during this process that each member should review mentally the teacher-student interaction models of Gordon, Dreikurs, and Glasser; values clarification, transactional analysis, behavior modification, and assertiveness, as well as the directional pathways and the Developmental Socialization Continuum. This review will help the member to decide what teacher methods and techniques would be the most helpful and how one can organize these behaviors systematically in relation to the power to be given the student or to be used by the teacher. Writing these possible solutions involves each member in these overt actions, and it means, in Glasser's sense, that the members have committed themselves to the problem-solving process.

B. Each member presents his or her ideas orally to the group. Each person reads in order, without any discussion. The discussion of ideas is held until later in order not to inhibit the free flow of each member's ideas.

C. Interaction among staff members now becomes of primary importance, as the members can fully discuss how their ideas are interrelated or have commonalities. The models in the various schools of thought (Relationship-Listening, Confronting-Contracting, and Rules/Rewards-Punishment), the directional pathways, and the overt techniques should be used as a framework for evaluating the solutions presented. The group might ask: "Do our solutions cluster into one model or school of thought? Do they suggest that we wish to begin with the pathway of minimum teacher power, maximum power, or shared power? Can the student's behavior be placed on the Developmental Socialization Continuum? Can educational changes or changes in time or space affect some or all of the problems?"

It is important in this step to understand that the teacher and staff members have progressed from the "personal wisdom" kind of speculative thinking where teachers try to solve problems by "stabbing in the dark." The constructs, methods, and procedures provided for teachers and school staffs have brought the professionals out of the "darkness" of functioning as limited technicians, and have provided a framework for scientific problem solving, which is characteristic of a true professional.

Hints to Timekeeper: Try to keep the group from talking or discussing each other's ideas until after the actions have been read by each member. Allow approximately five minutes for writing and reading and fifteen minutes for discussion.

> *Step 3:* Deciding on a plan of discipline: Commitment to action
> Time: 20 minutes
> Purpose: Step 3 is to decide on an orderly plan of action, to put the plan in writing, and for staff members to make a commitment to implementation.

Procedures:

A. Staff members discuss and decide upon an agreed-upon plan of action in which members will be responsible for carrying out the various segments of the plan.

B. The use of Form 15−1, The Staffing Plan, can organize the writing of the plan of action and the designation of responsibilities. The group should agree on who will take what actions and when they will be taken. Furthermore, the group should agree on the date of a followup meeting, and the information to be collected by that time to determine if student behavior has improved. These records can be made through observation, baseline data, or experimental data.

C. As in Glasser's view of commitment, each staff member is asked to sign or initial the written plan, and, by so doing, agrees to actively carry out the procedures agreed upon.

Hints to Timekeeper: Be sure that all members understand what they are to do by the end of the meeting and when they'll meet back. A simple reading of the entire plan with time for questions should be sufficient to check on understanding.

Step 4:   Set evaluation meeting
Time: 5 minutes
Purpose: To secure an agreement from all group members when they will meet again to review the progress of the plan and make subsequent revisions.
Procedures:

A. Members should discuss a time to have a followup meeting that will allow for sufficient implementation of the plan of discipline.
B. After time and date have been established, members should be reminded that at the next meeting, they will be asked to describe their own individual actions (as agreed to on the written plan) and individual progress with the student before an overall group determination is made of student progress and need for further actions.

STAFFING—A CASE STUDY

Benilde Rojas, high school science teacher, had become increasingly concerned with her student, Fred Wood. Fred was in her tenth-grade general science class and was failing the course. He was not completing his work, didn't appear to care about his grades, incessantly talked during class, came to class late, passed notes to other students, and caused a constant disturbance to the teacher. Benilde knew from talking to other teachers that Fred's misbehavior and indifferent attitude reached beyond her own classroom. The way he was going, he had little chance of graduating and would probably be expelled from school before the year was out.

Benilde decided to ask the other teachers who had Fred as a student as well as the school guidance counselor to meet with her to determine what might be done. Such a meeting received the endorsement of the school principal who concurred that Fred's frequent referrals to the principal's office for disciplinary actions indicated that most teachers were running out of patience with him. The guidance counselor and six of the seven teachers agreed to meet. At the last minute, one teacher had a scheduling conflict and couldn't be present. Teachers Benilde Rojas (science), John Trock (English), Margaret Hambleton (history), Bill Sanska (auto mechanics), Juan Dupree (algebra), and Sam Fayne (guidance counselor) sat down for a one-hour meeting. Benilde and Sam had decided not to involve Fred's parents in this first meeting as they wanted to see if a staffing plan of in-school action would work. Let's now take a look at how the meeting proceeded.

Benilde quickly reviewed the staffing agenda (Form 15–3) and Sam agreed to be the timekeeper. The meeting started.

Step 1: Benilde began the problem-definition step by mentioning her concerns with Fred and read information that she had gathered on the student background information form (Form 15–2). The other members offered their own pieces of information about the circumstances surrounding Fred's behavior. A picture of Fred emerged. He was an eighteen-year-old who had been retained in the twelfth grade for not passing third-year mathematics and fourth-year English, and he also had failed the required exit competency exam in mathematics. He had been a former wrestler and football player, but his eligibility period was over and most of his friends had graduated in what should have been his senior class. His parents wanted badly for him to stay in school, pass the competency exam, and graduate; Fred preferred to get a job. The teachers all commented on his indifferent attitude and disturbing behavior in their classrooms with the notable exception of Bill Sanska (auto mechanics). Bill said that Fred had been no trouble at all. Bill was his former wrestling coach and Fred appeared to enjoy working on automobile engines in Bill's class. During this first step of information gathering John mentioned, "Why don't we work out an incentive plan with auto mechanics? We could..." Sam, acting as timekeeper and regulator, gently interrupted John and reminded him that this was not the time for proposing solutions.

The group concurred that goals for improvement in Fred's behavior should be less talking, promptness to class, and a better attitude towards teachers' directions. After fifteen minutes, John told the group to move on to Step Two.

Step 2: In Step Two they began by quietly writing possible actions. When completed, they went around the group and read their proposals. Some of the possible actions that emerged were:

- Close door when bell rings, don't let him in, and have him make up missed work (logical consequences from Dreikurs's social discipline model).

- Have individual conferences with him and set up a mutual contract for his behavior in each classroom (contract from Glasser's reality model).
- Go over the rules with him and make him sign a statement that he will obey or go to the office (verbal limit setting and punishment from the Canters' assertiveness model).
- Speak with him in private, allow him the chance to talk about his beliefs about staying in school (value clarification exercises from Raths and Simon's valuing model and active listening from Gordon's supportive model).
- If he fails to follow teacher instructions more than once in a class period, set up a nonreinforcing isolation area in one of the classrooms for him to go to (isolation from the behavior-modification model).
- Reward him for good behavior by allowing him to assist Bill Sanska with lower-level mechanics classes or with the wrestling team (positive reinforcement from the behavior-modification model).
- Have all his teachers meet with Fred and his parents to discuss concerns and see what he suggests that we all do to help him get through the year and pass his courses and his competency exam (modified classroom meeting from Glasser's reality model).
- Have each teacher say hello and show personal interest and have friendly daily "chats" and "pep talks" (encouragement from Dreikurs's social discipline model).
- Incorporate mathematics competency-exam materials into an individual lesson plan for him in each of his classes (educational change from Glasser's reality model).

After discussing these alternatives, John reminded the group that it was time to move to Step Three.

Step 3:   Step Three began by group members determining which proposed actions were most realistic and likely to work. The group agreed that they should capitalize on Fred's fondness for auto mechanics, wrestling, and for his former coach Bill Sanska. They also agreed that they should show more personal concern for Fred and that they needed individually to remind him of their expectations. Together they agreed upon the following plan (see Form 15–4).

Step Four was quickly concluded. The group decided that a three-week implementation of the plan would provide enough time to determine if their actions were being helpful.

Student's Name: _____Fred Wood_____

School: _____Oakridge_____

Date of Staffing: _____February 5, 1984_____

I. *Student's Behavior*
   A. *General Concern:* Lateness, indifference to work, failure to follow teachers' instruction, incessant talking, failure to do assignment
   B. *Specific Improvements Desired*: Follow teachers' instruction and reduce talking

II. *Actions to be Taken*	*By Whom*	*When*
A. Conferences with Fred to review the rules and set up reward contract for all classes. (*contingency contract*)	All teachers	February 9
B. Implement contracts that will establish that for each class period he follows instructions and is told to stop talking no more than once, he will earn 1 point. By Thursday if he has earned 15 points from all his classes, he can assist Coach Sanska at Friday's wrestling meet or have an extra period of auto mechanics. (*token reinforcement*)	All teachers	February 13–17 February 21–24
C. Speak individually with him each day in a friendly and informal way. (*encouragement*)	All teachers	Everyday February 9–24
D. Have individual conference with him in English and mathematics to see what can be done to make the class more relevant and help him to pass his competency exams. Perhaps set up tutorial. (*educational change*)	John Troch Juan Dupree	February 13 meet February 15–24: implement plan

FORM 15−4. The Staffing Plan

III. *Evaluation of improvement*
A. Information to be collected:
amount of points he accumulates
for good behavior at the end of
each week; percentage of assignments
completed; his attitude towards the
contract.
B. Date of followup: meet to assess
progress on February 26 at 8:00 a.m.

Staffing Members
Juan Dupre _____
Sam Fayne _____
Margaret Hambleton _____
Benilde Rojas _____
Bill Sanska _____
John Troch _____

FORM 15–4.   The Staffing Plan (cont.)

SUMMARY OF STAFFING PROCEDURES AND AGENDA

The structured agenda with arbitrary procedures is a systematic or scientific problem-solving process loosely based on the six steps of problem solving described by Gordon in *TET Teacher Effectiveness Training* and attributed to John Dewey. Such techniques, of course, can be modified by a staff to fit its working style, but what is most imperative is the agreed-upon structure for the staff meetings. (Some schools will write these procedures for the staff on a large chart and place it on the wall in the meeting room.) The solution generated by the staffing procedures must rest on the foundation of understanding the various overt and covert techniques in each model, and how models cluster under various "schools of thought." There is also a need for understanding the use of power that these techniques imply, and how that power can be positioned. Additionally, an understanding of the severity of misbehavior and student social development gives a solid knowledge base from which teachers and staff personnel can make informed decisions. Finally, many educational changes will be made within the classroom or throughout the school in order to create a school atmosphere in which problem students become nearly nonexistent.

Introduction: Discipline and Classroom Management

"He's one of those get-tough-on-the-first-day types."

Cartoon by Ford Button

Nearly everyone who has sat in a classroom looking up at a teacher has had a "Mr. (or Mrs.) Bumbles." Whether passing out papers, giving an assignment, or asking a question of students, they appear disorganized. This disorganization keeps students waiting. When students wait, they become bored and restless, and soon become discipline problems. Such a teacher does not need help in discipline techniques, which involve actions towards students disrupting the education environment, but instead needs help in classroom management. Good classroom management is basic to the prevention of many minor discipline incidents.

Much research has accumulated on good classroom management. We briefly present it in Chapter 16 so that teachers may reflect on their own organization, gain an understanding of the basic elements of good management, and thus prevent many discipline incidents. Finally, Chapter 17 summarizes what has been learned from the various schools of thought, operational discipline models, overt and covert teacher behaviors, and ways of deciding appropriate discipline actions.

298

16

Classroom Management: A Preventive Process

We sit in a tenth-grade classroom. Ms. Wedgeworth's third-period American history class has begun. She has asked Fred to come to the front of the room and chart the Mormon migration on the map of North America. At the same time, she has asked the other students to do likewise on a blank map at their seats. She cues Fred with questions when he appears stumped by asking "Think now, where was John Smith imprisoned?" She turns to the class and at random asks other students questions: "Where did Brigham Young lead the group?" "Did they go directly from Nauvoo, Illinois to Utah?" Now Ms. Wedgeworth returns to watch Fred complete charting the route. While doing so, Susannah in the back of the room begins whispering to Samantha about the upcoming pep rally. Without missing a beat, Ms. Wedgeworth says "Susannah, I can hear you talking, please stop. Now, class, everyone put your maps up so we can see if you and Fred are in agreement." Susannah stops talking to Samantha and two other girls who were listening to Susannah join the rest of the class in following Ms Wedgeworth's directions.

Now we move next door to Mr. Turnstyle's American history class. He also is teaching about the Mormon migration with a section of tenth graders. Mr. Turnstyle is lecturing about the route taken to Utah. His back is to the class as he draws the path and explains the circumstances surrounding each stop. Most students are listening with their textbooks open to a similar map already diagrammed. Three girls, spearheaded by Sonya, have begun passing notes quietly around to the boys. The notes are insulting such as "You are a real blob, sterno." "Why are you so fat?" "John, word is out that you're a real nerd." Seeing the boys' amused reactions, the three girls increase their

299

writing campaign, trying to top their previous insults. Now twelve students are involved in passing notes. When Mr. Turnstyle faces the class, the students look up and pretend to be attentive and when he asks a question they raise their hands. They know from previous experience that raising their hand is the best way not to be called on. Mr. Turnstyle inevitably calls on the one student who is not waving enthusiastically. As this goes on, one note is passed into the hands of Jim Swift who has just broken up with Alicia, one of the girls in the class. The note says, "Jim, we know that you're a queer and a weirdo. Alicia says you're real short." Jim crumples the note and throws it with all his strength towards the girl who handed it to him. Mr. Turnstyle, seeing this, explodes: "Jim Swift, you get out of this room this minute! Who do you think you are?" Jim looks up and retorts, "I didn't do anything and I'm not leaving." The girls who began the note smirk to themselves; the rest of the class is anxious to see how Mr. Turnstyle is going to make Jim leave the classroom.

Unfortunately Mr. Turnstyle now has a discipline problem to handle. He might use parts of the Teacher Behavior Continuum: silently looking on, active listening, nondirective statements, questions, directive statements, reinforcement, physical modeling, isolation, or punishment to solve this problem. Ms. Wedgeworth, on the other hand, does not have a discipline problem and can continue with her lesson. The focus of this book is solving discipline problems and yet there are many discipline problems that could be prevented by sound classroom management practices. Without moving away from the central purpose of this book, we can state that it is necessary for a teacher to be aware of what research has shown to be good, preventive management techniques so that he or she will have a minimum of discipline problems to solve.

Remember, even the best classroom manager will still have students who misbehave, disrupt, and keep others from learning. Effective management allows the teacher to work with the real problem students. For example, Mr. Turnstyle is faced with a situation that Ms. Wedgeworth has avoided. The difference in the two is management. We will continue to contrast Ms. Wedgeworth's and Mr. Turnstyle's practices as we highlight what research has proven characteristic of all successful classroom managers.

A definition of management offered by Daniel L. Duke, editor of *Classroom Management*, the 1978 yearbook of the National Society for the Study of Education (1979), states that

> Classroom management constitutes the provisions and procedures necessary to establish and maintain an environment in which instruction and learning can occur.[1]

Some of those practices and procedures have been uncovered through the studies of Jacob S. Kounin in 1970[2] and added to by Carolyn M. Evertson and Edmund T. Emmer in 1982[3] and by others.[4] We will discuss Kounin's work, then the work of Evertson and Emmer, and conclude by providing a management checklist that a teacher can use to improve classroom behavior.

KOUNIN'S WITH-IT-NESS AND OVERLAPPING

Jacob Kounin has conducted research with several colleagues of kindergarten, elementary, secondary, and college classrooms. His most important findings have come from videotaping fifteen first- and second-grade classrooms and fifteen third- through fifth-grade classrooms. They were videotaped half-days for two months. Kounin followed with another study of fifty primary classrooms videotaped for a full day. For each classroom, he recorded the behavior of eight students chosen at random and one emotionally disturbed child. His concern was with finding teacher practices related to student work involvement and low student misbehavior. Kounin isolated the teacher practices and procedures of "with-it-ness," "overlapping," "smoothness and momentum," and "group alerting" as parts of classroom-management success. Teachers who were aware of what was going on throughout the class in terms of student behavior and student work and who showed their awareness to students had high student work-involvement and low student misbehavior. Kounin calls this awareness "with-it-ness." In other words, the teacher would pick up that several students did not understand their seatwork, that a student was not listening, or a student was reading a comic book and then would show awareness by such actions as moving over to the student, giving a quick reprimand, or asking the student a question. The teacher action showed the entire class that he or she was on top of what everyone was doing. On the other hand, if a teacher was not aware of such occurrences, then confused students would give up on their assignment and become agitated; students not listening to the lesson would tend to get other students away from the lesson; students reading comic books or passing notes would be seen by other students as getting away with inattentiveness; and others would begin to turn to nonacademic behavior of their own. The students knew which of their number were not paying attention, were "goofing off," or being disruptive, and unless the teacher dealt with those students, their misbehavior spread to others. Additionally, if a teacher blatantly showed his or her lack of awareness by reprimanding the wrong student for talking or the last person in a chain of students who had all picked up comic books, or by commanding one student to pay attention while other students were even more "off-task," then the class became further convinced that the teacher was not in tune with what was going on and that they could feel safe in continuing to be uninvolved in school work.

Kounin also found teacher "overlapping" was a complementary practice with the "with-it-ness" of successful classroom managers—attending to two events at the same time. A teacher who could instruct a group of students while responding to student concerns from outside of the group could keep an entire classroom working smoothly. On the other hand, a teacher who was in the habit of attending exclusively to students in the instructional group would lose the work-involvement and increase the misbehavior of students outside of the group. For example, let's consider the case of a teacher with a reading group having students recite; another student comes up to the teacher with a question about a seat assignment. If the teacher turns away from the reading group and focuses entirely on the student asking the question, misbehavior and off-task behavior will increase in the reading group. On the other hand, if the teacher ignores the student and the student goes back and sits down without direction, and the teacher continues to direct his or her attention to the reading group, then the questioning student is left without anything productive to do. He or she then starts talking with other students or exhibits other misbehavior that gets the attention of students who were working productively. The result of the teacher's ignoring one segment of the class is compounding misbehavior. We're reminded of a recent airport experience in which an airline agent showed overlapping behavior. The agent, the only one on duty, issued tickets, placed labels on baggage, and at the same time conversed on the phone with a distressed ticket holder. The line of twelve persons could easily have started grumbling, demanding, and complaining if the agent had ignored their needs to be checked through the line and instead talked on the phone. Similarly, the phone caller could have been upset if the agent had attended only to the waiting passengers. Instead, both were accommodated. The passengers reached their plane on time and the confused phoner was rerouted to a more desirable flight. The same type of simultaneous accommodations holds true for a classroom teacher who must juggle the competing demands of students and not just play to one student or one group.

Let's return to the classrooms of Ms. Wedgeworth and Mr. Turnstyle to understand how Kounin's categories of with-it-ness and overlapping explain Ms. Wedgeworth's preventive managment and Mr. Turnstyle's compounding discipline problems. Ms. Wedgeworth was "with it." She was engaging all students in an activity of tracing the Mormon route. The seated students were trying to chart the part on their maps while Fred was doing the work in front of the class. Ms. Wedgeworth was helping Fred while at the same time scanning the room and listening to what the other students were doing. She showed the class that she knew what was going on by immediately picking up on a new noise and telling Susannah to stop talking. On the other hand, Mr. Turnstyle showed the class his lack of being "with it" by not being aware of the note passing; a disruption occurred when he finally shouted at the victim, Jim, rather than at the students who caused the misbehavior. Mr. Turnstyle's error confirmed to the misbehaving students that they could continue to misbehave.

We can also understand how Ms. Wedgeworth kept students on task by using her "overlapping" abilities while Mr. Turnstyle aggravated the situation by putting total emphasis on the misbehaving student (the wrong student at that); this distracted those remaining students who were still doing the learning activity. Ms. Wedgeworth corrected Samantha and in the same breath asked the class to hold up their maps. She showed the class she could attend to two events together. Mr. Turnstyle stopped the lesson entirely to confront Jim. The class had nothing else to do now but to stop and watch the confrontation. When Mr. Turnstyle decided to return to the lesson, the students would have to refocus their attention and begin all over again.

Besides with-it-ness and overlapping, Kounin found some other classroom practices related to successful classroom management—smoothness, momentum, and group alerting. Smoothness is shown by the teacher continuing with the learning activity without going on a tangent, being distracted by some unplanned event, interrupting students from working, leaving a learning activity in midstream, or reversing directions. Smoothness is staying with the logical organization of a lesson. Those teachers who get easily distracted by such examples as beginning a mathematics lesson, showing the class how to do a calculation, and then saying such things as, "Did I pass back your homework? Oh well, then let's put away our books for a moment. Here's your homework, your scores mean . . ." or when students are quiet and working on seat work and the teacher says "Oh, I forgot to take lunch money—will those who are getting milk please come up here." Teachers who stray and break up the continuity of the lesson will have a higher incidence of student misbehavior and lower student attention than those teachers who organize their time so as not to interfere with the goal of the lesson.

Momentum is another critical factor in successful classroom management which relates to the organization and delivery of the lesson. Momentum is a concern for the pacing of instruction. The lack of momentum or a slowing down occurs when the teacher continues to elaborate on a point that students already understand. For example, the teacher gives a writing assignment and says, "Before you begin, make sure your margins are one inch on both sides. In this classroom I want you to all be in the habit of keeping the margins to one inch. Look at this paper I am holding up. Now I measure one inch on this side, and one inch on this side. We must have good writing habits. Margins are important . . ." By this time, the students who were ready to begin writing are impatiently waiting for the teacher to be quiet. Waiting students are prone to take up other noninstructional matters. Another example of lack of momentum is a teacher drawing out procedures by passing out papers, materials, and books one at a time via one person; instructional time is lost. Nagging students can be another loss of momentum; i.e., "Why is it that when I leave you alone, this class is so noisy? If you are going to be grown-up, you need to act like grown-ups. In this country, we give adults a lot of responsibilities. Part of growing up is knowing when to behave. When I was a student . . ." A final type of slowdown is when a teacher keeps students waiting on other students for something insignificant. Examples would be, "I want to meet with reading group C now. You are to come to the group one at a time, but only when I call your name. Sit with your heads down until you are called. OK, Fred, you come and sit down. Sara . . ." or "Now it's time for group projects. First put your math books away and look up when they are all in yours desks. Jerry, don't put your papers away yet until everyone has put their math books away. OK, now that everyone has put their math books away, let's put your papers away. Now, I didn't say anything about taking out your projects yet!" A teacher with momentum might instead say, "Reading Group C, come quietly up here with your materials in hand" and "Now it's time for group projects. I'll give you a minute to clear your math materials, get out projects and start thinking about what your group should be doing today." A teacher without momentum loses instructional time and causes student restlessness. A teacher with momentum capitalizes on transition times as short flowing times into the next activity.

Lastly Kounin found *group alerting* as another teacher practice highly related with effective classroom management. These are behaviors used to keep students in suspense and "on their toes" as to whether or when they will be asked to demonstrate their knowledge. Students are kept in suspense: they are called upon at random and often asked to recite as a total group. If a student tunes out from the lesson or does not keep up on the work, she or he can't avoid the high likelihood of being called upon. Nonalerting practices are those that protect a student from being accountable. A predetermined pattern of calling students, such as calling on only students with their hands up (or down) or in a clockwise manner are examples of nonalerting practices.

> Kounin found simply that teachers who . . . keep children alerted and on their toes are more successful in inducing work involvement and preventing deviancy than are teachers who do not.[5]

To summarize Kounin's important work on classroom management, a teacher can minimize misbehavior by

1. With-it-ness:
   - Keep constantly alert to sights and sounds around the classroom
   - Arrange students to be within sight at all times
   - Scan the classroom whenever attending to an individual or small group of students
   - At the first detection of misbehavior, use a brief acknowledgment to let the class know that you know of the misbehavior; i.e., "Felina, would you please get back to your work?"

2. Overlappingness
   - Attend to two events at the same time whenever necessary so as not to leave students waiting
   - When instructing one group, acknowledge difficulties that students outside of the group may be having but keep group instruction moving; i.e., "Marsha, keep explaining that logarithm out loud to us while I check on Petunia's problem. Now, Petunia, where do you need help—I see. Martha, check your logarithm with the rest of the group; then all of you do exercise B. Petunia, you're forgetting to invert the ratio . . ." Correct misbehavior but keep instruction moving; i.e., "Tom, it's your turn to read (teacher turns head to class in seats). There's too much noise. I can't hear Tom read. Tom, sound that word out by syllables: *for, tu, nate*. Good. Sam, get back in your seat. If you need help come over here. Sandra (who sits two seats from Tom in the reading group), please pronounce the same word that Tom just had . . ."

3. Smoothness
   - Preplan the lesson so that extraneous matters are taken care of beforehand; i.e., "Now that today's schedule and assignments are handed out, have we forgotten any other items? If not, let's give our full attention to Gothic design. Let's look on page 13, the picture of the Cathedral of Chartres. No, Sally, I'll pass back homework at the end of class. What do you notice about this cathedral that is different from Notre Dame? Bruce?"
   - Once students are absorbed in their work, do not distract them. Leave them alone to work and assist them individually.

4. Momentum
   - Keep the lesson moving briskly
   - Do not overdwell on a minor or already understood part of the lesson
   - Correct students quickly without nagging and return to the lesson

- Have students move from one activity to the next without having to wait for each other on each subpart of the transition (i.e., avoid saying "First everyone put your pencils away")
5. Group alerting
  - Call on students at random
  - Raise group interest by interspersing suspense between questions by saying "This is a tough one coming up." "Can you figure this one out?" "You haven't heard of this before." "I want you all to think hard before responding."
  - Have the entire group or class respond in unison
  - Physically move around the room and ask students to show what they have done
  - While asking one student to respond, look at other students

Kounin found that with-it-ness, overlapping, smoothness, momentum, and group alerting were the teacher practices most highly related to management success. With-it-ness, overlapping, and group alerting are focused teacher behaviors, verbal and nonverbal, in scanning and responding to students. Smoothness and momentum are focused on the organization of the lesson, presentation of instruction, and transitions between work activities. Next we will discuss the more recent work of Evertson, Emmer, and their colleagues that concurs with much of Kounin's work and also adds some critical elements to successful classroom management.[6]

EVERTSON AND EMMER

Evertson and Emmer[7] after collecting observations of twenty-seven self-contained third-grade classrooms (from twenty-five hours of observation during the first three weeks) and fifty-one junior high school mathematics and English teachers (fourteen one-hour observations) were able to find significant differences between practices of good and poor classroom managers as measured by student achievement, student on-task behavior, and the amount of disruptive student behavior.

With third-grade classrooms, they found that effective teachers at the beginning of the school year

- *Broke down* their classroom tasks into specific rules and procedures for students to understand and follow

- *Taught the rules* and procedures as an important classroom lesson consisting of presentation, examples, practice, and feedback
- *Predicted* procedures where students would have the greatest confusion and emphasized the teaching of those procedures
- *Monitored* and handled problems directly and immediately

The study of junior high school effective and ineffective teachers found differentiating practices similar to the elementary teachers. The findings were that effective managers:

- *Instructed* students in specific rules about appropriate behavior
- *Monitored* student compliance by consistently enforcing acceptable behavior
- *Made an accounting of student work* through precise record keeping of students' work accomplishment.
- *Broke down rules* from general "holisms" to specific do's and don'ts.
- *Organized* time so most classroom time was devoted to instruction (as with Kounin's terms smoothness and momentum).

What echoes throughout the Evertson and Emmer studies is that teachers break down the areas of expected student behaviors into specific classroom rules and procedures and then instruct their students in how to follow them.

Evertson and Emmer recorded the expectations and procedures of successful classroom managers. The reader who teaches in preschool or elementary school may wish to review Chart 16–1. The reader who teaches in junior/middle or secondary school may wish to review Chart 16–2.

After reading through these charts and considering Kounin's work, the teacher may think of some immediate classroom-management changes to make. Since the purpose of this book is to help teachers solve the discipline problems of individual students, the vast amount of literature and research on classroom management can only be briefly explored. Instead this discourse on management is to suggest that if a teacher finds discipline problems pervasive throughout the classroom, then further study and a change in management techniques may be needed before looking at ways to deal with individual students. A reader who wishes to pursue classroom management further can find excellent readings listed at the end of the chapter.

CHART 16–1 Expectations and Procedures for the Elementary School Classroom*

Area of Behavior	A Common Expectation or Procedure
A. Student use of classroom space and facilities	
1. Desks or tables and student storage space	Students are usually expected to keep these areas clean and neat. Some teachers set aside a particular period of time each week for students to clean out desks. Alternatively, straightening out materials could be a good end-of-day routine.
2. Learning centers/stations	Appropriate behavior at the center, access to the center, care of materials, and procedures for coming and going should be considered.
3. Shared materials, bookshelves, drawers, and cabinets	Access and use should be spelled out.
4. Teacher's desk and storage areas	Frequently these are off-limits to students, except when the teacher's permission is given.
5. Drinking fountain, sink, pencil sharpener, and bathroom	Decide when and how these can be used. Most teachers prefer not to have lines waiting at any of these locations.
B. Procedures concerning other areas of the school	
1. Out-of-class bathrooms, drinking fountains, office, library, resource rooms	Appropriate student behavior needs to be identified. Procedures for students coming to and going from these areas should be decided upon.
2. Coming and going from the classroom	Students need to learn how to line up properly and how to pass through the halls correctly. Consider such things as the condition of the room before lining up and whether talking is allowed.
3. Playground	Expectations need to be identified for coming from and going to the playground, safety and maintenance rules, and ways to get students' attention for lining up or listening. Some teachers use a coach's whistle.
4. Lunchroom	Expectations for table manners, behavior, and noise level should be identified.
C. Procedures during whole-class activities	
1. Student participation in class discussions	Many teachers require students to raise their hands to be called on before speaking during whole-class activities.
2. Student involvement and attention	Students are expected to listen to the person who is talking.
3. Assignments	Many teachers record assignments on a chalkboard or elsewhere or have students copy the assignments in notebooks.
4. Talk among students during seatwork	Some teachers require silence; others allow quiet talk (very soft whispering). Also, teachers sometimes use a cue or signal to let students know when the noise level is unacceptable. For example, a bell rung once means no more talking. Also needed are procedures for students working together, if this is to be allowed, and some procedure to enable students to contact the teacher if they need help. Typical procedures involve students raising hands when help is needed or, if the teacher is involved with other students or in group work, the use of classroom monitors.
5. Passing out books and supplies	Supplies that are frequently used can be passed out by a monitor. Students need to know what to do while they wait for their materials.
6. Students turning in work	Teachers frequently have a set of shelves or an area where students turn in assignments when they are finished. Alternatively, a special folder for each student may be kept.
7. Handing back assignments to students	Prompt return of corrected papers is desirable. Many teachers establish a set time of the day to do this. Students need to know what to do with the material when they receive it (place it in a notebook, or folder, or take it home).

Area of Behavior	A Common Expectation or Procedure
8. Make-up work	Procedures are needed for helping students who have been absent as well as for communicating assignments that must be made up.
9. Out-of-seat policies	Students need to know when it is acceptable to be out of seat and when permission is needed.
10. What to do when seatwork is finished	Some teachers use extra-credit assignments, enrichment activities, free reading, etc.
D. Procedures during reading groups or other small-group work	
1. Student movement into and out of group	These transitions should be brief, quiet, and nondisruptive to other students. Many teachers use a bell to signal movement from seatwork to small group. This works when there is a preset order that students know.
2. Bringing materials to the group	Students need to know what they are to bring with them to the group. One way to communicate this is to include a list of the materials along with posted assignments.
3. Expected behavior of students in the small group	Just as in whole-group activities, students need clear expectations about what behaviors are appropriate in small-group work.
4. Expected behavior of students not in the small group	Students out of the group also need clear expectations about desirable behavior. Important areas include noise level, student talk, access to the teacher, and what to do when the seatwork assignment or other activities are completed. Effective managers avoid problems by giving very clear instructions for activities of students out-of-group. Checking briefly between groups also helps prevent problems from continuing as well as allowing monitoring. Student helpers may also be identified.
E. Other procedures that must be decided upon	
1. Beginning the school day	Establishing a consistent routine, such as saying the Pledge of Allegiance, the current date, birthdays, an overview of the morning's activities; or passing back graded papers helps start the day while still giving time for late arrivals and for administrative matters to be accomplished.
2. Administrative matters	Such details as attendance reporting, collecting lunch money, and other recordkeeping must be done while students are in the room. Teachers can set aside a specific time of the day for performing these tasks during which the students are expected to engage in some activity. For example, ten minutes of quiet reading fills the time constructively while allowing the teacher to handle administrative tasks with little interruption.
3. End of school day	Routines can be planned for concluding each day. Straightening desks, gathering materials, singing a song, or reviewing activities and things learned during the day provide some structure for this major transition time.
4. Student conduct during interruptions and delays	Interruptions are inevitable and sometimes frequent. Students can be taught to continue working if interrupted, or to sit patiently and quietly otherwise.
5. Fire drills, and other precautionary measures	School procedures need to be identified and carefully taught to the children.
6. Housekeeping and student helpers	Most children love to help, and the teacher needs only to identify specific tasks. These are also a good way to help some children learn responsibility. Some possibilities: feeding classroom pets, watering plants, erasing chalkboards, acting as line leader, messenger, etc. A procedure for choosing and rotating responsibilities among students needs to be established.

Evertson, Carolyn M. and Emmer, Edmund T. "Preventive Classroom Management." In *Helping Teachers Manage Classrooms*, Daniel L. Duke, ed. Alexandria, Virginia: ASCD, 1982.

CHART 16–2 Expectations and Procedures for Junior High School/Middle School Classrooms

Area of Behavior	*A Common Expectation or Procedure*
A. Procedures for beginning class	
1. Administrative matters	The teacher needs procedures to handle reporting absences and tardiness. Students need to know what behaviors are expected of them while the teacher is completing administrative procedures. Some teachers begin the period with a brief warm-up activity such as a few problems or a brief assignment. Others expect the students to sit quietly and wait for the teacher to complete the routine.
2. Student behavior before and at the beginning of the period	Procedures should be established for what students are expected to do when the tardy bell rings (be in seats, stop talking), behavior during PA announcements (no talking, no interruptions of the teacher), what materials are expected to be brought to class each day, and how materials to be used during the period will be distributed.
B. Procedures during whole-class instructional activities	
1. Student talk	Many teachers require that students raise their hands in order to receive permission to speak. Sometimes teachers allow chorus responses (everybody answers at once) without hand raising, but the teacher then needs to identify and use some signal to students that lets them know when such responding is appropriate.
2. Use of the room by students	Students should know when it is appropriate to use the pencil sharpener, to obtain materials from shelves or bookcases, and if and when it is appropriate to leave their seats to seek help from the teacher or other students. Unclear expectations in this area result in some students spending time wandering about the room.
3. Leaving the room	Some procedure needs to be established for allowing students to use the bathroom, go to the library or school office, etc. Usually the school will have some specified system. We have noted that teachers who are free with hall passes frequently have large numbers of requests to leave the room.
4. Signals for attention	Frequently teachers use a verbal signal or a cue such as moving to a specific area of the room, ringing a bell, or turning on an overhead projector to signal to students. Such a signal, if used consistently, can be an effective device for making a transition between activities or for obtaining student attention.
5. Student behavior during seatwork	Expectations need to be established for what kind of talk, if any, may occur during seatwork; how students can get help; when out-of-seat behavior is or is not permitted; how to gain access to materials; and what to do if seatwork assignments are completed early.
6. Procedures for laboratory work or individual projects	A system for distributing materials when these are used is essential. Also, safety routines or rules are vital. Expectations regarding appropriate behavior should be established for students working individually or in groups, and when extensive movement around the room or coming and going is required. Finally, routines for cleaning up are suggested.

Area of Behavior	A Common Expectation or Procedure
C. Expectations regarding student responsibility for work	
1. Policy regarding the form of work	Procedures can be established for the placement of headings on the paper, for the use of pen or pencil, and for neatness.
2. Policy regarding completion of assignments	The teacher will have to decide whether incomplete or late work is acceptable, under what conditions, and whether a penalty will be imposed. In addition, some procedure for informing students of due dates for assignments should be established, along with procedures for make-up work for students who were absent.
3. Communicating assignments to students	An effective procedure for communicating assignments is to keep a list of each period's work assignments during a two- or three-week period of time. Posting this list allows students who were absent to easily identify necessary make-up work. Another useful procedure is to record the assignment for the day on an overhead projector transparency or on the front chalkboard, and require students to copy the assignment onto a piece of paper or into a notebook. Students who do not complete assignments in class will then have a record of what is expected when they return to the assignment at home or during a study period.
4. Checking procedures	Work that is to be checked by students in class can save the teacher time and provide quick feedback to students. Procedures should be established for exchanging papers, noting errors, returning papers, and passing them in to the teacher.
5. Grading policy	Students should know what components will be included in determining report card grades and the weight (percent) of each component.
D. Other procedures	
1. Student use of teacher desk or storage areas	Generally these are kept off-limits to students, except when the teacher gives special permission.
2. Fire and disaster drills	Students should be informed early in the year about what they are to do during such emergencies. Typically, the school will have a master plan and will conduct school-wide drills.
3. Procedures for ending the class	Expectations regarding straightening up the room, returning to seats, keeping a tolerable noise level, and signaling for dismissal may be established. When cleanup requires more than a few seconds, teachers usually set aside the necessary time at the end of the period to complete the task before the bell rings.
4. Interruptions	Students need to know what is expected during interruptions (continue working or sit quietly).

Evertson and Emmer, op. cit.

SUMMARY

Classroom management has been discussed as a preventive process for many discipline problems. Research by Jacob Kounin on "with-it-ness," "overlapping," "smoothness," "momentum," and "group alerting"; and the research by Evertson and Emmer on rules and monitoring provide insights to help teachers organize their classroom practice. It is our belief that management will reduce but not eliminate all discipline problems. Therefore, a teacher needs strategies and behaviors for both.

NOTES

1. Daniel L. Duke, ed., *Classroom Management: The Nineteen Seventy-Eight Yearbook of the National Society for the Study of Education, Part II* (Chicago, Illinois: University of Chicago Press, 1979), p. xii.
2. Jacob Kounin, *Discipline and Group Management in Classrooms* (New York: Holt, Rinehart, and Winston, 1970).
3. Carolyn M. Evertson and Edmund T. Emmer, "Preventive Classroom Management," in Daniel L. Duke, ed., *Helping Teachers Manage Classrooms* (Alexandria, Virginia: Association for Supervision and Curriculum Development, 1982), pp. 2–31.
4. Jere Brophy, "Teacher Behavior and Its Effects," *Journal of Educational Psychology* 71 (1979): 733–50. M. Dunkin and B. Biddle, *The Study of Teaching* (New York: Holt, Rinehart and Winston, 1974).
5. Kounin, *Discipline and Group Management*, p. 123.
6. L. Anderson, C. Evertson, and E. Emmer, "Dimensions in Classroom Management Derived From Recent Research," *Journal of Curriculum Studies* 12 (1980): 343–356. Jere Brophy and Carolyn Evertson, "Context Variables in Teaching," *Educational Psychologist* 12 (1978): 310–16. Jere Brophy and Carolyn Evertson, *Learning From Teaching: A Developmental Perspective*, (Boston: Allyn and Bacon, 1976). E. Emmer, C. Evertson, and L. Anderson, "Effective Classroom Management at the Beginning of the School Year," *Elementary School Journal 1980* (1980): 219–31. C. Evertson, J. Sanford, and E. Emmer, "Effects of Class Heterogeneity in Junior High School," *American Educational Research Journal* 18 (1981):219–32. T. L. Good, "Teacher Effectiveness in the Elementary School: What We Know About It Now," *Journal of Teacher Education* 30 (1979): 32–64. J. Stanford and C. Evertson, "Classroom Management in a Low SES Junior High: Three Case Studies, " *Journal of Teacher Education* 32 (1981): 34–38.
7. Carolyn M. Evertson and Edmund T. Emmer, "Preventive Classroom Management," p. 17.

REFERENCES

Cruickshank, Donald and Associates. *Teaching is Tough*. Englewood Cliffs, New Jersey: Prentice-Hall, Inc., 1980.

Curwin, Richard, and Medler, Allen. *The Discipline Book: A Complete Guide to School and Classroom Management*. (Reston, Virginia: Reston Publishing Co., 1980).

Duke, Daniel L., ed. *Helping Teachers Manage Classrooms* Alexandria, Virginia: Association for Supervision and Curriculum Development, 1982.

Emmer, E. E., Evertson, C. M., Sanford, J. P., Clements, B. S., and Worsham, M. E. *Classroom Management for Secondary Teachers* (Englewood Cliffs, New Jersey: Prenctice-Hall, Inc., 1984).

Evertson, C. M., Emmer, E. E., Clements, B. S., Sanford, J. P., and Worsham, M. E. *Classroom Management for Elementary Teachers* (Englewood Cliffs, New Jersey: Prentice-Hall, Inc., 1984).

Good, Thomas, and Brophy, Jere, *Looking in Classrooms* New York: Harper & Row, Publishers, 1978.

Kounin, Jacob S. *Discipline and Group Management in Classrooms* New York: Holt, Rinehart, and Winston, 1970.

Tillman, Murray. *Troubleshooting Classroom Problems* Glenview, Illinois: Scott, Foresman and Co., 1982.

17

Conclusion: A Better Tomorrow

Recall the story about Mr. Erelan with which we began the book. When we left Mr. Erelan (see Chapter One), he had little hope. Previously, he had been an effective teacher with years of experience in using a single approach of stern commands to disruptive students. He now finds this approach ineffective with Sophia, yet he has little training or knowledge for changing his behavior. Therefore, he has continued an approach that has accelerated Sophia's misbehavior. What hope does he have for a better tomorrow?

How does a teacher break this cycle of despair? Many well-meaning supervisors or colleagues will advise "to be patient and everything will improve." Such advice is of little use to a teacher who needs help. He or she wants to know what actions to take. Hoping for a miraculous change without implementing a concrete plan of action would be an exercise in fantasy. It is our belief that Mr. Erelan and other teachers want the very best for their students These educators are intelligent and capable persons who, if given the knowledge base and tools, will make informed changes for the better. This book has attempted to provide the knowledge base and many of the tools to achieve these changes.

KNOWLEDGE AND CHOICES FOR TODAY'S TEACHER

The teacher who has read this book will be aware of the following three schools of psyhological thought when disciplining students:

1. *The Relationship-Listeners*, who believe a student must learn to discipline himself or herself through the facilitation of his or her inner rationality.
2. *The Confronting-Contractors*, who believe a student learns discipline from the interaction of his or her desires with those of the outside world.
3. *The Rules/Rewarders-Punishers*, who believe a student learns appropriate behavior as a result of the influences of the outer environment.

Within each school of thought there are specific authors of various teacher-student interaction models who suggest specific teacher practices. Each of those practices has been interpreted along the Teacher Behavior Continuum. (See Figure 17—1.) At one end of the continuum, strategies are used whereby the child has the most control of his or her behavior and the teacher has minimal control (capital *C*, lowercase *t*), and at the other end the teacher subsumes the child's power (lowercase *c*, capital *T*).

The Relationship-Listening models stress the minimally controlling behaviors at the left of the continuum, the Confronting-Contracting models emphasize the teacher behaviors in the middle, and the Rules/Rewards-Punishment models stress the behaviors at the right of the continuum.

The popular advocates of discipline models, corresponding to schools of thought, are:

Relationship-Listening	
Thomas Gordon	Supportive model
Eric Berne	Communication model
Thomas Harris	
Louis E. Raths	Valuing model
Merrill Harmin	
Sidney B. Simon	
and others	
Confronting-Contracting	
Rudolf Dreikurs	Social model
William Glasser	Reality model
Rules/Rewards-Punishment	
Saul Axelrod	Behavior-modification model
Lloyd Homme	
and others	
Lee and Marlene Canter	Assertiveness model
James Dobson	
Siegfried Engelmann	Behaviorism-with-corporal-punishment model

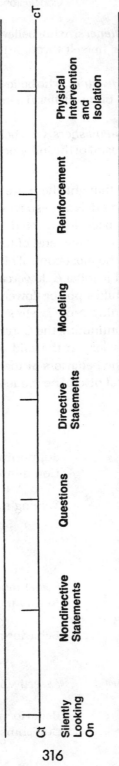

FIGURE 16–1. Teacher Behavior Continuum (TBC)

Ct | Silently Looking On | Nondirective Statements | Questions | Directive Statements | Modeling | Reinforcement | Physical Intervention and Isolation | cT

Each of the models provides specific *overt* and *covert* teacher behaviors. The teacher can immediately choose from such behaviors as "active listening" (Gordon), to "social questioning" (Dreikurs), to "off to the castle" (Glasser), to "saturation" (behavior modification), to "demands" (Canters). However, for a more consistent, long-range plan, a teacher can choose a combination of the elements of various models. The teacher can choose to work from student control to teacher power, from teacher control to student power, or from share power. The teacher can make decisions based on the seriousness of the student's behavior, the social development of the student, or the wisdom of a professional team. Classroom management can be used to minimize the amount of student misbehavior that a teacher must solve. The ultimate goal of all teacher decisions is to have the student be able to exercise control over his or her own behavior.

The various choices a teacher can make are illustrated in Figure 17–2.

Another important element to consider is the school personnel who can be used to help the student. The misbehavior may be beyond the classroom teacher's *spheres of competency*. He or she might use a school *staffing* to develop an *individualized education plan* or to seek outside professional help.

THE PROFESSIONAL TEACHER

Many choices have been provided for the teacher. The authors have purposely refused to give a single "recipe" for action. Instead, the schools of thought, models, and pathways have been presented as information for the teacher to act on in his or her own way. Strengths and limitations of each model were presented, not to influence, but instead for the reader to consider the consequences of all the choices presented. The belief that has re-echoed throughout this book is that *there is no one approach to discipline or interaction that will be successful for all students*. In today's age of heterogeneity and pluralism, teachers will be most effective by diversifying and individualizing their approaches.

In the final analysis, we believe teachers will make wise choices. It is our contention that every teacher desires the best for his or her students. Within their own classrooms, only they truly know their students. If provided with a knowledge base for using the alternative "tools" of discipline, they can make the appropriate applications.

A teacher is a professional. A professional can make decisions based on careful observation and analysis. A medical doctor, when confronted with an

FIGURE 16–2. Teacher Choices

ill patient, will listen to the patient, monitor the body mechanisms, and observe the symptoms. The doctor will then not only use his or her past experience, intuition, or former training to determine a treatment, but he or she will add the knowledge acquired by having kept abreast of the latest research or theory. From this total picture, the physician will then decide what treatment is most suitable. If he or she is proven to be wrong, then the process begins again. Patients have confidence in a doctor who is knowledgeable, experienced, current, and intelligent. The patient's confidence in the doctor often helps in the cure; so it is with the student's confidence in the teacher. Confidence comes from knowing and being able to apply alternative remedies. Helplessness comes from not knowing what else to do.

A BETTER TOMORROW

The teacher who has read this book can be optimistic for good reasons. If current teacher behaviors with a disruptive student are unsuccessful, there are many other actions that can be taken. Mr. Erelan, whom we left leaning aganst the wall, can straighten up, "clear his head," reassess the situation, and decide on further action. He now has a range of strategies, models, and pathways to use. He and Sophia have every reason to expect a "better tomorrow."

Appendix

Moral Reasoning:
From Seven Years
To Adulthood

Jean Piaget,[1] the noted child psychologist, was instrumental in providing the basis for Lawrence Kohlberg's[2] later work in the area of moral development. Piaget demonstrated that it was not until the child was eleven years old, or older, that he or she became intellectually able to evaluate abstract moral dilemmas. The values in such issues as future roles or occupations, sexual relationships, acceptance or rejection of religious principles, and relationships to figures of authority have little meaning to the young child. Piaget, and later Kohlberg, discovered that what a kindergartener or first-grade child thinks is "naughty" and what an adolescent thinks is right or wrong are dramatically different. An understanding of how reasoning varies among students can help the teacher who wants to communicate with a variety of students. The teacher is ordered by an understanding of moral growth in deciding what disciplinary techniques will best lead children to make more mature moral decisions about what is right or wrong and what, in turn, affects their actions towards others.

Let us provide an example of such divergencies in student reasoning. Piaget interviewed many children across different age levels to gather their responses to common dilemmas. One of Piaget's typical dilemmas reads as follows:

A. A little boy (or a little girl) goes for a walk in the street and meets a big dog who frightens him very much. So he then goes home and tells his mother he has seen a dog that was as big as a cow.

B. A child comes home from school and tells his mother that the teacher has given him good marks, but it was not true; the teacher had given him no marks at all, either good or bad.[3]

Piaget then asked the various youngsters which child was the naughtiest. He found that children younger than first-grade age (prerational period) simply could not understand the problem and therefore could not give an intelligible response. However, students in the early elementary grades did have a definite point of view. Their reasoning was generally of this manner.

Fel (Age 6)

Which of these two children is naughtiest?—The little girl who said she saw a dog as big as a cow.—Why is she the naughtiest?—Because it could never happen. —Did her mother believe her?—No, because there never are (dogs as big as cows).—Why did she say that?—To exaggerate.—And why did the other one tell a lie?—Because she wanted to make people believe that she had a good report.—Did her mother believe her?—Yes.—Which would you punish most if you were the mother?—The one with the dog because she told the worst lie and was the naughtiest.

Bug (Age 6)

Which is the naughtiest?—The one with the cow.—Why is he the naughtiest? —Because it isn't true.—And the one with the good marks?—He is less naughty. —Why?—Because his mother would have believed, because she believed the lie.[4]

The replies are typical of boys and girls in *early* elementary school. "Naughtiness" or lying is measured by the degree of its credibility to adults. The lie about the good marks is "not so bad" because the mother will be easily taken in by it. Piaget demonstrated through these types of stories that the refinement of moral judgment and reasoning is a developmental process. Not until the ages of eleven or older does moral reasoning begin to change from being centered on "those more powerful adults" (believable to mother or father) to reasons of intent and justice when living cooperatively with others. The following are the responses of older children to the same vignettes.

Kei (Age 10)

Which is the naughtier?—The lie about the teacher.—Why?—Because he deceived his mother.—But so did the other.—But he (the one of the teacher) had said something the teacher hadn't said.—The other one too had said something that wasn't true. (Our counter-suggestions, no matter how insistent, are ineffectual.)—He had told a great big lie. The teacher hadn't said he was good. —Why is it naughtier than the lie about the dog?—Because you can see better that it (the lie about the dog) is not true. You can't tell with the lie about the teacher.—Why did he say he had seen a dog as big as a cow?—To make them believe he had seen something marvelous.[5]

What teachers should infer from the information just given is that, based on the child's experience and maturing intellectual abilities, what students understand as right or wrong will be dramatically different at different ages. If this developmental growth process is disregarded, teachers will be making demands on students to evaluate behavior and problems that they do not yet have the intellectual abilities to fully understand. Also, teachers will be using techniques and methods that may inhibit or retard the moral growth of students.

LEVELS OF MORAL REASONING

The work of Lawrence Kohlberg has followed Piaget's findings with more exact stages of reasoning.

In the Developmental Socialization Continuum (DSC), one can see how Moral Levels I through VI are further substages of the two stages, social interaction through language and conceptualization through language. All moral reasoning levels begin at the rational age of seven years.

Moral Level I—Punishment and Obedience Orientation

Characteristic of early elementary grade students, this is a level where reasoning is based on the physical consequences of an act. The determination of goodness or badness is made regardless of the person's intention or motive. For example, let's look at two situations:

Tommy is helping his mother to set the table, and accidentally the door closes on him as he is passing through it and it knocks the plates from his hands; all twelve plates break.

Jimmy wants to get a cookie from the cupboard while his mother is away. He climbs onto a chair and attempts to get to the cookies that are on a high shelf. He bumps one cup, and it falls and breaks.

A child with Moral Level I reasoning would say that Tommy was the "naughtiest": he broke twelve items and Jimmy only broke one item. The Moral Level I child could judge and declare that Tommy should receive harsh *physical* punishment.

Moral Level II—Instrumental-Relativist Orientation

It is not until around the ages of nine to eleven that students begin to understand motive. With the two stories just described, the Moral Level II child would suggest that Tommy was only helping and should not be punished for an accident. On the other hand, Jimmy was "bad"; he was doing something he knew was wrong. The Moral Level II child would further suggest that Jimmy should be punished by having to pay the logical consequence (Dreikurs). Jimmy might give up his allowance or do extra work at home to pay for a replacement. This logical consequence at Moral Level II is for the sole purpose of re-establishing the social order: "If things are broken, one must work to replace them."

Moral Level III—The Interpersonal Concordance or "Good Boy-Nice Girl" Orientation

Towards adolescence, moral reasoning reaches a stage of conforming to an image of what one should do based on what others will think. A good boy or girl of Level III would not knowingly take the cookies when told not to; therefore, Jimmy was wrong because he had disappointed his mother. This is the age of "peer review," when one reasons according to what classmates as well as adults might think, and it can be seen in conformity in dress and mannerisms among students of this age, in order to measure up and be "one of the gang," or a "good boy-nice girl."

Moral Level IV—Law and Order Orientation

Reasoning now shifts from what others might think to the unquestioned need for rules and regulations to sustain the social order. Jimmy attempted to "steal" the cookies, and stealing is against the law. What he did was wrong. It made no difference if he broke one cup or a hundred; his actions were illegal. Correct behavior in Level IV is obeying and upholding societal standards of conduct as rules for the common good. If everyone disobeyed the rules, there would be no society.

Moral Levels V and VI—Social-Contract Legalistic Orientation and Universal-Ethical Principles Orientation

According to Kohlberg, very few people ever reach Moral Levels V and VI. Right actions are defined in terms of general *individual* rights and standards based on a concept of democracy that overrides incompatible laws and orders. In Moral Level VI, reasoning is based on one's universal, self-chosen principles of what is good. Such a sense of justice transcends not only current law and order but also conventional concepts of government. In both Levels V and VI, the individual reasons to the rightness or wrongness of an act, not from selfish interests or standards upheld by authority, but rather on considerations of what is forever in the best interest of all people.

NOTES

1. Jean Piaget, *Moral Judgment of the Child*, trans. Marjorie Gabain (New York: Free Press, 1965).
2. Lawrence Kohlberg. "The Cognitive-Developmental Approach to Moral Education," *Phi Delta Kappan*, ed. Stanley M. Elam, 56(1975); 10.
3. Piaget, *Moral Judgment of the Child*. p. 148.
4. Piaget, *Moral Judgment of the Child*. pp. 150–151.
5. Piaget, *Moral Judgment of the Child*. p. 158.

Index

Adler, Alfred, 17, 85
Adult. *See* Transactional Analysis
Alberti, R.E., 152
Assertive Discipline (Canter and Canter), 152
Assertiveness model, 152−153, 161, 199−202, 225, 243, 244. *See also* Rules/Rewards-Punishment
  instructional media for, 162−163
  and the TBC, 154 (Fig. 9-1), 155−160. *See also under categories of teacher behavior*
Attention getting, student goal of, 86, 88, 90−91, 96
Authority, Gordon's types of, 36−37
Axelrod, Saul, 20, 23, 131
Axline, Virginia, 18

Bandura, Albert, 131, 141
Behavior. *See* Students; Teacher behavior; Teachers
Behaviorism, 17
Behaviorism/punishment model, 167−169, 202−205, 225, 243. *See also* Rules/Rewards-Punishment
  instructional media for, 179−180
  and the TBC, 169−176, 177. *See also under categories of teacher behavior*
Behavior modification, 129−133, 197−199, 225, 243. *See also* Reinforcement; Rules/Rewards-Punishment
  instructional media for, 148−149
  and the TBC, 136−145, 146. *See also under categories of teacher behavior*
Beliefs on Discipline Inventory, 10−12, 209
Bereiter, Carl, 166, 173
Berne, Eric, 47, 48−49. *See also* Transactional Analysis

Blackham, Garth, 20, 131, 133
Body gestures, 53
Born to Win (James and Jongeward), 47
Broken-record method, 158
Bruner, Jerome, 17

Canter, Lee and Marlene, 20, 23, 152, 161. *See also* Assertiveness model
Child. *See* Transactional Analysis
Child development, theories of, 15−18
"Chip on the Shoulder," 61
Class council meetings, 93−94
Classroom:
  democracy in, 93−94
  environment, modification of, 40, 43
  heterogeneous, 3
  management of. *See* Classroom management
  as social unit, 275
  time, organization of, 40, 43
Classroom management, 298−301
  Evertson and Emmer on, 306−311
  Kounin on, 301−306
Classroom meetings, Glasser's, 118−122
"Clown," 61
Coercive/legalistic model, 240, 244
Communicating, Gordon on, 30. *See also* Door openers; Language; Listening; Roadblocks
Communication model. *See* Transactional Analysis
Competency, spheres of, 275−277
Conditioning, 20. *See also* Behavior modification; Reinforcement; Rules/Rewards-Punishment
Conflict, Gordon's definition of, 37
Conflict resolution, Gordon on, 37−38, 41. *See also* Method III (no-lose); Ownership of the problem

Confronting-Contracting, 17−19, 39−40, 189−192, 216, 225, 240, 242. *See also* Reality model; Social discipline model
   case study in (Plan III), 231−235
   as a starting point (Plan 3), 223
   and the TBC, 22−24
Consequences. *See* Natural/logical consequences
Contingency contracting, 142−143
Contracting. *See* Confronting-Contracting; Contingency contracting
Crises, degrees of, 238−244

Dare to Discipline (Dobson), 166
Decision making, 208−211
   eclectic, 209, 213−216
   team, 211
Demands, 157−158
Democracy, classroom, 93−94
Developmental psychology, 17
Developmental Socialization Continuum (DSC), 251−253
Developmental theory, 246−256
Dewey, John, 39
Dinkmeyer, Don, 97
Directive statements, 21, 225. *See also* Teacher Behavior Continuum
   and behavior modification, 138−140
   and Berne and Harris's Transactional Analysis, 58−59
   and Canters' assertiveness model, 157
   and Dreikurs's social discipline model, 88−93
   and Engelmann and Dobson's behaviorism/punishment model, 170−171
   and Glasser's reality model, 111−112
   and Gordon's T.E.T., 33−36, 42
   and Raths and Simon's values clarification, 75−76
Dobson, James, 20, 23, 166, 168, 169, 176, 178. *See also* Behaviorism/punishment model
Door openers, 30−31, 33−34, 43
Dreikurs, Rudolf, 19, 23, 39, 85−86, 97, 98, 172, 176. *See also* Social discipline model

Eclecticism, 209, 213−216
Ego, 47, 49, 52
Emmer, Edmund T., 306−311
Emmons, M.L., 152

Encouragement, Dreikurs on, 94, 96−99
Engelmann, Siegfried, 20, 23, 166, 167, 176, 178. *See also* Behaviorism/punishment model
Ernst, Ken, 47, 61
Evertson, Carolyn M., 306−311

Facial expressions, 53
Freed, Alvyn M., 47, 60
Freedom, areas of, 39−40
Freud, Sigmund, 16, 47−48. *See also* Psychoanalysis

Games, 60−62
Games People Play (Berne), 47
Games Students Play (Ernst), 47
"Gear shifting," 216
Gestalt psychology, 17
Glasser, William, 19, 23, 39, 109−110, 172, 176. *See also* Reality model
Glickman, Carl D., 10n.
Goals. *See* Student goals
Gordon, Thomas, 18, 23, 27, 29−43, 96. *See also* T.E.T.: Teacher Effectiveness Training
Grey, Loren, 98

Harmin, Merrill, 18, 23, 69, 70, 71
Harris, Thomas, 18, 23, 47, 60. *See also* Transactional Analysis
Helplessness, student goal of, 86, 88, 92, 96, 98
Homme, Lloyd, 20, 131, 142
Humanism, 16

"I" message:
   Canters on, 157
   Gordon on, 33, 34, 38, 43
I'm OK—You're OK (Harris), 47
Individualized Discipline Plan (IDP), 215−216, 224
   case studies of, 224−235
   from Confronting-Contracting (Plan 3), 223
   matrix for (Chart 12-1), 225
   from Relationship-Listening (Plan 1), 217−222
   from Rules/Rewards-Punishment (Plan 2), 222−223
   worksheet for, 226−227
Individualized Educational Plan (IEP), 283
Interactionalism, 17−18, 19

Intervention. *See* Crises, degrees of; Physical intervention and isolation
Isolation. *See* Physical intervention and isolation

James, Muriel, 47
Jongeward, Dorothy, 47

Kohlberg, Lawrence, 320
Kounin, Jacob S., 301–306

Language. *See also* Verbal aggression; Verbal clues
  positive and punitive, 139
  social interaction and conceptualization through, 251–253, 270–274
  use of, in behavior modification, 138–140
Learning theory, 14–18
  application of, 18–20
Listening. *See also* Relationship-Listening
  active, 31–34, 38, 43. *See also* Non-directive statements
  Gordon on, 30, 33–34, 43
Looking on. *See* Silently looking on

Madsen, Charles and Clifford, 20, 131
Mainstreaming, 3, 281
"Make Me," 61–62
Maslow, A.H., 28, 237–244
Meetings:
  class council, 93–94
  Glasser's classroom, 118–122
Memory processes, research on, 48
Method III (no-lose), 38–43
Modeling, 21, 225. *See also* Teacher Behavior Continuum
  and behavior modification, 140–141
  and Berne and Harris's Trasactional Analysis, 60
  and Canters' assertiveness model, 158–159
  and Dreikurs's social discipline model, 93–94
  and Englemann and Dobson's behaviorism/punishment model, 171–172
  and Glasser's reality model, 113
  and Gordon's T.E.T., 40–43
  and Raths and Simon's values clarification, 76–77
Moral development, 246–256
Moral reasoning, 320–324
Moustakas, Clark, 18

National Education Association (NEA), 2
Natural/logical consequences, Dreikurs on, 94–96
Needs, Maslow's hierarchy of, 237–244
Nondirective statements, 21, 225. *See also* Teacher Behavior Continuum
  and behavior modification, 138–140
  and Berne and Harris's Transactional Analysis, 56
  and Canters' assertiveness model, 157
  and Glasser's reality model, 111
  and Gordon's T.E.T., 31–34, 38, 42
  and Raths and Simon's values clarification, 73
Nonverbal clues, 53

Overlapping, 301–306
Ownership of the problem, 33–34, 37

Parent. *See* Transactional Analysis
Pavlov, I., 130
Peers, modeling of, 140
Penfield, Wilder, 48
Physical intervention and isolation, 21, 225. *See also* Teacher Behavior Continuum
  and behavior modification, 144–145
  and Berne and Harris's Transactional Analysis, 60
  and Canters' assertiveness model, 160
  and Dreikurs's social discipline model, 99–100
  and Engelmann and Dobson's behaviorism/punishment model, 173–176
  and Glasser's reality model, 116–118
  and Gordon's T.E.T., 41, 42
  and Raths and Simon's values clarification, 77
Piaget, Jean, 320
Power and control, student goal of, 86, 88, 91, 96
Power relationship, teacher-student, 22–24, 37–38. *See also* Teacher Behavior Continuum; Win-lose methods
Praise, Dreikurs on, 97–99
Problem ownership. *See* Ownership of the problem
Problem resolution, Gordon's Method III for, 39–43
Psychoanalysis, 16, 47–48, 109–110

Psychology, educational, 14–18
  application of, 18–20
Punishment, 134, 145. *See also* Reinforcement; Rules/Rewards-Punishment
  Canters on, 159, 160
  Dreikurs on, 95–96
  physical, 166. *See also* Behaviorism/
  punishment model

Questions, 21, 225. *See also* Teacher
  Behavior Continuum
  and behavior modification, 138–140
  and Berne and Harris's Transactional
    Analysis, 56–58
  and Canters' assertiveness model, 157
  and Dreikurs's social discipline model,
    87–90
  and Glasser's reality model, 112–113
  and Gordon's T.E.T., 30–34, 42
  and Raths and Simon's values clarification, 73–75

Raths, Louis, 18, 23, 69, 70, 71. *See also*
  Values clarification
Reality model, 109–110, 193–196,
  225, 242. *See also* Confronting-
  Contracting
  instructional media for, 125–128
  and the TBC, 110–118, 123 (Fig. 7-1).
  *See also under categories of teacher
  behavior*
Reality Therapy (Glasser), 110
Redl, Fritz, 7
Reinforcement, 20, 21, 133–136, 225. *See
  also* Rules/Rewards-Punishment;
  Teacher Behavior Continuum
  in behavior modification, 131–136,
    142–144
  and Berne and Harris's Transactional
    Analysis, 59
  and Canters' assertiveness model, 159
  and Dreikurs's social discipline model,
    94–99
  and Engelmann and Dobson's be-
    haviorism/punishment model, 172–
    173
  and Glasser's reality model, 113–116
  and Gordon's T.E.T., 36–40, 42
  and Raths and Simon's values clari-
    fication, 77
Relationship-Listening, 16, 18–19, 71, 96,
  100, 181–182, 216, 225, 240, 241. *See
  also* T.E.T.: Teacher Effectiveness

Training; Transactional Analysis;
  Values clarification
  case study in (Plan I), 228–229
  as a starting point (Plan 1), 217–222
  and the TBC, 22–24
Revenge, student goal of, 86, 88, 91, 96, 98
Rewards. *See also* Rules/Rewards-Pun-
  ishment
  Canters' use of, 159
  Dreikurs on, 97–99
Roadblocks:
  Canters on, 156
  Gordon on, 31, 32, 35–36, 41
Rogers, Carl, 16, 18, 27–28
Rules/Rewards-Punishment, 17, 19–20,
  36, 40, 196, 216, 225, 240, 243.
  See also Assertiveness model; Be-
  haviorism/punishment model; Be-
  havior modification
  case study in (Plan II), 230–231
  as starting point (Plan 2), 222–223
  and the TBC, 22–24

Saturation, 144–145
"Schlemiel," 61
Schools Without Failure (Glasser), 110, 122
Self-concept, 29
Shaping, 143–144
Silberman, Adolph, 20, 131, 133
Silently looking on, 21, 225. *See also*
  Teacher Behavior Continuum
  and behavior modification, 136–138
  and Berne and Harris's Transactional
    Analysis, 52–56
  and Canters' assertiveness model,
    155–156
  and Dreikurs's social discipline model,
    87
  and Engelmann and Dobson's be-
    haviorism/punishment model, 169–
    170
  and Glasser's reality model, 110–111
  and Gordon's T.E.T., 29–30, 33, 42
  and Raths and Simon's values clarifi-
    cation, 72–73
Simon, Sidney, 18, 23, 69, 70, 71. *See
  also* Values clarification
Skinner, B.F., 17, 130
Smith, M.J., 152
Social development, 246–256
Social discipline model, 84–86, 192–193,
  225, 242. *See also* Confronting-
  Contracting

instructional media for, 103–106
and the TBC, 86–102, 101. *See also
under categories of teacher behavior*
Social learning theory, 14–18
application of, 18–20
Social psychology, 17
Social "transaction," Berne's, 48–49. *See
also* Transactional Analysis
Staffing, 282–285
agenda, 285–291
case study of, 291–295
Stand Up, Speak Out, Talk Back (Alberti
and Eamons), 152
Statements. *See* Directive statements;
Nondirective statements
Stimulus and response, 130. *See also*
Conditioning
Stroking, 52
Students:
crises of, 238–244
faulty goals of, 85–86. *See also* Attention getting; Helplessness; Power
and control; Revenge; Social discipline model
misbehavior, Raths's types of, 70
needs of, 237–244
passive, 256–262
physically aggressive, 266–270
and problem ownership, 33–34
social and moral development of, 210,
246–256
time, organization of, 40, 43
and Type II authority, 36–37
verbally aggressive, 266–270
"Stupid," 61, 62
Superego, 47, 49, 52
Supportive model. *See* T.E.T.: Teacher
Effectiveness Training
Suspension, 117
Systematic exclusion, 160

TA for Tots and *TA for Kids* (Freed), 47
Tamashiro, Roy T., 10n.
TBC. *See* Teacher Behavior Continuum
Teacher behavior, 13–14, 20–24. *See also*
Teachers
categories of, 21. *See also* Directive
statements; Modeling; Nondirective
statements; Physical intervention
and isolation; Questions; Reinforcement; Silently looking on
continuum. *See* Teacher Behavior

Continuum
overt and covert, 41–43, 225
Teacher Behavior Continuum (TBC), 5, 7,
22–24, 209, 225. *See also* Teacher
behavior, categories of
and behavior modification, 136–145,
146
and Berne and Harris's Transactional
Analysis, 52–64, 63
and Canters' assertiveness model, 154,
155–160
and Dreikurs's social discipline model,
82–102, 101
and Englemann and Dobson's be-
haviorism/punishment model, 169–
176, 177
and Glasser's reality model, 110–118,
123
and Gordon's T.E.T., 29–43, 42
and Raths and Simon's values clarification, 71–78, 79
T.E.T.: Teacher Effectiveness Training,
27–29, 182–186, 225, 241. *See also*
Relationship-Listening
related readings and films on, 43–45
and the TBC, 29–43, 42. *See also under
categories of teacher behavior*
Teachers:
areas of freedom of, 39–40
behavior of. *See* Teacher behavior
competency of, 275–277
demands of, 157–158
power of, 22–24, 37–38
as professionals, 6–7
as values clarifiers, 71
Team approach, 211, 279–282. *See also*
Staffing
Theory, psychological, 14–18
application of, 18–20
Threats, 157–158
Time, organization of, 40, 43
"Time out," 144
Transactional Analysis (TA), 47–52, 186–
188, 225, 241. *See also* Relationship-
Listening
instructional media for, 65–67
and the TBC, 52–64, 63. *See also under
categories of teacher behavior*
Types I and II authority, 36–37

"Uproar," 61

Values clarification, 34, 68—71, 188—189, 225, 241. *See also* Relationship-Listening
   instructional media for, 80—83
   and the TBC, 71—78, 79. *See also under categories of teacher behavior*
Verbal aggression, 249—251, 266—270
Verbal clues, 53

Vocal tones, 53

Walker, James E., 131
When I Say No I Feel Guilty (Smith), 152
Win-lose methods, 37—43
With-it-ness, 301—306
Workman, E.A., 142n.